The Lost Southern Chefs

A HISTORY *of* COMMERCIAL DINING
in the NINETEENTH-CENTURY SOUTH

Robert F. Moss

The University of Georgia Press
ATHENS

Frontispiece: Hancock's Restaurant, Washington, D.C.
(Library of Congreess Prints and Photographs Division)

© 2022 by the University of Georgia Press
Athens, Georgia 30602
www.ugapress.org
All rights reserved
Designed by Erin Kirk
Set in ITC New Baskerville
Printed and bound by Sheridan Books
The paper in this book meets the guidelines for
permanence and durability of the Committee on
Production Guidelines for Book Longevity of the
Council on Library Resources.

Most University of Georgia Press titles are
available from popular e-book vendors.

Printed in the United States of America
26 25 24 23 22 P 5 4 3 2 1

Library of Congress Cataloging-in-Publication Data

Names: Moss, Robert F., 1970–, author.
Title: The lost Southern chefs : a history of commercial
    dining in the nineteenth-century South / Robert F. Moss.
Description: Athens : The University of Georgia Press,
    [2022] | Includes bibliographical references and index.
Identifiers: LCCN 2021037127 | ISBN 9780820360850
    (paperback) | ISBN 9780820360843 (ebook)
Subjects: LCSH: Cooking, American–Southern style. |
    Cooking–Southern States.
Classification: LCC TX715.2.S68 M67 2022 |
    DDC 641.5975–dc22
LC record available at https://lccn.loc.gov/2021037127

THE LOST SOUTHERN CHEFS

For Charlie

CONTENTS

ACKNOWLEDGMENTS

Big thanks are due to Hannah Ayers and Lance Warren, the directors and producers of the documentary film *The Hail-Storm: John Dabney in Virginia*, from whom I learned of Wendell Dabney's manuscript autobiography and its detailed information about his father's career in Richmond. Professor Ethan Kytle of California State University, Fresno, kindly shared with me a copy of Mrs. Francis Porcher's letter about the Nat Fuller Feast, which he unearthed in the collections of the South Caroliniana Library and which solved a mystery that had long had me stumped.

As always, my wife, Jennifer, has been extremely supportive of my research and fairly tolerant of the many hours I spent holed up in my office instead of taking her to lunch.

Finally, this book wouldn't be possible without the scholarly work and kind assistance of Professor David Shields of the University of South Carolina. His pioneering work in this field is the reason why we even know the names of many of the figures who appear in this book. While working on his book *The Culinarians*, which was published in 2017, Shields compiled profiles of hundreds of once-famous and now-forgotten caterers and chefs from the nineteenth and early twentieth centuries. He generously shared his material with me while his book was still in manuscript form, including many profiles that ended up not making the cut for his finished volume. That material helped get the ball rolling for the research behind this book, providing some of the most crucial pieces of information of all: the names to look for. From there I was able to go back and retrace Shields's tracks, starting with the sources he had identified and then digging deeper for additional newspaper articles, census records, city directory entries, and archival documents. In the process, I was able to flesh out the individual biographies, correct a number of ambiguities and red herrings, and begin to connect the many dots into my own interpretation of how commercial dining evolved in the American South.

But the story of southern restaurants and bars—and the larger picture of southern cuisine in the nineteenth century—is far too rich a field to be addressed in just one or two books. Following in the footsteps of Professor Shields, I hope I have beaten back a few more bushes and limbs and made the path clearer for others to follow. I anticipate that many more writers will continue to refine and correct the story as they find new dots of their own and connect them in ever more revealing ways. We've only scratched the surface.

THE LOST SOUTHERN CHEFS

INTRODUCTION

On an April evening in 2015, I was fortunate to be one of eighty guests invited to attend a remarkable celebratory dinner in Charleston, South Carolina. It was the Nat Fuller Feast, a commemoration of the 150th anniversary of a culinary event that, until just a few months before, I hadn't even known had happened.

I grew up in South Carolina. By 2015 I had been studying southern food culture for a good two decades, digging deep into the rich history of the region's foodways—first barbecue, then the full southern culinary canon, and especially the long traditions of my adopted hometown of Charleston. How could it be that I had only recently heard the names of the once-famous caterers and cooks being honored that night—Nat Fuller, Tom Tully, and Eliza Seymour Lee?

The dinner's organizers had, of necessity, made a lot of educated guesses. They did not know the exact date of the original feast, just that it appeared to have occurred in April 1865, so they picked April 19 for the commemoration. Nor did they know the names of the guests or any of the dishes that were served. All they had to go on was a single line from a letter written by one Mrs. Francis J. Porcher, a wealthy white Charlestonian. "Nat Fuller," the line read, "a Negro caterer, provided munificently for a misce-genat dinner, at which blacks and whites sat on an equality and gave toasts and sang songs for Lincoln and Freedom." Mrs. Porcher, for the record, was not amused.[1]

David Shields, an English professor turned food historian, and Kevin Mitchell, a chef and culinary instructor with a deep interest in southern food traditions, resorted to a sort of culinary forensics to stage the dinner. From scattered newspaper accounts and archival materials, they pieced together the repertoire of Nat Fuller as well as his protégé Tom Tully and Fuller's culinary mentor Eliza Seymour Lee to synthesize a likely bill of fare. Through historical triangulation they determined how the tables were likely to have been set and that the service likely would have been *à la Russe*, with each course brought to the table sequentially, already individually plated. They even surmised what could have been said during the rounds of toasts that closed the meal. It was quite a feat of extrapolation, spinning a rich, compelling narrative from scant scraps of evidence. It wasn't until several years later that I realized exactly how scant that evidence was. In fact, the event that we were commemorating that night had never actually happened—or, at least, it hadn't happened in anything like the form in which it was reconstructed.

That such speculation and extrapolation were required reflected the state of research into southern professional cookery in 2015. Hundreds of books and thousands of articles on southern food had been published in the preceding decades, but the names of the great caterers of Charleston—and of Richmond, Louisville, and Washington, D.C.—appeared nowhere in them. Those caterers are central characters in one of the great untold stories of the South's cultural past, a story that is very different from the more familiar one about daily cooking on plantations or in family kitchens. It's not a story about fried chicken, grits, and cornbread, as delicious as those traditional southern dishes are. It's about a separate, parallel mode of dining, one that was public and commercial. That mode elevated southern cooking to the ranks of high art, and it earned fame and even fortunes for its most accomplished practitioners. And yet their names have been all but forgotten.

They were overlooked for many reasons. Very little of the lives of these culinary pioneers was captured in the historical record. Nineteenth-century chefs didn't write memoirs, and they didn't leave their business records to museums or archives. Many couldn't even read or write. Only a handful of menus from their restaurants and banquets survive—ephemera in the truest sense of the word. For those who died while still at the top of their craft, obituaries are often the fullest (if somewhat unreliable) sources of biographical detail. The many who died in obscurity left only scattered traces, crumbs sprinkled across newspaper ads, city directory entries, and court records.

But there is another factor at play. These early culinary professionals don't fit nicely into the narratives that have long been favored by those who tell the story of southern food. For decades, southern food writing was the province of misty myth and clever anecdote. Even writers who approached the subject respectfully had a tendency to assume an overriding European origin—especially English and French—for the region's foodways. In recent years, scholars and food writers have begun to correct the many distortions and omissions. It is now widely recognized, for instance, that many of the essential ingredients in the southern pantry originated in West Africa and arrived on American shores through the forced migration of the slave trade. More recently, we have begun to recognize the central role that people of color played in shaping and defining southern cooking over the centuries, as writers like Jessica B. Harris, Toni Tipton-Martin, and Michael Twitty have shown that African American talents, skills, and cultural traditions underlie almost every aspect of this great regional cuisine.[2]

The overall picture of those contributions, however, remains incomplete. Most discussions of nineteenth-century southern cooking start and end on the farms and plantations of the rural South, ignoring the towns and cities. This focus is to some degree understandable, for the region's economy was largely agricultural until well into the twentieth century, and the great majority of the population—more than 90 percent—lived in rural areas. But a lot was going on in the South's growing cities during the economic expansion that occurred between 1830 and 1860 as well as during the civic and commercial upheaval of Reconstruction and the New South years. Those developments transformed what people throughout the region were eating, both in the cities and out in the countryside. In the process, the South developed a modern mode of fine dining, with dishes and customs that are quite different from those that appear in the standard narrative today.

The men and women who helped shape the business of food were frequently of African descent, and they didn't advance their craft behind the scenes as nameless hands in the kitchen. Instead they were right out in front as hosts, chefs, and business owners. Their efforts commingled with those of immigrant entrepreneurs—another underappreciated facet of the story. When food writers discuss the European influence on southern cooking, they typically look to the home kitchen and focus on Europeans who arrived during the colonial period, especially the Huguenots in South

Carolina and the French colonists of Louisiana. When it comes to commercial cooking, though, the relevant window is considerably later. Though the number of immigrants to the South in the nineteenth century was relatively small, the successive waves of migration that transformed northern and midwestern cities—first Germans, Swiss, and French, followed by Italians, followed by Greeks and Eastern European Jews—had an outsized influence on the foodways of the South, too.

This isn't the usual cast of characters when it comes to southern culinary history, which has tended to enlist a romanticized version of plantation life to explain everything. In 1977 the election of President Jimmy Carter prompted a surge of interest in all things southern, including a flurry of articles in northern and midwestern newspapers that introduced the region's cooking to curious readers. "There is a particular down-home goodness about Southern cooking," a columnist for the *Evansville Courier* explained. "It was developed by generations of plantation owners and their servants. The bounty of the great plantations set the basic flavors: ham, chicken, corn, beans, rice, sweet potatoes, black-eyed peas, greens and grits."[3]

Those are indeed some of the basic flavors of the southern table. But here are some others: green turtle soup, Maryland terrapin stew, canvasback duck, Madeira wine, and broiled shad. We should add mint juleps made with peach brandy, not bourbon. And oysters, too—raw, fried, stewed, and steamed. None of these foods and beverages were "developed by generations of plantation owners," but they are an important part of the story nonetheless.

This book details the evolution of commercial dining in the American South over the course of the nineteenth century. By "commercial dining" I mean meals that were purchased and consumed outside the home in places like restaurants, saloons, and hotel dining rooms as well as at large feasts and banquets staged by caterers in exchange for money. Businesses like boardinghouses and bakeries as well as informal, often underground, enterprises like cookshops do qualify at least partially as commercial dining, but this study by necessity touches on them only briefly, for they are more accurately categorized as semiprivate dining or food sold for home, not public, consumption. Defining "the South" is a tricky proposition, too, but here it includes Kentucky and Maryland as well as Washington, D.C., all of which shared similar cultural roots, including legalized slavery. From a culinary perspective, furthermore, D.C. and Maryland were linked with Virginia by the shared bounty of the Chesapeake Bay. The geographical reach stops somewhat arbitrarily at the Mississippi River, so Texas and Arkansas are not addressed, but many of the same patterns found in cities like Nashville and Louisville would apply west of the Mississippi.

If you've dipped into the previous scholarship on southern commercial dining, you might expect the story to start out something like this: *Once upon a time, American restaurant food was very, very bad, and it was especially bad in the South.* Restaurant historians have long maligned the quality of commercial dining in early America, and there undoubtedly was plenty of miserable fare to be found in eating houses and taverns, especially on the frontier. Travelers from more sophisticated places—especially imperious Britons—recorded all manner of eminently quotable complaints in their diaries and travelogues. Joe Gray Taylor collected many of these in 1982 in *Eating, Drinking, and Visiting in the South,* one of the first histories to treat southern dining in detail. He opens his chapter "Eating Away from Home" by declaring that "the antebellum southerner did not care for commercial hospitality." Taylor paints a portrait of grubby roadside taverns and rude boardinghouses where guests suffered through "common fare from a common table."[4]

But commercial cuisine in the South was far from universally poor. The notion of what we today would call fine dining arrived early on, and it flourished throughout the region as its towns and cities grew from frontier outposts into thriving commercial centers. Too many commentators have mistakenly treated the "antebellum period"—that is, everything between the American Revolution and the start of the Civil War—as if it were a single era with a consistent, shared set of foodways and dining norms. It's tempting to draw a straight line, as Taylor does, from a traveler's being served "rancid fish, fat salt pork, and bread made of Indian corn" in the late eighteenth century to William Howard Russell, passing through Holly Springs, Mississippi, in 1861, eating breakfast "at a dirty table on most execrable coffee, corn bread, rancid butter, and very dubious meat." It's also tempting to ignore the cities altogether and perpetuate a romantic image of a southern society that is uniformly genteel and agrarian. Social histories like Taylor's portray a culture of hospitality in which southern gentlemen avoided lowly taverns and hotels, preferring instead to "stop along the way with friends and relations." That genteel culture is depicted as having had little need for commercial cooking, but if you pause to think about it, *somebody* must have been staying at all those taverns and hotels and keeping them in business.[5]

It was actually quite easy for travelers to dine well in southern cities, provided they had the means. The South's commercial centers were undergoing a multidecade boom, and with each passing year southerners who loved to eat had an increasing array of options—hotel dining rooms, restaurants, oyster houses, confectionery stores, coffeehouses, and free lunches in saloons. This flourishing of culinary businesses resulted from a convergence of social and economic forces. It involved advances in transportation, especially improved roads and canals, interior shipping routes, and the rise of railroads, which made treasured delicacies available in parts of the country where they had never been seen before. Equally important were inventions like improved cookware and stoves, which replaced fireplace cookery and brought more fine-tuned control of heat. Chemical leavening allowed cooks to make "quick breads" without waiting hours for yeast to rise their dough, and the advent of the ice trade brought the ability to cool everything from pastry dough to alcoholic drinks and made possible cold confections like ice cream and sherbets.

The institutions of commercial dining looked very different at the end of the nineteenth century than they had at the outset. The old "restorator" or "restaurat" became the restaurant, though in southern cities they often went by names like "eating house" or "dining saloon." Taverns and boardinghouses evolved into hotels, and hotels became increasingly grand, growing from modest two- or three-story buildings into elaborate palaces of marble and granite. The quality of the food they served, both in their dining rooms for overnight guests and in their ballrooms for banquets and special events, became important marks of distinction. Food took on increased importance in drinking places, too. Taverns evolved into coffeehouses and saloons—terms that were almost interchangeable, for rare was the coffeehouse that sold more caffeinated beverages than alcoholic ones. As the kitchens in these establishments increased in importance, platters of oysters and free turtle soup gave way to full restaurant menus.

More than anything, the story of commercial dining in the South is the story of people and personalities. By the 1840s, any southern city of reasonable size had not one but several famous caterers. These figures helped define and codify the conventions of public dining. They staged grand feasts in their cities' finest hotels and banquet halls, and they often operated their own dining rooms where the public could obtain meals throughout the day. When elite social organizations like fraternal clubs and militia units gathered for celebrations, they turned to their local caterers to provide the most up-to-date, fashionable fare.

These men and women were accomplished cooks, but they were much more than that. They fully embodied the title "chef," for they were the chiefs of their kitchens, hiring and directing entire teams of cooks and waiters. They were masters of logistics, able to stage events for hundreds of guests because they had amassed large inventories of flatware, stemware, and china. They were masters of supply chains, too, establishing broad networks of suppliers in distant cities, for the ability to procure the very best ingredients was perhaps even more important than the skill with which one cooked them. A surprisingly large percentage of these culinary professionals were African Americans or recent immigrants from Europe.

In the middle part of the century, some caterers and coffeehouse keepers transitioned into restaurateurs, while others became chefs at the South's grand urban hotels or elite summer resorts, forging careers as practitioners of the high mode of cuisine. These men and women (and more than a few were women) were chefs in a mode that we might recognize today, with notable parallels to the current phenomenon of the celebrity chef. They started out as hardworking cooks but parlayed their talents into something more ambitious. They were adept at media relations, treating the local press to free samples of their fare and ensuring their names appeared regularly in print. They established business empires, became real estate investors, and helped protégés get started in the business. They were entrepreneurs in the truest sense of the word.

Like today's celebrity chefs and restaurateurs, the nineteenth century's were public figures, and they walked a fine line when expressing political opinions or becoming involved in social activism. Today's celebrity chefs, like Tom Colicchio and Andrew Zimmern, routinely air their political views on social media, and they are frequently criticized for doing so and told to "stick to cooking." The same thing happened more than a century ago, only the medium was letters to the editors of newspapers instead of posts or tweets. It is remarkable how well connected some of these early restaurateurs and caterers became, and not just in their relationships with suppliers and business associates. Many played a central role in the abolitionist movement before the Civil War and in the civil rights movements that followed. They were intimate with the nation's leading politicians and social reformers. Some even became politicians themselves.

These remarkable figures have long been overlooked in southern food histories, but we are now finally starting to recover their names. Once we learn those names, we can begin to piece together their stories and weave them into the larger narrative of dining in the South. Home cooking and "vernacular cuisine" are essential parts of that story, but there is more to its full, rich sweep. The complete picture connects antebellum cookery to the fine dining of the present in unexpected ways. It's a tale of artistry and ambition laced with frustration and despair, and it's essential for understanding our shared culinary past.

 CHAPTER 1

Commercial Dining in Early Nineteenth-Century Charleston

We'll start in Charleston, South Carolina, for the culinary evolution in that city was an early indicator of the changes that were about to occur throughout the South. Charleston was among the first southern cities to transition from colonial-era taverns and boardinghouses to more modern hotels and restaurants. It also saw the early emergence of other important institutions in urban culinary life, like confectioneries and oyster houses. From the earliest days of professional cooking in Charleston, the trade involved people from many different cultures and backgrounds, including native-born whites but also free persons of color and immigrants from Europe. These latter two groups played outsized roles in shaping the city's culinary life.

Until 1800, when it was eclipsed by Baltimore, Charleston was the largest city in the South, and it remained the richest in the country for several more decades because of the extraordinary wealth amassed by rice planters during the colonial era. The city's ports connected it with the Caribbean and Europe, making it a hub of international trade. As the nineteenth century opened, though, Charleston was coasting on its past successes, and its economy and culinary life were both in transition. The emergence of hotels, saloons, and restaurants created a new set of occupations—caterer, bartender, waiter, chef—that had not existed in the days of taverns and boardinghouses, and it expanded the roles of cooks. More than anything, it laid the groundwork for a new form of southern cuisine, one prepared not by home cooks nor by enslaved domestic servants who worked without pay. It was a professional cuisine, prepared by men and women who cooked in exchange for money.

The colonial tavern and the antebellum hotel served similar purposes—to provide room and board for travelers as well as food and drink for local residents—but they had very different physical forms. Apart from a small sign hanging outside, a tavern or inn could scarcely be told from a private house. Most taverns, indeed, started out as private residences and were converted to take in lodgers. The typical tavern bar was just a wooden cage from which liquor was dispensed, and it would be locked up when the proprietor retired for the night. Most guests slept in common rooms, sharing beds with strangers, though many taverns had a few private bedchambers for guests of means. Lodgers ate three meals a day at taverns, but they did so on the proprietor's terms. Meals were served at a fixed hour, and guests sat together at a common table and ate whatever fare the owner or his or her cook had decided to prepare that day. Boardinghouses operated on largely the same principle, though they typically lacked the common room with the caged bar that was the focus of the tavern's social activity.[1]

In the early decades of the nineteenth century, the features of the modern hotel began to emerge throughout the United States, and they became more standardized as buildings were constructed expressly for the purpose of being hotels instead of being converted from houses or stores. These features included a large entryway on the ground floor with a desk to welcome visitors—what we today would call the lobby—as well as a separate room to house the bar, which, like today, generated a sizeable portion of the business's income. Separate eating spaces, typically called just "dining rooms" or "dining parlors," were essential, too. The kitchen where the meals were prepared was generally located in the back of the building or in a separate outbuilding behind it.

But this was still a time of transition. For much of the nineteenth century, there weren't strict delineations among hotels, restaurants, and bars—or saloons, as they were more frequently called—and most establishments served all three functions simultaneously. Those that were primarily places of lodging might have a formal lobby, a front desk, and numbered guest rooms arranged along corridors, but they invariably had a bar and "dining saloon" as well. Others were drinking establishments first and foremost, but the proprietor might have a separate dining room attached and a few private rooms on the upper floors where patrons could rent a bed. In some of these operations, the barroom did double duty as the lobby, with the bar top serving as the front desk and the proprietor receiving new guests while mixing toddies or slings. Even businesses that advertised themselves as restaurants might take in a few boarders on their upper floors.[2]

Charleston had various establishments operating under the name "hotel" as early as the 1780s, but these seem to have been standard boardinghouses and not something we would recognize today as a hotel or restaurant. More in the modern vein was Jessop's Hotel, which opened in 1799 at 63 East Bay Street. Its proprietor, Jeremiah Jessop, emphasized public dining, especially in his long room, which could be engaged for parties. He kept a marine book with detailed entries of ships' comings and goings to assist "citizens engaged in commerce." He also sold "ice creams and ice punch" and had private rooms available "for the accommodation of ladies" who wished to enjoy the frozen treats. From its earliest days, commercial dining in the South was sharply divided into male and female spheres. Respectable women did not dine alone in rooms that catered to men—especially when alcohol was served, as it usually was. Men had their exclusive dining spaces, and women had theirs, but men could generally dine in "the Ladies Dining Room" if they were accompanying a woman.[3]

In 1800 the St. Mary's Hotel opened for business in "a commodious house" on the corner of Meeting and Queen Streets. It was named not for a saint but rather for its proprietor, Francis St. Mary, and he advertised he would accommodate gentlemen with boarding and lodging together, or with boarding alone. His board included "Breakfasts, dinners, etc. Soup every day—and suppers, beef steaks and oysters every evening." St. Mary had private rooms for parties, but he was emphatically not operating a restaurant where customers could walk in off the street and order something to eat. In January 1801, St. Mary announced that he wished "to confine his business to his friends and the respectable Clubs and Societies" and at three o'clock each day "dinner will be upon the table, at which none will be admitted but those presented by his boarders."[4]

Despite its name, St. Mary's Hotel, like Jessop's, was more of a precursor than a true modern-style hotel. Charleston's first business to fit that category actually evolved out of St. Mary's establishment. In 1803 James Thompson took over the business and renamed it the Planter's Hotel. His main order of business was to provide "Country Gentlemen and their Families with Boarding and Lodging." This early hotel had a total of fourteen rooms, and serving meals to the public was an important part of Thompson's plan. His early ads noted that he "proposes to entertain Societies and furnish Public Dinners, as his rooms can contain upwards of one hundred gentlemen." Early on Thompson drew the patronage of the Jockey Club, the stockholders of the South Carolina Cotton-Company, and the Hibernian Society, an Irish benevolent society that would build the massive structure known as Hibernian Hall on Meeting Street in 1840.[5]

Unfortunately, we don't know what Thompson served at those public dinners. The language of his advertisements reflects an emerging set of conventions that would persist for most of the nineteenth century, in which restaurant fare was routinely described in vague generalities that assert the quality of the fare without providing any clues as to what that food actually was. "His Larder will always be furnished with the best the markets afford," promised one of Thompson's notices. "And his Liquors will be genuine and of the first quality." Phrases like "the best the markets afford" were the nineteenth-century equivalent of today's "grilled to perfection"—ubiquitous clichés that sound lofty but tell the poor diner nothing. We can identify at least one dish served at the Planter's Hotel, though. In September 1806, Thompson advertised that "a large fine Green Turtle" would be dressed that day at the hotel, and "Steaks may be had, if applied for early this morning."[6]

Here we see the great commercial delicacy of the early nineteenth century: green sea turtle. "Dressing a turtle" meant butchering it and portioning it to use in various dishes. Typically that involved killing the creature, removing its head, and hanging the carcass to drain the blood. Next, the top and bottom shells were removed, then the meat was taken off the bones, scalded in boiling water, and cut into bits, with the various organs reserved for frying or other use. The "steaks" referenced in Thompson's ad were the turtle's fins, which would be scaled to remove the rubbery outer skin and then sliced. Also common was turtle forcemeat—lean meat, fat, seasonings, and sometimes eggs that were ground together, rolled into balls, and fried. The rest of the meat from the carcass was incorporated into turtle soup, an American favorite since the colonial era.

In Thompson's day, cooks started their turtle soup with a rich beef or veal stock and added sliced turtle meat along with the broth reserved from scalding the meat and boiling the shell. The mixture was seasoned with herbs and aromatics like parsley, thyme, and onions and with spices like mace, cloves, and black and cayenne peppers. After simmering for hours until the meat was tender, the soup was generally thickened with flour and finished with a generous dose of Madeira—the sweet, complex fortified wine from the island of Madeira that was favored by southerners for most of the nineteenth century.[7]

Southerners made soup from all sorts of turtles—generic cooters, the famous diamondback terrapin of the Chesapeake—but the most prized of all was green turtle soup, which was made from gigantic green sea turtles. Throughout the nineteenth century, hoteliers and saloon keepers would publish notices in the local newspapers each time they received a particularly large turtle. These could weigh several hundred pounds and were always delivered live, generally arriving on schooners from Nassau or other parts of the West Indies.

James Thompson soon faced competition from other commercial hoteliers and cooks. In October 1806, William Robinson took over the "large and commodious house" at 60 East Bay Street, which had originally been owned and operated as a tavern by Edward McCrady. Fifteen years earlier, in 1791, McCrady had hosted President George Washington in his Long Room as the guest of the Society of the Cincinnati. The tavern had changed hands several times after McCrady's death in 1801, and Robinson promised patrons that he had thoroughly updated the building. Like James Thompson of the Planter's Hotel, Robinson was an early adherent of another irritating nineteenth-century restaurateur's convention: assuming that the reader already knows everything about you. "My mode of providing is so universally known," Robinson announced, "that, to enlarge on the subject, would appear superfluous." Superfluous, perhaps, in a town the size of Charleston, which in 1806 had fewer than twenty thousand residents, but not to those trying to reconstruct restaurant history. Did Robinson's establishment qualify as a hotel instead of a tavern? We simply don't know.[8]

In 1806 the Planter's Hotel was purchased by Alexander Calder, a cabinetmaker, and his wife. In 1809 they moved the business to a new building at the corner of Church and Queen Streets, the first in the city to be purpose-built as a hotel. Opening in late November, the hotel was, the Calders boasted, "superior to any establishment of its kind in the Southern States." The building featured a lobby with stucco and woodwork by the noted craftsman William Purvis and a grand staircase in the lobby that ascended to a drawing room on the floor above. The new hotel had separate bedrooms for each guest, newly furnished and with a fireplace in each. Addressing a long-running complaint of guests at their original hotel—the

Entrance to McCrady's Tavern, Charleston, South Carolina, 2010. (Brian Stansberry under the Creative Commons Attribution 3.0 Unported license)

lack of fresh drinking water—their new location boasted "a never-failing Cistern of Water, allowed to be the best in the State."[9]

Visitors to Charleston can still see that original lobby today, for, unlike almost every other hotel and restaurant discussed in this book, the building is still in use. It was enlarged over the years. Wrought iron balconies supported by limestone columns were added around 1835, and the structure eventually encompassed what are essentially six separate buildings. During the Depression, the Works Progress Administration converted it into the Dock Street Theatre, and it was thoroughly renovated again in 2010. The original lobby and staircase serve today as the entryway to the theatre.

Front view of the Planter's Hotel, Charleston's first purpose-built hotel building, which now houses the Dock Street Theatre. (Library of Congress, Prints and Photographs Division)

Though the Planter's Hotel soon gained significant rivals, for the next half century it remained among the principal hotels in Charleston, serving a regular clientele of plantation owners and seafaring merchants as well as the occasional traveler. Charleston finally had a modern hotel.

➤⸎⸺ Jehu Jones Becomes a Hotelier

A few years after the Calders moved the Planter's Hotel to Church Street, another local family decided to try their luck in the hospitality business. What distinguished this family from previous ones in the trade was that they were free persons of color.

Jehu Jones was born into slavery in 1769 and learned the craft of tailoring. By 1798 he had earned enough money to buy his freedom for £100 sterling. Jones set up a tailor shop on Broad Street, and in 1809 his son, Jehu Jr., joined him in the business. Tailoring and barbering were the two most common occupations for free persons of color in the South, and both became closely linked to the culinary trades. Many caterers and cooks got their start as barbers or tailors, which were fairly low-cost trades to enter, and invested their savings in the equipment and property needed to launch a culinary and hospitality business.[10]

In 1809, the same year his son joined his tailoring firm, the elder Jones purchased a house next to St. Michael's Church on Broad Street and began operating it as a hotel. Three years later he handed the tailor shop over to his son and focused on his hotel full time. He seized a chance to expand in 1815, when the owner of the property next door to his hotel died. Jones bought the three-and-a-half-story wooden mansion and converted the rooms to accommodate boarders. In the rear was a two-story brick building with rooms that he rented to professionals such as lawyers to use for offices. In 1820 the painter and future telegraph inventor Samuel F. B. Morse set up his "painting room" in the rear building, where he did a brisk business producing portraits of wealthy Charlestonians. The lot also contained separate outbuildings that served as the kitchen, stable, and outhouse along with a cistern that supplied water for the premises. Once Jones moved into the new building, he promptly sold his old one next door to the congregation of St. Michael's Church, which knocked it down and extended the churchyard.[11]

No menu or description of the meals served in Jones's dining room survives, but visitors' accounts suggest the fare rose above that of the typical tavern or boardinghouse. Thomas Hamilton, a Scottish soldier and author, traveled through the South in the early 1830s, and while in Charleston he stayed at Jehu Jones's establishment. "Every Englishman who visits Charleston," he wrote in 1832 in *Men and Manners in America*, "will, if he be wise, direct his baggage to be conveyed to Jones' hotel. It is a small house, but every thing is well managed, and the apartments are good." Hamilton had arrived in Charleston after a long journey from New Orleans, most of it by stagecoach through Alabama and Georgia, and he was relieved to find "clean tablecloths and silver forks" and to exchange "salt pork and greasy corn cakes, for a table furnished with luxuries of all sorts. . . . After the privations of a journey from New Orleans, the luxury of Jones' iced claret might have converted even Diogenes into a gourmet."[12]

The 1820 census shows that Jones' Hotel was staffed primarily by enslaved African American women. These early records do not list individuals by name but instead tally the number of residents by gender and age group. The record for Jones's household shows six free persons of color—presumably Jones and his family—along with a single enslaved male and twenty-one enslaved women between 14 and 26 years of age, plus two more women between 27 and 45. The enslaved residents were not necessarily owned by Jones himself, for it was a common practice in Charleston and other southern cities for slaveholders to apprentice their slaves to a hotelier or caterer for training or to hire them out to generate income. Indeed, an advertisement in the *Southern Patriot* in April 1826 offered for sale "a Mulatto man who is an excellent house servant. He was brought up by Jehu Jones, by whom on an application his character and certifications will be made known."[13]

The nature of the early hotel and restaurant business was shaped by seasonal variations. Those who made a living catering to the wealthier ranks structured their lives to follow their clientele as they traveled throughout the year, though the timing and destinations varied from city to city. In Charleston the commercial and social calendar was dictated by the rice trade, the engine of wealth that drove the economy. The social season began in the fall, when planters brought their newly harvested crop into the city to sell. Winter was the great social season, a time of dances, balls, and private dinner parties. The city teemed with life during the cooler months. Summer was a different story. Charleston was still a fetid, unhealthy city, occupying a narrow peninsula between two rivers and crisscrossed by brackish creeks and low-lying marshes. Conditions were particularly unhealthy during the sweltering summers. As the thermometer rose in May and June, wealthy Charlestonians headed across the harbor to the beaches at Sullivan's Island, and the proprietors of Charleston's hotels followed.[14]

In the summer of 1807, Mrs. Calder of the Planter's Hotel opened an auxiliary house on Sullivan's Island to take in boarders, who could use the main hotel's facilities free of charge while visiting in town and then at night escape by boat to the cooling ocean breezes on the island. Around 1814, Jehu Jones purchased several buildings on the west end of the island, the side closest to Charleston, near the landing at which boats from the city arrived. The main building had two large public rooms and ten private chambers, each lathed and plastered. Two large piazzas offered sweeping views of the harbor. A smaller building had two additional rooms and five bedchambers, and the property also included a stand-alone kitchen, stable, and carriage house. Jones typically opened up his beach operation in early May and ran it until September, when he returned to the city and his hotel on Broad Street.[15]

⇒)⊯← Confectioners and Pastry Chefs

Another line of business that was a precursor to southern restaurants was confectionery and pastry. These businesses started out primarily as retail shops, preparing a range of sweets for customers to purchase to take home and eat. Over the course of the nineteenth century, confectioners began selling entire meals, sometimes as part of catering services for functions in private homes and banquet halls but increasingly for customers to eat right there in the shop. The art of the caterer, pastry chef, and restaurateur remained tightly intertwined for decades to come.

Two of the first pastry chefs in Charleston were Adam Prior and Charles Moore. Both were raised and trained in England, and they arrived in Charleston in the 1780s and opened shops specializing in cakes, French pies, "patties" (that is, pâtés), trifles, and meat pies. Another early figure was a Frenchman named Gaston about whom little is known. In 1804 Gaston announced to the public that he had recently arrived from France and was commencing business. That business lasted only briefly, but his advertisements offer a glimpse of an early confectioner's repertoire. It includes a range of pastries and desserts "in either the English or French mode," including jellies, blancmange cakes, and ice creams. Gaston's offering went beyond sweets to sausages, salted meats, and "beef a la mode, to keep on long voyages." Notably, Gaston also announced that he would "take some young negroes, as apprentices," for one of the important functions of Charleston's early confectioners and pastry cooks was to train enslaved workers in the culinary arts so that they, in turn, could serve in the kitchens of the city's private homes and as well as in plantation houses in the countryside.[16]

Essential to supporting a full confectionery trade was the availability of ice, which was not only used for making ice cream and flavored ices but also for cooling dough to allow it to be worked and for keeping dairy products from spoiling. In the eighteenth century, icehouses could be found only in the upper parts of the South like Maryland and northern Virginia, which had cold winters and were close to lakes that would freeze solid. They were rarer further south, and it took the development of a coastwise ice trade—ships delivering ice from northern ports—to ensure a reliable supply. Charleston had some of the first icehouses in the lower South, which helped confectionery blossom earlier in that city than elsewhere. In 1798 Jeremiah Jessop of Jessop's Hotel constructed an icehouse "at a considerable expense," and he used its contents to make ice creams and iced punches, but he couldn't make a go of it and put the equipment up for sale in October 1800. Similar short-lived ventures followed, and it took until 1817 for an enduring ice business to be established. That year Frederic Tudor, a Bostonian who had recently launched a successful trade with Cuba, built an icehouse on Fitzsimmons's Wharf and filled it with his first shipload of frozen water cut from Massachusetts ponds. Charlestonians could buy ice for 8½ cents a pound and take it home wrapped in blankets, which they could buy at the icehouse for a dollar apiece.[17]

Tudor extended his ice business to Savannah and New Orleans in the years that followed, and plenty of competitors entered the trade. During the 1820s icehouses became larger and better insulated, making ice cheap and widely available in all of the South's port cities. In 1828 Phineas Pierce built a new icehouse on Meeting Street at the cost of $15,000. It could hold the cargoes of four ships. Pierce sold his ice for a penny a pound—the same price as in northern cities. The ice was essential for many aspects of Charleston's culinary trade, from storing meat to cooling drinks, and it made possible the production of flavored ices, ice creams, and delicate pastries on a commercial scale.[18]

As in the hotel business, the city's most prominent practitioners in the confectionery trade were from a family of free persons of color. Sally

Seymour was born into slavery and became the mistress of a white planter named Thomas Martin, the father of her three children. Seymour trained with Adam Prior and then, after being manumitted in 1795, opened her own pastry shop on Tradd Street. Two of her children, William and Eliza, started working there as well. Many of the other workers in the shop were enslaved apprentices, for Sally Seymour became the instructor preferred by Charleston slaveholders for training their young house servants in the art of pastry and meat cookery.[19]

In 1823 Seymour's daughter Eliza married John Lee, a free person of color who had a tailoring shop on Broad Street, not far from Jehu Jones's hotel. The Lees embodied the complex and contradictory status of mixed-raced persons in early nineteenth-century Charleston. John Lee was a member of the Brown Fellowship Society, which had been founded in 1790 as a funeral society with a goal of establishing a separate cemetery for Charleston's "brown" men—that is, mixed-race males—and supporting their widows and surviving children. The society's founders were all free persons of color who attended St. Phillip's Church but could not be buried in the church's white-only cemetery. With a steep fifty-dollar initiation fee, the society was exclusive by design, and almost all its members were light skinned, with the exception of a few darker-skinned individuals with naturally straight hair. (In 1843 a group led by Thomas Smalls created an alternative organization called the Society for Free Blacks of Dark Complexion, which established its own cemetery.)[20]

Like Jehu Jones and Sally Seymour, John and Eliza Lee owned slaves. In 1823 Seymour sold two enslaved persons named Flora and George to her daughter for five dollars. When she died in 1824, Sally Seymour's estate was valued at $1,645.75 and included two slaves, a man named Felix and a "servant woman" named Jenny. This practice was by no means confined to the Lee family. David Shields has identified at least seven other free persons of color in Charleston during this period who were pastry cooks and owned slaves.[21]

After Seymour's death, Eliza Lee took over her mother's establishment as well as her mantle as the city's most in-demand pastry chef. In her shop on Tradd Street, she sold pastries and cakes and hosted private dinners for organizations such as the Medical Society of South Carolina and the Society of the Cincinnati. Lee also succeeded her mother as the city's leading culinary instructor. In this era there were no formal cooking schools or published manuals for commercial chefs. Professional cooks in the nineteenth century learned the trade through apprenticeship. In Charleston, at least, that was a rather formal process. Apprentices typically got started when they were in their early teens and received upwards of five years of instruction. Slaveholders regularly sent their enslaved domestic servants, both male and female, to serve an apprenticeship with Eliza Lee. Through this avenue she ended up training an entire generation of cooks. Most of her apprentices went on to work in the kitchens of planters' town houses, but a few managed to become independent craftsmen, following in their teacher's path and opening their own businesses.[22]

>⋇– Cooks, Chefs, and Caterers

It's worth pausing to discuss the various roles that existed in the South's emerging culinary industry. Today we tend to use the word "chef" to refer to any skilled cook, but the term actually has a more precise meaning. The chef is literally the "chief" of the kitchen, the manager at the top of the hierarchy of staff. In the nineteenth century the term was more commonly used in connection with the staff of aristocratic houses than it was with hotels or restaurants. The public face of a restaurant or other eating establishment—the person who interacted with diners and received laurels from the press—was more commonly termed a caterer.

That word derives from the French *acatour*, meaning "buyer"—an apt term, for a nineteenth-century American caterer was indeed a master of procurement. As we shall see, the single most important factor in a caterer's success was his or her ability to procure the best ingredients not just from local farmers, fishermen, and merchants but from suppliers in a wide network of trade that, in the early decades of the century, might span hundreds of miles and, later, many thousands. For most of the nineteenth century, this skill in purchasing was advertised and noted even more prominently than the skill or technique with which the provisions were prepared.

Sometimes a caterer might be the one working the stoves and ovens in the kitchen, but that role was more typically the province of a cook, of which there were various grades. A "plain cook" was a sort of moderately skilled generalist, while "meat cook" and "pastry cook" were used to describe those who had attained specialized skills in one of the two main lines of cookery. A "complete cook"—the most prized—was someone who had mastered both meat and pastry. In Charleston as well as the rest of the South, the great majority of these cooks were people of color, and most were enslaved. Hundreds of advertisements from Charleston newspapers offer for sale persons described as either plain cooks or pastry cooks, and most of these are women. Numerous enslaved men, though, are described as "confectioners."

In 1821 a notice from T. Barksdale offered a reward for the capture of "A Negro girl named Phyllis, stout and short; well known in town as a pastry cook." She had run away from her place of employment the week before, which may have been a private home or one of the city's several pastry shops. One notable advertisement shows the interrelated nature of Charleston's culinary businesses and the training of enslaved workers for domestic service. In April 1817 an unnamed seller advertised a private sale of "a young negro woman, and her female child, about 2 years old." The woman was described as "a complete Pastry Cook" who "has served a regular apprenticeship under Sally Seymore—she formerly belonged to Mrs. Calder, and lived several years in the Planters' Hotel." After the hotel, the woman had apparently been put to work in a private residence in the city, for the ad noted she was being sold "for no fault, only not liking to do all kinds of House Work."[23]

The conditions in commercial kitchens were harsh for enslaved cooks, as can be seen at the Planter's Hotel. A visitor to Charleston who lodged there in 1832 noted that among the guests "very little wine is drunk, and rather too much brandy." The hotel by this point was owned by Horatio G. Street, who had purchased it from the Calders in 1828. The guests, men and women alike, dined at a long table, with Mrs. Street seated at the head and her husband at the foot. James Stuart, who lodged at the hotel in 1830, recorded that the dinner served "was very good" and consisted of turtle soup, fish, and "an abundance of food." He also noted that when he returned to the hotel after nine o'clock, he found the male servants—which is to say, enslaved African American men—lying down for the night in the hallways, fully clothed, having neither beds nor bedding for sleep.

"Mrs. Street treated all the servants in the house in a most barbarous manner," Stuart recorded. Not a day passed during his visit when he didn't hear Mrs. Street "whipping and ill using one of her slaves." On one occasion she became so exhausted during a particularly long session of beating that she insisted that her barkeeper, a Scotsman by the name of Ferguson, continue the punishment in an adjoining room while she took his place behind the bar. The bartender, having no stomach for such things, cracked the whip on the walls instead of the poor woman's back, while she in turn "bellowed lustily." Mrs. Street later learned of Ferguson's leniency and summarily dismissed him.[24]

Even worse was the experience of the Planter's Hotel's enslaved cook. Two years before Stuart's visit, the unnamed cook, "a great robust fellow," had been put up for sale along with his wife and two children. Mr. Street purchased the cook while someone else bought the rest of the family. "Though he was living in the same town," Stuart learned, "he was never allowed to see them;—he would be beaten within an ace of his life if he ventured to go to the corner of the street." It's hard to know how typical the Streets' barbaric behavior was in early southern hotels, for most accounts mention the enslaved workers only in passing—if, indeed, they mention them at all. Those accounts in which the workers do appear, however, contain numerous references to their being whipped and otherwise mistreated. The cruelties of slavery were as much a part of city restaurant and hotel life as they were on rice and cotton plantations.[25]

⇥✳⇤ Ambiguous Hospitality

The situation was a little different for free persons of color in the hospitality and culinary trades, which offered a rare avenue for achieving not only a limited amount of autonomy but even prosperity, both in terms of wealth and of reputation. That free African Americans could find such work serving a white clientele is not particularly surprising, for the culinary trades were closely linked to domestic service. The other occupations commonly held by free persons of color—tailoring, barbering, and coach or hackney driving—were also in the service sector. What is more remarkable is that a few African Americans not only made a living in the culinary trades but were able to establish large, prosperous businesses that employed numerous other workers. In some cases they earned quite a significant income doing so.

John and Eliza Lee, for instance, purchased a considerable amount of property in the 1820s, including several lots with houses that they rented out for income. They also accumulated property in the form of human beings. The 1830 federal census listed twenty-three slaves in John Lee's household. It is unclear how many of those slaves were owned by the Lees themselves and how many had been apprenticed by their owners to Eliza Lee's pastry business, but records indicate that John Lee purchased at least two slaves—a man named George from Sarah Ralston for $1,000 in 1839 and the following year a man named Edwin for $700.[26]

Charleston's free persons of color walked a precarious line. On the one hand, they were entrepreneurs who managed to stake out prominent positions in the city's commercial life. Many not only were slaveholders themselves but, as the instructors of generations of enslaved domestic workers, directly contributed to the expansion of enslaved work in the city. At the same time, as persons of color, they were not full and free members of society, and their businesses and personal liberty were constantly at risk. Over time, the "free" part of "free person of color" was steadily chipped away amid increasing fear among whites over the stability of their slaveholding society. In June 1822 officials in Charleston heard rumors of a planned slave revolt. Among the alleged ringleaders were Denmark Vesey, a carpenter and free person of color, and several other leaders of the newly formed African Methodist Episcopal Church. Vesey was swiftly tried, convicted, and hanged on July 2. Some thirty-five other alleged conspirators were executed in the days that followed. Citing the danger of "religious fanaticism," city leaders ordered the African Church burned to the ground, and the state legislature passed a series of measures that greatly restricted the rights of free persons of color. One provision required every free Black male over the age of fifteen to have a white guardian or "trustee." Another severely curtailed the movements of free persons of color, prohibiting them from returning to the state once they left its borders.[27]

This latter provision proved disastrous for Jehu Jones and his family. Earlier in 1822 his wife, Abigail, and stepdaughter, Ann Deas, had traveled to visit family in New York, and the new laws, passed while they were absent, prohibited their return. Jehu Jones, who had stayed back in Charleston, was required to name a trustee, and the individual he selected was perhaps the most influential white citizen he could pick: John Lyde Wilson, a Charleston lawyer and the sitting governor of the state. In December 1823, Wilson petitioned the state senate on Jones's behalf, noting that "his wife and family now abroad and prevented from returning to this State, under penalty of the late act," and requesting that Jones be permitted to visit his family in New York and return to South Carolina afterward.[28]

The petition languished in the senate, and Jones may well have been thinking of leaving the state permanently if it did not get approved. In April 1826, just before the summer resort season opened, he put the property he owned on Sullivan's Island up for sale, but he appears not to have found a buyer. Two months later he announced that he was again opening the establishment for the season. Adjoining that ad was a notice that "Mrs.

Jones" was moving her boardinghouse in New York City from 300 Broadway to a "handsome and commodious house" on the corner of Broadway and Beaver. During her enforced absence, it seems, Abigail Jones operated a lodging establishment in New York that catered to visitors from Charleston. Jehu Jones meanwhile had engaged Eliza A. Johnson, another free person of color, to assist him with running "the female department" at his two Charleston hotels.[29]

Jones struggled financially during his wife's absence. On several occasions in the late 1820s and 1830s, the building and lot he occupied on Broad Street were seized by the sheriff and ordered to be put up for auction to satisfy lawsuits by various creditors, one of which was the South Carolina Society, a charitable and social organization. For a while Jones was able to resolve the debts and retain ownership, but the property was finally sold, and Jones was forced to lease it back from the new owners.[30]

➤✳— From Coffeehouses to Restaurants

Culinary historians have long asserted that the presence of French Huguenots in Charleston gave a French inflection to the city's cuisine. A small number of Huguenots had indeed arrived way back in the 1680s, fleeing religious persecution after King Louis XIV revoked the Edict of Nantes, which had allowed the French Protestants to worship within a Catholic nation. But a far stronger influence on the food culture of Charleston came from a new wave of European immigrants who arrived in the early nineteenth century, and it was through the city's coffeehouses and confectioneries that these new arrivals' presence was first felt.[31]

Among their ranks was a Frenchman named Rémy Mignot. Born in Normandy in 1801, Mignot was reportedly "strongly attached to the imperialist cause" as a teenager. He fled France around 1818 amid the political turmoil following the fall of Napoleon and the restoration of the Bourbon monarchy, and he ended up in Charleston. By 1823 he had opened a coffeehouse on East Bay Street, and a few years later he moved to a more fashionable location on King Street, where he operated a confectionery that sold ice cream, Roman punch, tea cakes, and other sweets. After his first wife died, Mignot married Théonie de la Rivière, the daughter of a French exile. Her father was a baron who had escaped the French Revolution by fleeing to Haiti and then escaped the Haitian Revolt of 1804 by fleeing to Charleston, where he established himself as a successful grocer.[32]

In 1837 Rémy Mignot partnered with two other Frenchmen, Louis Lefeve and Alexis Galliot, to open the United States Coffee House at 129 East Bay Street. They offered lunch and refreshments throughout the day and "an Ordinary or Table d'Hote" at 2:30 p.m. "in the style of the Parisian and New York Restorat." This appears to be the first appearance of the term "restorat" or "restaurant" in connection with a Charleston business, though it had been in use for several decades in cities further north. In 1793 Jean Baptiste Gilbert Payplat, known as Julien, had opened "The Restorator" on Leverett Street in Boston, modeling it after the Parisian-style eating houses that were famous for their soups. The name "restorat" or "restaurant" derived from the broth's purported restorative properties.[33]

In these early days of professional cookery, terms like "restaurant" and "eating house" were slippery, for the conventions of the trade were still coalescing. One characteristic that distinguished what were increasingly called restaurants from the older taverns or boardinghouses was that patrons could arrive whenever they pleased and be served on their own schedules. The phrase "meals served at all hours" appeared more and more frequently in advertisements for eating houses in the 1830s and 1840s. This did not mean twenty-four hours a day—though most restaurants were open quite late, many until midnight or one a.m.—but rather that the meals weren't served at a fixed time announced by a clanging bell. This feature became increasingly important with the rise of railroad travel, and restaurants near train stations often advertised their late hours and willingness to accommodate newly arrived travelers "at short notice." Another restaurant innovation was to replace the communal table of the boardinghouse with separate tables where diners could sit by themselves or in small groups. Patrons had more flexibility in choosing what to eat, too, as establishments began allowing them to order à la carte from a menu instead of just taking the meal of the day—or, to use the term borrowed from the French, the table d'hôte.

Charleston's first official "restorat" was short lived. Just a year after it opened, Mignot's partnership with Lefeve and Galliot collapsed in a tangle of lawsuits, and the building and kitchen equipment were sold in a sheriff's sale. The Mignots bounced around to several other ventures for a few years before relaunching a confectionery in their old location on King Street, which quickly became a fixture of the city's social season. At Christmas they offered rock candy, sugarplums, and an extravagant selection of toys imported from France and Germany.[34]

Théonie de la Rivière (left) and her sister Hortense,
in an undated daguerreotype.

These early European immigrants readily adopted the trade practices
of the slaveholding society in which they found themselves. It is unclear
whether the Mignots owned any of their workers, but Louis Eude, another
of the city's early French caterers and also a native of Normandy, certainly
did. Eude arrived in Charleston in 1830 and opened the French Coffee
House. Less than two years later he posted a notice in the *Charleston Courier*:
"Ran away yesterday, from the subscriber, my mulatto man Henry." Eude
noted that Henry was "lately from North Carolina," suggesting he had

purchased an enslaved man who had only recently been brought to the city. Eude's use of enslaved workers seems more the rule than the exception, for European immigrants throughout the South routinely staffed their restaurants with enslaved labor.[35]

➤❊— "The Worst and Most Detestable Purlieus of Charleston": Oyster Houses

Before we leave Charleston, we must note one more form of southern commercial dining that emerged during this period: the oyster house. These establishments were modeled upon a style made popular in New York City, especially along Canal Street, though in New York they tended to be located below street level and were called "oyster cellars." There, hungry Gothamites could step down a short flight of stairs and feast on freshly shucked bivalves that were served raw with a little salt, pepper, and lemon juice or stewed in the shell over a wood fire. Diners could wash their oysters down with porter or ale served from a bar that inevitably stretched along one end of the room.

Charleston's version of the oyster house was found at street level instead of in a cellar, but the fare was essentially the same. Two of Charleston's longest-running houses were David Truesdell's New-York Oyster House at the corner of Queen Street and Philadelphia Alley and S. B. Burdges's Carolina Oyster House one block further down Queen at the corner of State Street. At least three others—the King Street Oyster House, Markey's Oyster House, and James McClean's Oyster and Eating House on Church Street—were in operation around the same time. These were strictly male gathering places where ale and liquor flowed freely, and as such they had rather unsavory reputations. A correspondent for the *Charleston Courier*, in the course of defending "fashionable amusements" like dancing and playing whist, argued that such pastimes strengthened the social contract and allowed young people to enjoy leisure time together. "The destruction of all places of amusement," he warned, "fills the tavern—the oyster house, and all the worst and most detestable purlieus of Charleston—Is this desireable?"[36]

Despite such reprobation, the proprietors of Charleston's oyster houses were serious about the quality of the bivalves they served. They sourced their shellfish primarily from Carolina waters. Both Truesdell and Burdges regularly received large shipments of between six hundred and one thousand bushels on sloops arriving down the coast from Beaufort, North Carolina, and up from the May River near Bluffton. The oyster trade was seasonal, hewing to the age-old convention of months with an *r*, and Charleston's oyster houses shut their doors once warm weather arrived in May. In 1825 David Truesdell announced that he was offering terrapin soup in place of his normal oysters and would remain open for the summer, but this experiment must not have paid off, for he closed the New-York Oyster House each summer in the years that followed.[37]

By the 1830s, Truesdell had become Charleston's undisputed oyster king. He experimented with creating a hybrid of local "raccoon oysters" and New York varieties. In 1834 Truesdell advertised that he was "negotiating for a Mill Pond for the cultivation of Oysters." Should he succeed, Truesdell noted, he would be able to serve "as good an article as can be procured in any of the Northern cities." The pond approach didn't work out, but he soon landed on a better one. Around 1836 Truesdell acquired two hundred acres of marshland on the eastern end of Sullivan's Island and transformed them into a flourishing oyster farm. Borrowing techniques from rice planting, he built brick abutments with floodgates to control the flow of the tide into his beds, which allowed him to cultivate and harvest even during high tides. Truesdell's beds were a tempting target for poachers, and the oyster farmer was reported to have stood guard over his crop with a blunderbuss and a brace of pistols each night when the tide was low.[38]

Truesdell's Charleston business was so good that he opened an outpost of the New-York Oyster House in the state capital, a hundred miles inland. "How little do the gourmands at Columbia," William Gilmore Simms wrote in 1849, "conjecture the toil, the care, the watchful anxiety with which he has reared these young and artless creatures, that they may minister to the delights and appetites of the Statesman and the Politician."[39]

So here we have, in Charleston, the foundational elements of the South's commercial culinary life: pastry shops, coffeehouses, hotels, and oyster houses, many owned by European immigrants and free persons of color and staffed largely by enslaved cooks. The same patterns could soon be found in cities across the South. By the 1830s, hotels and coffeehouses and saloons were flourishing in Richmond, Baltimore, Mobile, New Orleans, Savannah, and the nation's capital, Washington, D.C. Boardinghouses were still common places of accommodation, and plenty of taverns and inns were still around, looking not much different than they had in colonial days. But the South had begun its transition to a new era of dining.

CHAPTER 2

Early Commercial Dining
in the Mid-Atlantic

On the night of April 11, 1835, in Washington, D.C., a mob of angry, drunken laborers—"mechanics," as they were then called—descended upon the Epicurean Eating House on Pennsylvania Avenue in the heart of the capital's dining and lodging district. The mechanics were looking for the restaurant's proprietor, Beverly Snow, a man famous for his skill in cooking game birds—pheasants, partridges, woodcocks, and, more than anything else, the prized trophy of the Chesapeake region, canvasback duck. But it wasn't a fine dinner the crowd was after.

The mob had gotten wind that the restaurateur, as one newspaper put it, might have "used very indecent and disrespectful language concerning the wives and daughters of Mechanicks." Fortunately, Snow had been warned by friends and was nowhere to be found. The mob proceeded to roam the city, searching the homes of Snow's associates in a fruitless attempt to find the restaurateur. Finally they returned to the eating house, where they cut down the restaurant's sign and "broke and destroyed most if not all of the furniture in the house," as one newspaper put it, "not forgetting to crack a bottle of the 'old Hock' now and then."[1]

The members of the mob were white, many of them Irish immigrants. Beverly Snow was Black, a free person of color who had been born in Virginia. It's unlikely that any of the men who ransacked Snow's eating house had sampled the cuisine that made Snow famous.

Capital Cuisine

In its early days, Washington was a highly transient city. Like Charleston, it had a pronounced seasonality to its culinary life, but in Washington's case that seasonality was driven by the political calendar, not an agricultural or commercial one. The city teemed with life when Congress was in session, which usually started the first week of December, and it largely shut down in the summer and fall once members went back home to their districts. Boardinghouses dotted Capitol Hill, offering lodging and meals in a largely male environment, though typically overseen by a housemother, often a widow. Meals were eaten at a common table and served at fixed times: breakfast at six, dinner at noon, supper in the early evening, each announced by the ringing of a bell or gong. Because of the transient population, catering emerged as an important business in the District. Like the elected officials, many government bureaucrats resided in the city just half the year, and most left their families at home and stayed in boardinghouses or rented rooms. For the latter, caterers delivered two boxed meals per day, breakfast and dinner, for a set monthly fee.[2]

Those who wanted more upscale accommodations sought out the city's two most fashionable hotels, Gadsby's and Brown's. John Gadsby literally bridged the tavern and hotel eras, for he got his start operating Gadsby's Tavern in Alexandria between 1796 and 1808. He moved across the Potomac to Washington in the early 1820s and operated a boardinghouse for a few years before buying a row of Federal-style town houses on Pennsylvania Avenue and converting them into an establishment he named the National Hotel. Most Washingtonians called it simply Gadsby's. As was the case with the city's other early hotels, Gadsby's grew piecemeal as the proprietor acquired various smaller buildings and tacked them together. He eventually added new facades, merging the disparate buildings into what appeared from the street to be a single structure. After various expansions both in width and in height, Gadsby's by 1857 would be transformed into a single building, five stories tall and stretching half the length of the block.

Well before this transformation, Gadsby's dining room became famous for the breadth and quality of its fare, especially its terrapin dinners and rare wines. The proprietor imported the highly prized Madeira by the "pipe"—a long, distinctively shaped barrel—and bottled it for his guests to enjoy at his table. A correspondent for the *Boston Atlas* in 1835 described Gadsby's as "the centre of attraction to all visitors at Washington." In those days guests still dined at fixed hours on the table d'hôte plan, and the rapid pace of Gadsby's meals seems on a par with those encountered by travelers elsewhere in the South. Dinner was announced by "a vociferous bell" rung by "one of his sable myrmidons," and once the doors were opened

Gadsby's National Hotel, Washington, D.C., from an engraved billhead and receipt, ca. 1840. (Library of Congress, Prints and Photographs Division)

The famed canvasback duck of the Mid-Atlantic, from *Fifth Annual Report of the Commissioners of Fisheries, Game and Forests of the State of New York, 1899.* (Courtesy of Freshwater and Marine Image Bank, University of Washington)

"the mob rush in like ravenous hyenas . . . chairs are secured with amazing alacrity, and the first course of cold soup disappears like enchantment." Guests ate together at a single long table, and Mr. Gadsby himself stood at the head, pausing until his waiters delivered the next course on covered trays. "With an affecting and interesting pause between the two words," the correspondent noted, the host would command, "Remove—covers!!!" and then announce the bill of fare of the day: "Roast beef, mutton, lamb, fish, turkey, ham, chicken—and Canvas-Backs."[3]

Those "Canvas-Backs" were a prized breed of ducks, the famed specialty of the Mid-Atlantic, and they would play an increasingly important role in southern fine dining as the decades progressed. Wild ducks of all varieties—mallards, redheads, wood ducks—were popular with diners of the era, but the canvasback was in a class of its own. Its breeding grounds were on the prairies of the Dakotas and Canada, and huge flocks migrated south to the Chesapeake Bay each winter. There they fattened themselves on the wild water celery that grew abundantly along the rivers, which connoisseurs insisted imparted to the meat a flavor unlike any other game bird's. The ducks beneath the silver covers on Gadsby's table likely came from just a few miles away, for the Potomac teemed with canvasbacks in the late fall and early winter.

A block west on Pennsylvania Avenue stood Brown's Hotel, Gadsby's great rival. Purchased by Jesse B. Brown in 1820, it was commonly known as the Indian Queen—a name attached to many other hotels around the country at this period—thanks to the brightly colored picture of Pocahontas that graced its swinging sign. Like Gadsby, Brown himself presided over the dinner table, dressed in a large white apron, though he greeted his guests at the door and escorted them to their seats before moving to the head of the table to carve and serve the featured roast—and to hype the virtues of the day's selection. "I have a delicious quarter of mutton from the Valley of Virginia," one account captured Brown saying. "Let me send you a rare slice, Mr. A. . . . Mrs. D., there is a fat and tender mongrel goose at the other end of the table. Joe, pass around the sweet potatoes. Colonel E., will you help to that chicken pie before you?" To accompany their meals, guests could purchase fine Madeira for three dollars, or help themselves at no charge to decanters of brandy and whiskey placed on the table.[4]

Brown and Gadsby were native-born, but many of those feeding the city's lawmakers and diplomats were recent immigrants from Europe. Joseph Boulanger was born in 1791 in Belgium, but as far as Washingtonians were

BROWN'S INDIAN QUEEN HOTEL,
WASHINGTON CITY

North side of Pennsylvania Avenue about midway between the Capitol and the Presidents House, a few doors east of the Centre Market. The front is an imitation of Free stone. The Proprietor has recently purchased this extensive Establishment and made many large additions consisting of a spacious Dining Room equal if not superior to any in the U.S. Parlors more front on the Avenue & Chambers all of which are Elegantly furnished. Every attention will be paid to those who may honor him with a call. The General Stage Office is immediately East of the principal Entrance. Equal Stables is attached to the Hotel.

Brown's Indian Queen Hotel, Washington, D.C., from a hand-colored lithograph, ca. 1832. (Library of Congress, Prints and Photographs Division)

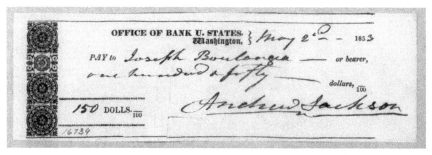

Check from President Andrew Jackson to his steward, Joseph Boulanger, 1833.
(Library of Congress, Manuscript Division, Andrew Jackson Papers)

concerned, he was French. Boulanger trained in Paris at Maison Chevet, the renowned restaurant and catering establishment in the Palais Royal. He spent the early years of his career in the service of various noble British families as they traveled through Europe, including the diplomat Sir Charles Richard Vaughan. In 1825 Vaughan was appointed ambassador to the United States—or, as the office was modestly called at the time, Envoy Extraordinary and Minister Plenipotentiary—and Boulanger accompanied him to Washington, D.C., to serve as his steward.[5]

In 1831 Vaughan fell ill and returned to England on a leave of absence, but Boulanger stayed on in his adopted city and soon secured the prestigious position of steward to President Andrew Jackson. The steward's role encompassed far more than just the kitchen. Boulanger greeted guests and shepherded those with appointments to see the president. He directed the household staff, managed the accounts, and procured supplies from local merchants. Receipts in the Andrew Jackson Papers record Boulanger ordering everything from oats and vinegar to brandy and port wine, and for banquets and balls he purchased long lists of delicacies like ladyfingers, ice cream, and molded ices from local confectioners. To pay for these purchases, Jackson reimbursed Boulanger with checks drawn on his personal bank account, for in those days the president was expected to fund official entertaining from his own pocket.[6]

At the other end of Pennsylvania Avenue in the Capitol Building, hungry and thirsty congressmen needed refreshment, too. One of the first to provide it was Joseph Letourno, a French Canadian who had immigrated to Philadelphia in 1812 and operated a public entertainment resort called Vauxhall Garden, named for the famed pleasure gardens in London.

Letourno moved to Washington in the early 1820s, and he briefly operated a hotel and restaurant on 10th Street before moving closer to the Capitol and leasing a building known as the Fountain Inn. Located on the south side of Pennsylvania Avenue at 6th Street, it was in a prime location, just a block away from the Capitol and conveniently across the street from Gadsby's and Brown's hotels.[7]

Letourno quickly learned an important lesson for those who catered to the appetites of the political classes: the trade could be lucrative, but it was hard work. In 1827, just a year after taking over the Fountain Inn property, Letourno found himself dreading the pending return of the political hordes to the city. In August he announced that he was putting the Fountain Inn up for rent, explaining that "the fatigues of an increased business, which is anticipated during the ensuing unlimited session of congress, are likely to be too arduous for my aged frame." He apparently had no takers, for he kept operating the establishment on Pennsylvania Avenue, commonly called Letourno's, for another five years. Around 1830 his wife opened a complementary establishment next door, called Mrs. Letourno's.[8]

Finally, in the fall of 1832, Letourno found a buyer. George W. B. Blackwell, who previously had worked at Brown's Hotel across the street, purchased the restaurant and renamed it Congress Hall Hotel and Refectory. Letourno moved on to bigger and more ambitious things. Rather than having the politicians come to his house to dine, he decided to go to theirs, and he secured a concession to operate in the basement of the U.S. Capitol what he called a refectory, borrowing a term more commonly used for the dining room in a boarding school or a monastery.[9]

A correspondent for the *Northampton Courier* visited Letourno's Refectory in 1837 and was surprised by how small and dark it was. In a basement room measuring about ten by fifteen feet, Letourno presided at a small circular bar in one corner "with his busy sugar stick," graciously welcoming guests while mixing juleps, slings, and wine bitters. On the opposite side of the room, several African American workers opened oysters on a long bench. Raw steaks, game birds, and sausages hung from the ceiling in all directions, "ready to be impaled upon the spit or stretched upon the gridiron." The cooking was performed right there in the small room, where several more African American cooks roasted the meats and stewed oysters in a fireplace. At any one time, the tiny refectory would be crammed with twenty to thirty customers, ranging "from the dignified Senators and

Representatives down to the smallest errand boy of the Capitol." Still more guests ate their meals in the adjoining dining room, which was dimly lit and had a long common table in the middle and smaller tables in alcoves along the walls. During evening sessions, the reporter noted, "often-times successive glasses of strong drink are carried up to the Representatives' Chamber, to refresh certain members while giving utterances to their windy and miserable declamation."[10]

Letourno ran his basement restaurant in the Capitol until 1838, when he was succeeded first by John West and then by John Foy, the former proprietor of a hotel on D Street. Foy operated "John Foy's Refectory, at the Capitol" for six years, becoming famous for his witty sayings. After losing the concession in 1848, Foy moved over to a house near the South Gate, where he promised to serve the "same viands, flesh and fowls" as he had in the Capitol proper. He gave that establishment up after a few years and returned to operating his hotel on D Street. Restaurants have been in operation in the basement of the Capitol Building ever since, though today they are somewhat larger and better lit. The House and Senate dining rooms are reserved for legislators and their staffers and guests, but up to four hundred visitors at a time can dine at the Capitol Café on burgers, hot dogs, pizza, and salads. No oysters or beefsteaks are served these days, and nothing alcoholic to drink, either—though the speeches of congressmen are no less windy or miserable.[11]

As in Charleston, free persons of color were instrumental in shaping Washington's commercial dining market. Thousands of free African Americans made their way to the capital during this period, including Beverly Randolph Snow, who had been born into slavery in Lynchburg, Virginia, around 1799 on the plantation of Captain William Norvell. In his will, Norvell bequeathed Snow to a daughter with the proviso that he be manumitted at the age of thirty. While still enslaved, Snow began operating a small oyster house on Lynch Street in Lynchburg, keeping a portion of the profits for himself, and he married a free person of color named Julia.[12]

In November 1829, Snow was freed according to the provisions of Captain Norvell's will, and he and Julia decided to try their fortunes in Washington. In 1831 Snow opened a restaurant on 7th Street and arranged to be supplied by steamboat with fresh fish and game birds. The following year he moved into a new three-story brick building at the corner of 6th Street and Pennsylvania Avenue, strategically located between Gadsby's and Brown's

Advertisement for Beverly Snow's Epicurean Eating House, in the *Daily National Intelligencer*, October 11, 1833.

hotels. Snow took on William Walker, another free person of color, as a partner, and the two men gave their establishment a most ambitious name: Snow's Epicurean Eating House and National Restaurateur.

Snow's repertoire included what was fast becoming the standard for southern gourmands: game birds, including canvasback ducks, pheasants, partridges, and woodcocks, along with fresh venison, "Norfolk fish," and oysters. Snow's advertisements highlighted his use of "all the necessary articles to give the epicurean finish to the luxuries of his larder," including chafing dishes and plate heaters. From time to time the steamers that chugged up the Potomac from Norfolk delivered a green sea turtle, and when they did, Snow made turtle soup. Though Gadsby's and Brown's hotels were both highly regarded for their cooking, Snow was soon drawing more customers to his dining rooms than either of his neighbors.[13]

Lynch Wormley was another free person of color who moved to the city from Virginia, and his family would go on to play a prominent role not just in the city's culinary life but in its politics. Wormley and his wife, who most likely was named Cleo, arrived in Washington around 1814, having purchased their freedom for $400. Wormley had not received the certificate of freedom that was required for persons of color to engage in business in the District, so in 1815 he hired Francis Scott Key, a prominent D.C. lawyer who penned national anthems on the side, to sue his former owner and obtain the necessary documentation. It took five years, but in 1820 Wormley finally received his certificate and was able to enter the livery business.[14]

In the years that followed, Lynch Wormley drove hacks for some of the city's most prominent politicians and businessmen, and his eldest son, William, joined the business once he reached his teens. That trade not only earned the family lucrative tips but also put them in regular contact with the city's movers and shakers. Early on, William Wormley became active in educational causes and the nascent abolitionist movement. He was one of the two original Washington agents for William Lloyd Garrison's influential and incendiary abolitionist newspaper the *Liberator*, and he used the proceeds from his thriving livery business to pay for his sister Mary to attend the female seminary in Philadelphia operated by Sarah Mapps Douglass, a prominent African American educator and abolitionist.

Mary Wormley returned to D.C. in 1830 and began conducting classes in a schoolhouse that William paid to have built near the corner of Vermont Avenue and I Street. Her health was failing, though, and the school was taken over first by an Englishman named Calvert and then by William Thomas Lee. Among the first class of students they taught was James Wormley, younger brother of Mary and William.[15]

These efforts to educate the city's young African Americans came at a time when the demographics of Washington were shifting. By the 1830s, free persons of color outnumbered slaves in the city for the first time, and they were increasingly establishing themselves in the few lines of business allowed to them—driving horse-drawn taxis, working as government messengers, and running restaurants and catering operations. As the number of African Americans grew, tensions rose among resentful white residents, and the government began imposing new limits on African Americans' freedoms. In 1808 the city had passed a series of so-called Black Codes that imposed fines for African Americans caught playing cards or dice or being on the streets after ten p.m. Free persons of color were required to carry documents, and each free family had to post an annual cash bond that they would forfeit if they broke any laws.

Things worsened after Nat Turner's rebellion in 1831, which unnerved the city's white community. Those fears were heighted by the growing abolitionist movement, and in particular by the appearance in the city of the *Liberator*, which William Wormley was helping distribute. Hardliners urged new rounds of legislation to restrict the movement and assembly of African Americans, both enslaved and free. Tensions were particularly high between African Americans and the "mechanics"—poor white manual laborers, many of them young Irish immigrants. These laborers increasingly were competing with African Americans for jobs, and they believed their wages were being undercut when well-off white Washingtonians hired enslaved workers at lower rates.

The spark came on August 4, 1835. That night, an enslaved man named Arthur Bowen spent the evening drinking with friends and stumbled home late to the house of his owner, Anna Thornton. Bowen later testified that he was too drunk to remember what happened, but somehow he picked up an axe and carried it into the bedroom where Thornton, her elderly mother, and Bowen's own mother all slept. The women awoke to find Bowen standing over them, staring straight ahead and silently holding the axe. Anna Thornton slipped from the room and ran to the neighbors for help, while Bowen's mother rushed to her son, snatched the axe from his hands, and pushed him down the passage and out the back door. A furious Bowen pounded on the door, insisting, "I've got just as much right to freedom as you," then stumbled away through the back garden and disappeared down an alley.

Though Bowen had not committed actual violence, the idea of a Black man entering a white woman's bedroom with an axe had more than enough echoes of Nat Turner to send panic through the white community. Their fears were fanned by local papers, which portrayed Anna Thornton as "a kind and indulgent mistress" who had "just been saved from butchery in her own chamber." Bowen was said to be part of a group of slaves being egged on by white abolitionists to raise an insurrection.[16]

The rage was most intense among the mechanics, and soon a crowd of angry white laborers, most of them drunk, surrounded the city jail. They "swore they would pull the jail down," a free person of color named Michael Shiner recorded in his diary, and "get Mrs. Thornton's mulatto and hang him without judge or juror." The city's police force numbered just ten constables, so Francis Scott Key, who had been named district attorney in 1833, called in a detachment of marines armed with bayonets to disperse the mob. The rumors of a pending slave revolt remained high for the next several days, and Key was determined to take decisive action. On August 10 he ordered constables to search the office of Reuben Crandall, a young botanist and doctor from New York who was said to possess abolitionist literature. They uncovered a box containing copies of the *Anti-Slavery Reporter* and the *Liberator* and arrested Crandall on charges of sedition, locking him in the jail along with Arthur Bowen.[17]

This turn of events only enraged the mechanics further. Prevented by armed marines from lynching Bowen and Crandall, they set out looking for new targets. On April 11 the rumor of Beverly Snow's disrespectful remarks brought the mob descending upon his restaurant. Later that night, after trashing the Epicurean Eating House, the mechanics headed for John F. Cook's church and the Wormleys' school on I Street, where they destroyed books and furniture and set fire to the buildings before being dispersed by the militia. Cook borrowed a friend's horse and fled to Pennsylvania, and William Wormley and William Thomas Lee left the city as well.[18]

Beverly Snow, it turned out, had fled to his former hometown of Fredericksburg, Virginia, where he went to the local sheriff and asked to be locked in jail for his own protection. From his cell, Snow wrote an impassioned letter to the editors of the *National Intelligencer*, declaring himself innocent of uttering insults to white women or to anyone else. Asserting that the allegations had delivered "a death blow to all that I hold dear to me in this world, my character and my liberty," he pleaded for the newspapers to interview Washingtonians familiar with his character and pronounce his innocence.[19]

Snow's career in Washington was finished. On August 24, less than three weeks after the riots, he and William Walker dissolved their partnership and put the contents of their restaurant up for sale. Snow remained absent from the city for a full year, but one Friday night in August 1836 he was spotted walking on Pennsylvania Avenue. As word spread, a mob began to form, and Snow once again surrendered to a constable and was put in jail for his own safety. He claimed that he had returned to the city only to discharge old obligations related to his former business. Snow paid his outstanding debts, was released from jail, and left the city for good. He and his wife moved to Canada, where they opened a series of successful coffeehouses and saloons in Toronto, including one named—in a wistful echo of his heyday in D.C.— the Epicurean Recess. Beverly Snow died in Toronto in 1856.[20]

The Snow Riots took a severe toll on the Wormley family, too. The schoolhouse that William Wormley built was repaired, but the persecution "was so violent and persistent," as one historian put it, "that his health and spirits sank under its effects." Once "one of the most enterprising and influential Colored men in Washington," Wormley watched his business collapse after the riots, and he spent the remainder of his life in shabby poverty. Even worse was the fate of Arthur Bowen. Despite the protestations of his owner Anna Thornton that he had committed no crime, Bowen was sentenced to hang. A distraught Thornton composed an impassioned letter to President Andrew Jackson, begging clemency for Bowen. Jackson delayed the execution twice and finally, on the Fourth of July, pardoned Arthur Bowen. Thornton sold Bowen for $750 to a friend of the president, who trained the enslaved man to be a servant on a steamboat and took him from the city, never to return.[21]

➤✳︎— The State of American Fine Dining in 1842

If southern food writers have largely ignored the region's restaurants, it's not surprising those restaurants don't appear in histories that are more national in scope. Most accounts of commercial dining in the nineteenth century focus overwhelmingly on the urban Northeast, and especially on New York City, where a great many food writers and historians happen to live. There's long been a standard line that advances New York's legendary Delmonico's restaurant as the singular progenitor of fine dining in America—the indispensable French restaurant that taught boorish Americans how to eat. "In the United States there was very little dining out," Paul Freedman wrote in 2016 in *Ten Restaurants That Changed America*, "apart from taverns, lodging houses, and stands selling street food such as oysters. What was available was hardly luxurious. European travelers were often taken aback by the crudeness of the new country's culinary offerings." Redemption supposedly came in 1827, when two Swiss brothers named John and Peter Delmonico opened a simple pastry shop on William Street in Manhattan. Three years later they added a restaurant next door that served an array of elegant French dishes. "With its fine French food, immense menu, efficient service, and gracious atmosphere," Freedman explains, "Delmonico's seemed a revelation."[22]

The great English novelist Charles Dickens has been enlisted by numerous writers as a sort of culinary barometer to chart the evolution of American dining, and Delmonico's is the hero of the tale. The basic story goes something like this: when Dickens first visited the United States in 1842, he was feted at countless public dinners and balls, but he returned home appalled by the culture and manners he had witnessed, singling out for particular abuse the "barbarous" food in America. He captured those impressions in a 1842 nonfiction travelogue titled *American Notes* and in fictional form in 1844 in *Martin Chuzzlewit*. In a much-quoted passage from the latter, Dickens depicts an alarmed Martin's first boardinghouse dinner, at which twenty or so guests bolt their way through turkey, ducks, and fowl, stewed and pickled oysters, and "great heaps of indigestible matter" that melt away "as ice before the sun . . . a solemn and awful thing to see."[23]

A quarter century later, in failing health and in need of income, Dickens returned to America for a second reading tour. He turned down countless dinner invitations from hosts who were hoping, as Andrew P. Haley puts it in *Turning the Tables*, "to demonstrate that the United States of 1867–68 was a very different place from the young country Dickens had encountered in 1842." The great author consented to attend only a single public dinner, and it was held at Delmonico's, "the nation's most European restaurant, where French cuisine—and only French cuisine—was served." Dickens was so impressed by the fare, the story goes, that at the end of the meal he retracted his previous criticism. "This testimony," he promised, "so long as I live . . . I shall cause to be republished as an appendix to every copy of those two books of mine in which I have referred to America."[24]

These neat anecdotes about Dickens and Delmonico's are enticing, but they by no means capture the real story. As important and influential as Delmonico's was, it was just one of many notable restaurants that shaped the trajectory of American public dining, and many of those restaurants were found considerably further south than Manhattan. Charles Dickens's two visits to the United States did not actually play out quite the way they are frequently portrayed. Even on his first visit in 1842, the evidence suggests, the famous British author dined quite well—including in Washington, D.C.

The American capital offered visitors like Dickens a wealth of fine dining options in the 1840s. Remarkably, the Snow Riots were not the end of the Epicurean Eating House. Less than three months after the violence, Snow's former partner William Walker announced that he had fitted up the cellars in the very building that previously housed their restaurant and was reopening under a new name, the National Eating House. Walker believed he was positioned to succeed through his "long and practical experience in this department" as well as "his acquaintance with those that supply this market," and he turned out to be right. Over the course of the next decade, he groomed a broad network of suppliers who brought to the city an ever finer and more diverse array of fish, game, and provisions than the city had yet seen.[25]

In February 1839 Walker announced that he had just received via the steamer *Columbia* the first fresh shad of the season along with another delicacy rare to Washington: Lynnhaven Bay oysters. Both of these seasonal southern delicacies are worth examining in detail. American shad, the largest member of the herring family, grow as big as eight pounds. They spend most of their lives in the ocean but spawn in freshwater rivers. Each spring, once the waters warm to between 68 and 70 degrees, shad begin their runs up the river to their spawning grounds. In the nineteenth century, before their progress was blocked by dams, those runs might take the schools a hundred miles or more inland. This behavior inspired the *Alexandria Gazette* to declare the shad to have "innate politeness," for unlike "churlish oysters" they "come up the river themselves, that they may be caught at the very door" of restaurants. If only they had legs, the paper added, they might walk right into the kitchen and jump upon the gridiron to broil.[26]

Because spawning is triggered by rising water temperatures, shad runs begin first in the far South and roll their way week by week up the Atlantic Coast. In the 1830s and 1840s, shad were commonly caught in the Savannah River just after Christmas. Further up the coast in Richmond and D.C., the runs usually started in late March. The shad runs of this era were extraordinarily abundant, and the fish was one of most commercially valuable on the Eastern Seaboard. Diners prized shad for its sweet white meat, which is high in oil and takes particularly well to broiling over a fire on a gridiron, dressed only with butter and a little salt. "No fish that swims has the peculiar lusciousness of a fine shad," the *Boston Daily Times* exulted in 1839. Shad eating, though, was a specialized skill, for the fish's complex skeletal structure includes free-floating L-shaped bones that make it difficult to fillet. "The long elastic bones," the paper explained, lie "in rows among the muscles. By taking a little patience to examine the anatomical structure . . . it is quite easy for a practiced eye and hand to leave all these little matters on the table."[27]

The increased availability of ice and the invention of steamships allowed the South's restaurateurs to extend their reach and bring the first shad of the season to diners earlier and earlier. Richmond newspapers in the 1840s repeatedly expressed amazement that shad were available in early March, weeks sooner than in previous decades. The shad William Walker received via steamer in February likely came from North Carolina rivers, where for several months each year fishermen made a handsome return dragging gigantic nets—some as long as a mile in length—across the rivers to snare the surging silver hordes.

The other seasonal delicacy Walker received on the steamer *Columbia*, Lynnhaven oysters, were also rising culinary stars in the Mid-Atlantic. In the

Illustration captioned "Shad fishing in the James River opposite Richmond, Virginia," *Harper's Weekly*, May 9, 1874.

early part of the century, oysters tended to be a very localized product, but advances in shipping were changing that. The Lynnhaven River, an arm of the Chesapeake near Virginia Beach, was just one of the bay's many estuarial rivers whose name became attached to oysters, but Lynnhaven's bivalves were held in higher esteem than any other's. Large and sweet, their quality was attributed to the tidal ebb and flow of the river, which flushed the beds with fresh water when the tide went out and bathed them again in a dose of mineral-rich salt water when the tide came in. In the decades that followed, Lynnhavens would be shipped ever farther and wider, becoming perhaps the most treasured of the Chesapeake's many fine oysters.[28]

Chesapeake oysters were a favorite at Andrew Hancock's restaurant at 1234 Pennsylvania Avenue, which opened in 1840 and quickly became a popular haunt for Washington's political set. In the early years, Daniel Webster, Henry Clay, and John C. Calhoun were among the many notable statesmen and politicians who dined there. If Walker's National Eating House aspired to gastronomic excellence, Hancock's was more homey and eccentric. Its proprietor had developed a fondness for what the *Washington Post* termed the "queer and curious in art," and he began assembling a collection of knickknacks and ephemera that would later earn his establishment the nickname the Old Curiosity Shop. These items included Andrew Jackson's umbrella, the tall white hat worn by General Zachary Taylor at the Battle of Okeechobee in 1837, and a pair of slippers purportedly belonging to George Washington.[29]

Hancock's was a thoroughly male establishment, with no separate dining room or accommodations provided for women. In the early days, liquor was a bigger draw than the food. It was at Hancock's that Dick Francis, one of Washington's most notable bartenders, first came to the public's attention. Born Richard Francis in Surry County, Virginia, in 1827 to a free family of color, by 1848 Francis had come to Washington and found employment behind the bar at Hancock's, where he mixed toddies and whiskey smashes and devised the secret recipe for Hancock Punch. Only in his early twenties, Francis would play an increasingly prominent role in the city's sporting and culinary life in the years to come.[30]

William Walker soon gained a new rival at the head of Washington's emerging fine dining scene in the person of Joseph Boulanger, who had formerly served as the steward of Andrew Jackson's White House. The frontier-born president had not cared much for his steward's mode of European cuisine—"Boulanger did not cherish flattering recollections of General Jackson's taste," one commentator remembered—but the aspiring restaurateur seems to have had more faith in the taste of the city's bon vivants. In January 1837, shortly before the end of Jackson's final term, Boulanger left the White House and opened the American and French Restaurant on the south side of Pennsylvania Avenue, just across the street from Gadsby's Hotel and Walker's National Eating House. The establishment's name emphasized the dual national identities of the restaurant's fare, described in early advertisements as "all the luxuries of a French *Cuisine*, combined with the solid comforts of an American one." At first Boulanger put more emphasis on the French side. "Members of Congress and strangers from all sections of the Union," a notice promised in February, "will doubtless pay their *devoirs* to his *Potages*, his *Bouillis*, his *Rots*, his *Volaille*, and his *Gibier* . . . his *Salmis* and *Sautés* of poultry and game, flavored with the exquisite truffle and the delicate mushroom."[31]

But Boulanger's customers gravitated to the solid comforts of American cuisine. By January of the following year, admitting that he "has not met the encouragement which he expected" and "can no longer devote the whole of his establishment to a restaurant," Boulanger converted some of his dining rooms into chambers for boarders. He began highlighting a different slate of dishes on his menu: rump of beef (plain or garnished), rolled sirloin of beef, hot or cold ballotines of mutton, plus "soups of all kinds, by the pint, quart or gallon." He also began procuring oysters, terrapin, and game birds like pheasant and partridge. In March 1841, declaring that he was "desirous to discontinue his French style of cookery," Boulanger put up for sale his elaborate French plated dinner service, which was sufficient to serve up to sixty diners. (There appear to have been no takers, for Boulanger advertised the set for sale several more times in future years.) That July, the restaurateur advertised for the first time that he was serving the supreme icon of the American table: green turtle soup.[32]

Boulanger remained in demand for catering diplomatic dinners and banquets for local militia troops like the National Blues. "Here in Washington," a correspondent for the *Daily Picayune* explained to New Orleans readers, "an entertainment to potentates always brings into requisition Monsieur Boulanger, Monsieur Favier, and various other dignitaries of the spit, who have been bequeathed to this metropolis at divers times by departed ambassadors, in order to teach Uncle Sam's family how to eat." (Favier operated a confectionery and restaurant on 19th Street.) Looking back on Washington dining before the Civil War, the journalist Benjamin Perley Poore recalled of Boulanger, "his soups were gastronomic triumphs, and he was an adept in serving oysters, reed birds, quails, ortolan, and other delicacies in the first style of culinary perfection."[33]

One of the many visitors to Washington who dined at Boulanger's tables was none other than Charles Dickens, "Boz," who passed through the city twice during his 1842 reading tour of America. On March 14 the Washington correspondent for the *Baltimore Patriot* wrote: "The Boz dinner came off this evening at Boulanger's, on the Avenue." Hosted by a city club, the event's menu and the names of the thirty guests attending were not recorded, but the *Patriot* noted that the meal was "served up in the style in which a Frenchman always excels" and that there was "an abundance of everything in the way of eating and drinking."[34]

So exactly how dreadful did Boz find the food he was served at Boulanger's—food prepared by a chef trained at Maison Chevet in Paris, with the full bounty of the Chesapeake at his disposal? Dickens's writing offers no clue one way or another. He had no shortage of beefs with American culture. He singled out in particular the foul habit of tobacco chewing and, worse, tobacco spitting ("Washington might be called the head quarters of tobacco-tinctured saliva," he sniped in *American Notes*). He had plenty to say about the geography of the American capital, too, which he judged to be in a permanent state of semicompletion. The long, wide streets were unpaved and weed-choked in unexpected places, and one might come across a cluster of handsome marble buildings on one block and a few rough wood-and-plaster ones on the next. "It is sometimes called the City of Magnificent Distances," he wrote in *American Notes*, "but it might with greater propriety be termed the City of Magnificent Intentions."[35]

But Dickens's travelogue scarcely mentions the food that he ate in the United States, and the few times it does are in no way disparaging toward its quality. Dickens does note that a guest in Boston "is certain to see, at every dinner, an unusual amount of poultry on the table; and at every supper, at least two mighty bowls of hot stewed oysters," though this seems more an observation than a criticism. He laments "the awful gong" that was struck before each meal in the hotels where he stayed, but he doesn't address whether the meal itself was any good. This may be the reason why all the commentators looking to tee up Dickens as a detractor of American cuisine (before his later conversion by Delmonico's, of course) trot out the same passage from *Martin Chuzzlewit*, a satirical novel. That passage notably depicts a meal not in a restaurant but in a boardinghouse, a long-standing butt of jokes even among American writers.

Dickens does capture in *American Notes*, however, that as his train crossed the Great and Little Gunpowder Creeks outside Baltimore en route to Washington, he saw that "the water in both [creeks] was blackened with flights of canvas-backed ducks, which are most delicious eating, and abound hereabouts at that season of the year." It's all but certain, given that it occurred in early winter, that the banquet at Boulanger's would have featured canvasbacks.[36]

Boulanger may have been Washington's leading practitioner of haute cuisine, but the Belgian chef remained ambivalent about his prospects in the city. During a bout of ill health in 1841, he put the American and French Restaurant up sale, but it took a full three years to find buyers. Joseph Jewett and P. H. King renamed the business Congress Hall and Eating Saloon (apparently no relation to the previous Congress Hall that opened in 1832). Boulanger remained in Washington, though. Two years after selling his restaurant, he announced that he was still "desirous of removing from the city" and put his French dinner service up for sale (again) along with two brick houses he owned in the First Ward. Not long after, an unknown miscreant broke open the gate to the garden at the chef's residence and let in six cows, which over the course of the night "destroyed a splendid collection of trees, shrubbery, and flowers," many of which Boulanger had brought from Europe and personally nurtured for years. That cruel act of vandalism can only have increased his desire to quit town, but a full year later he had still not managed to sell his property, even after putting his houses up for public auction.[37]

Joseph Boulanger never did escape Washington's culinary scene. Two days after Christmas in 1847, he announced that he was reopening the American and French Restaurant. This time around, it was located not on the main commercial strip of Pennsylvania Avenue but rather on G Street, just northwest of the White House and directly across 17th Street from the War Department. It was Joseph Boulanger's fate to cater to the stomachs of America's political classes.[38]

CHAPTER 3

Commercial Dining in Old New Orleans and the West

No discussion of commercial dining in the antebellum South can omit New Orleans. The Crescent City is famous today for its vibrant and distinctive local cuisine. Visitors flock to New Orleans from around the world to experience its highly lauded restaurants, which range from humble poor boy sandwich shops to elegant bistros serving a long-entrenched canon of French-Creole classics. Food writers and historians generally treat New Orleans as something of a glorious exception in American culture, especially in its food culture. That exceptionalism is routinely attributed the city's long ties to France and Spain, under whose alternating colonial rule it remained until the Louisiana Purchase made it American territory in 1803.[1]

Curiously, though, when we examine the evolution of the restaurant and commercial cooking scene in New Orleans, we find that in the early years it had far more in common with Charleston and Washington than it had differences. The chefs—or, to use the more appropriate term, caterers—who emerged as the city's premier practitioners of haute cuisine did not hail from old French families who had been in New Orleans for decades, which is to say they were not Louisiana Creoles. Instead they came from the ranks of new arrivals, some of them recent immigrants from Europe, others migrants from different parts of the United States, especially the Eastern Seaboard. These newcomers established a restaurant cuisine that wasn't particularly Creole. It leaned heavily on the same early standards, like oyster, fish, and game preparations, that were found in cities further east. It was not until the closing decades of the nineteenth century that the distinctive blend of Creole and African American cooking that characterized the city's home kitchens began to find its way into hotels and restaurants.

What set New Orleans apart before the Civil War was the sheer number of restaurants and the wide variety of their fare. New Orleans was much larger than most other southern cities, standing neck and neck with Baltimore in population. Both cities had eclipsed one hundred thousand residents by 1840, while the next largest, Charleston, had only thirty thousand. Like Baltimore, New Orleans was a great nexus of trade, and during the 1830s and 1840s visitors streamed into the city from the surrounding countryside to conduct business. Today New Orleans is known as the Big Easy and is celebrated for its laissez-faire spirit and easygoing pace, but in the 1830s and 1840s what are now old, elegant buildings with stucco walls and elaborate iron scrollwork were considered new and up to date. Far from a languorous culture, New Orleans saw itself as a city on the move, a buzzing hub of commerce and trade.

Most southern cities boasted a handful of coffeehouses by the 1830s. In New Orleans they were ubiquitous. The city's now-legendary restaurant culture, in fact, evolved to a large degree out of that coffeehouse tradition. In New Orleans the term "café" was always something of a misnomer. "Though their usual denomination is 'coffee-house,'" one visitor noted in 1833, "they have no earthly, whatever may be their spiritual, right to such a distinction; it is merely a 'nomme de profession.'" Many took on the designation "exchange," too, for the city's coffeehouses were as much locations to conduct business as to socialize. Men of commerce gathered there to read the commercial papers and shipping news, negotiate deals, and buy and sell goods. And they needed to eat while doing so.[2]

The most famous of the city's early coffeehouses was the Exchange Coffee House, which changed hands numerous times. It opened in 1806 in a two-story brick building on Conti Street and served as the city's first commercial exchange as well as a meeting place, a gambling house, and an auction hall where everything from ships and real estate to cotton and enslaved people was sold. In 1811 the Exchange moved from Conti Street to the corner of Chartres and St. Louis Streets, where it was operated by a man named Bernard Tremoulet. Over the next fifteen years the business changed hands several more times, passing from Tremoulet to Pierre Maspero to Harvey Elkins and finally, in 1825, to a man named John Hewlett, who promptly renamed it Hewlett's Exchange.[3]

The British-born Hewlett enlarged the building and transformed it into the finest barroom in New Orleans. Travelers were wowed by its "dazzling array of glasses and decanters." At the café's tables, men drank sangaree (port wine mixed with water, sugar, and spices) while reading newspapers or playing dominos, all the while continually puffing on their "eternal segars." They could enjoy a solid dinner there, too. The former owner Bernard Tremoulet had instituted an ordinary—that is, a set daily meal—that cost one dollar, and Hewlett expanded upon it, creating a dining room separate from the bar. Hewlett's Exchange was just one of many such establishments in New Orleans. One visitor estimated there were a hundred coffeehouses in operation in the city in the 1830s.[4]

Hotels were the other great progenitor of New Orleans's restaurants. For many years Bishop's Hotel, a five-story structure extending between Camp and Common Streets, was the city's largest. Henry Durell visited New Orleans in 1835, and his description of the midday dinner at Bishop's is virtually identical to those of Gadsby's in D.C., emphasizing the unbridled speed at which the meal was consumed. The gong rang promptly at 3:00 p.m., and the doors to the dining room were thrown open. The guests immediately began elbowing and shouldering their way to their chairs, and the air was quickly filled with "the clashing of knives and forks, and the other collaborators of mastication." It took mere minutes for most to bolt their dinners, then they turned their attention to more pressing activities, like sipping wine or brandy and talking commerce.[5]

New Orleans in the 1830s was a boom town. Serving as "the great emporium of trade," as Henry Durell put it, for the entire Mississippi Valley, it linked the American interior to the rest of the world via the Mississippi and the Gulf of Mexico. Strolling along the riverbanks, visitors could count forty or more steamboats at any time, and more than a thousand flatboats routinely lined the levees. Those flatboats brought flour, corn, meat, and barrels of Monongahela rye and Bourbon County corn whiskey from the Ohio River Valley along with bale after bale of cotton from the newly planted farmlands of the Lower Mississippi.

After the Louisiana Purchase in 1803, Americans began arriving in droves from other parts of the United States. The French-speaking residents tended to cluster in the city's older section, known today as the French Quarter, while English speakers moved into the new neighborhoods south of Canal Street. That area was originally known as Faubourg Sainte Marie but soon was being called the American Sector. (It's known drably today as the Central Business District.) The population more than doubled in the space of a decade, surging from forty-six thousand in 1830 to more than one hundred thousand in 1840, not counting tens of thousands of transient residents who streamed into the city during the busy season to sell cotton and produce, buy supplies, and spend their newly earned cash.[6]

As the city grew, the demand for accommodations far outstripped what Bishop's and other small hotels could provide. The old Hewlett's Exchange was likewise proving too small to handle the immense volume of social and commercial transactions. In March 1835 a group of English-speaking businessmen announced plans to construct a grand new hotel called the St. Charles in the heart of the American Sector. An alliance of French-speaking Creoles promptly announced their own plans to erect a rival hotel in the French Quarter, to be called the St. Louis.

The St. Charles was completed first. Built at a cost exceeding $800,000, it featured a large portico fronting St. Charles Street, with marble steps and six Corinthian columns. Guests stepped from the portico into a soaring gallery topped by a forty-six-foot-diameter dome, with marble staircases curving around each side. That gallery became the city's de facto cotton exchange, and guests could dine in the Gentleman's Ordinary on the first floor, the octagonal barroom in the basement, or, if there were women in the party, in the ladies' dining room.[7]

A traveler's description of the Gentleman's Ordinary in 1851 sounds not unlike Durell's portrait of dining at Bishop's Hotel, but on a much larger scale, for the St. Charles's dining hall could seat some three hundred guests. A diner entering the room at three o'clock in the afternoon was greeted by "a hum of voices and a clash of knives and forks and spoons." Frantic waiters were "darting here—darting there; provisions everywhere for an army, surely." Downstairs in the octagonal barroom, where "Emperor Appetite and King Alcohol hold their court," the fare included "gombo soup, and the ham, and the punch and julep" along with "soups, and plates of fish, and game, and beef and loaves of bread." That fare is essentially the same as that found in saloons and eating houses from Richmond to Louisville, with the very notable exception of the "gombo" or gumbo—perhaps the first of New Orleans's distinctive local specialties to become a commercial dining staple.[8]

The St. Louis Hotel got off to a rockier start than the St. Charles. Hampered by the financial panic of 1837, it opened in 1838 in a form somewhat reduced from the original plans, and it burned to the ground less than two years later. The company promptly rebuilt, and by 1842 the hotel was back open for business, competing head-to-head with the St. Charles. A four-story building with a dome modeled after the Capitol in Washington,

Exterior of the St. Louis Hotel, New Orleans, in the 1870s, from *Le Tour du Monde: Nouveau Journal des Voyages*, 1876.

the St. Louis was where the city's elite Creoles met to eat, drink, and conduct business. Like the St. Charles, it served as a cotton exchange and auction room, and starting at noon its domed rotunda echoed with the din of auctions conducted in English, French, and Spanish until 3:00 p.m.—whereupon the famished businessmen retired for a big midday dinner.[9]

Both the St. Charles and the St. Louis were known for their cuisine, though the identities of the cooks were not advertised. The management of the St. Charles noted only that its kitchens were "supplied with the best French talent." We do know the names of a few of the men who made those dining rooms famous, for the hotels served as something of a training ground for the city's professional cooks. The businesses they launched after setting out on their own were instrumental in shaping the early restaurant cuisine of the city. One of these early restaurateurs, Walter Van Rensselaer, was born in New York around 1817 and moved to New Orleans while still in his teens. He made a name for himself as the caterer of Bishop's Hotel, becoming so popular that he achieved one of the city's badges of culinary honor—being known solely by his first name, Walter. In 1839 the managers of the St. Charles Hotel hired Walter away from Bishop's, and he remained there for four years before opening his own establishment, which was variously called the Crescent Restaurant and the Crescent Coffee House.[10]

The most celebrated single name in New Orleans restaurants, though, was not Walter but Victor. Two French-born brothers, Victor and Jules Martin, arrived in Louisiana around 1838 and opened a restaurant at 15 Madison Street, near the old French market and a block north of the Place d'Armes, which was renamed Jackson Square in 1851. They called their restaurant Victor's, and they moved locations several times during the early years as the commercial districts of the Faubourg Ste. Marie grew, drawing them steadily "uptown." The city's unique geographic lingo follows the flow of the Mississippi River instead of the compass, so "uptown" means to the south and west toward Canal Street. In 1844 the Martins leased a "mouldy, old Spanish building," as one commentator put it, overlooking the Place d'Armes, where the restaurant became "a famous resort of the bon vivants of our city," who ranked a breakfast or dinner at Victor's equal only to dining at the magnificent St. Charles Hotel.[11]

Five years later the Martins moved again, to 27 Toulouse Street, where they took a much larger space that included private dining saloons and would be their home through the closing days of the Civil War. Few details have survived about the fare served at Victor's during its first two decades, but we do know that it was French in character and was widely regarded as the best in the city. When announcing the restaurant's move to Toulouse Street, the *Daily Picayune* commented: "Victor's restaurant is famed throughout this community as second to none in New Orleans." In 1877 a *Daily Picayune* writer looking back at the restaurant's legacy declared that during its heyday in the 1840s and 1850s, Victor's was widely regarded as the best French restaurant in the United States and that its reputation "far exceeded Delmonico's famous establishment in New York."[12]

The construction of the St. Louis Hotel displaced John Hewlett from Hewlett's Exchange, for the builders bought him out and knocked down the building housing his popular coffeehouse. But Hewlett was far from finished in New Orleans. He moved over into the American Sector, where he opened Hewlett's Restaurant inside Banks' Arcade on Magazine Street. There diners could eat beneath a high glass ceiling, served by a dozen African American waiters in formal attire. In 1843 Hewlett took over the building formerly occupied by Bishop's Hotel, which had struggled after the St. Charles and St. Louis opened, and renamed it Hewlett's Exchange. "Everything is new—but his wines," the *Daily Picayune* announced. Those were taken from his prized old stock from his prior establishments. Hewlett hired as his cook a young Frenchman named John Marie, but the specialties of the house—turtle soup, broiled pompano, boiled capons with oyster sauce, and roast beef—were more American than Gallic.[13]

Confectionery also boomed alongside the cotton market in New Orleans. As in Charleston, the establishment of icehouses led to a surge of ice cream and sorbets. By 1848 New Orleanians could satisfy a sweet tooth at the Jenny Lind Ice Cream Saloon on St. Charles, at James Durno's in the gardens at the Carrollton Hotel, or in Armory Hall's Fashionable Ice Cream Saloon. At Gabriel Julien at 30 Rue de Conde and M. Serreau at the corner of Chartres and St. Louis, they could indulge in bonbons, brandied and sugared fruits, chocolates, and flavored syrups. In 1850 M. V. Lefort, "The King of Confectioners, Late from Paris," set up shop on St. Charles Street just opposite the Charles Theatre, where he offered pastries, cakes, and candies along with "flower pictures, statues, fancy goods, fruits, toys, etc. in pure sugar, which have never before been seen in this city."[14]

➤✳︎ Pompano and Oysters

Like Charleston, where the wealthy summered at the beach on Sullivan's Island, New Orleans developed resorts of its own during this period. These clustered along Bayou St. John, which reached southward from Lake Pontchartrain toward what was then the northern edge of the city. In 1832 steam engine service commenced on the Pontchartrain Railroad, which ran along what is now Elysian Fields Avenue from the east side of the French Quarter north to Milneburg at Lake Pontchartrain. The engines' infamous exhaust left a thick layer of black soot on passengers' clothes when they exited at Milneburg, earning the line the nickname Smoky Mary, but the railroad transformed the former fishing village into a popular resort. At the mouth of Bayou St. John, the abandoned fortifications known as Old Spanish Fort soon became the site of summer resorts, too. By the 1840s, between the months of May and September, thousands of vacationers from the city would sit out on the verandas at restaurants and enjoy the cool breeze coming in off the lake while they ate seafood dinners.[15]

One of the first cooks to cater to the resort crowds was Miguel Brisolara. Italian-born and Spanish-trained, he immigrated to Louisiana, took up a career as a fisherman, and then was hired on as a cook at the Arcade, a Lake Pontchartrain summer house. Later he and his wife, herself an accomplished cook, opened the Phoenix House in Milneburg, which became known simply as Miguel's. The restaurant, described by one newspaper as "unpretentious," was noted for its fish preparations, which covered, as the *Daily Picayune* put it, "every variety of dish from plain fry to the most delicious of courtbouillons." Novelist William Makepeace Thackeray dined at the Phoenix House in the spring of 1853 "when the orchards were flushing over with peach-blossoms, and the sweet herbs came to flavor the juleps" and declared, somewhat ponderously, "we had a bouillabaisse than which a better was never eaten at Marseilles."[16]

Brisolara had plenty of competition out at the lake. In 1843 the French-born Lucien Boudro opened the Shell Road Hotel at the West End, near the terminus of the railroad from the city. Five years after it opened, the hotel was destroyed by fire, but the following year Boudro opened a new establishment called the Pavilion in a great wooden structure with large piazzas. Back east along the Chesapeake the prized fish was shad, but in the Gulf region it was pompano. Boudro grilled the delicate white fish over a charcoal fire and slow-simmered it in a rich court bouillon. Close by to Boudro, Charles L. Bell operated the Washington Hotel and Restaurant. Bell's newspaper advertisements promised as standard fare eels, flounder, soft-shell crabs, and croaker. In the fall of 1846 he was receiving daily "those delicious birds known as Caille de Laurier," or wood thrush, New Orleans's answer to sora (a prized game bird on the East Coast) or ortolan.[17]

In 1843 a correspondent for the *Daily Picayune* recounted what had become his annual tradition of a "first-frost dinner." On October 29, well after most of the lake resorts had closed for the season, the writer and five companions took a pleasant ride out of the city on the Pontchartrain railroad and sauntered about the grounds at Bell's at the Lake before settling in for a long dinner. It began with two or three oysters dressed in lemon juice followed by a bowl of Bell's turtle soup, which they declared to be "what a turtle soup should be," with delicate flavor but not so rich that it spoiled the appetite. The main courses included sheepshead fish "baked aux huitres"—that is, with oysters—"and slightly flavored with tomatoes," followed by tenderloin of trout, beefsteak aux truffes, broiled blue-wing teal, and an omelet soufflé, "the best we ever ate in New Orleans." The writer reserved his highest praise not for the seafood or meats but for the vegetables—delicious green peas, delicate potatoes, and a salad with crisp and tender leaves "rejoicing in the sweet, emollient admixture" of dressing. The meal closed as did any large dinner of the period with several rounds of "exotics"— cheese imported from Europe, "golden fruits ripened in foreign climes," and a selection of wines that included Madeira and a pale sherry that the party determined to be far and away the best of the lot.[18]

In the months when they weren't out at the lake eating seafood, diners in 1840s New Orleans were gripped by the same oyster mania that had snared the East Coast a decade before. St. Charles Street was transformed into the Crescent City's new oyster row, with saloons modeled after those found in Baltimore and New York. The pioneer of these establishments was a man named Anthony Holbrook. In September 1843 he opened Holbrook's Oyster Saloon at 96 St. Charles Street, adjoining Murphy's bar. It was enough of a novelty to gain the notice of the *Daily Picayune*'s editors, who observed that it was "undoubtedly the first establishment of the kind in the city." A seasonal business, Holbrook's operated through the winter and closed once the waters warmed in the spring. In September of 1844 Holbrook reopened for the season in a new location, a little further up the block at 46 St. Charles Street in a building adjoining the Crescent, Walter Van Rensselaer's saloon and eating house. Accordingly, Holbrook christened this iteration of his business the Crescent Oyster Saloon.[19]

That season, Holbrook had competition. Thomas Miles, formerly of Hewlett's Restaurant in Banks' Arcade, announced that he was opening an oyster house directly across from the St. Charles Hotel. Being next door to the American Bar-room, he naturally named it the American Oyster Saloon. Two years later Walter, the charismatic proprietor of the Crescent, decided to get in the game. He booted Holbrook out of the space at 46 St. Charles and launched an oyster saloon of his own. To manage the establishment, he hired J. F. Tepell, who had overseen Florence's House in New York City, though he assured his friends that "Walter will be constantly on hand to render the visits of his customers pleasant and agreeable, and to see that 'all goes right.'" The displaced Holbrook moved his oyster saloon back up the block to 97 St. Charles, advising his patrons that "those persons employed before as oyster-openers, waiters &c are still with him" and that there was "no connection with the former stand, at No. 46 St. Charles St." By this point, two more competitors—Antonio Caytano's Oyster House and Lazzaro Dancevich's Palo Alto Oyster Saloon—had opened nearby.[20]

As was the case in other culinary lines, oyster houses competed primarily on their ability to source high-quality provisions. "To procure the best,"

Advertisements for Walter's Grand Oyster Saloon and Holbrook's Oyster Saloon, in the *New Orleans Crescent*, November 11, 1848.

the *Daily Picayune* noted, "is, of course, the first and great duty of him who sells oysters. Next to this, is providing all accessories which can render a symposium of oyster eaters luxurious." Anthony Holbrook engaged directly with operators of boats that harvested oysters and clams "from the differ-ent parts of the Lakes," while Thomas Mills at the American Oyster Saloon promised to serve bivalves "fresh from the best beds of the Gulf and the Lakes." Walter Van Rensselaer ranged even farther, boasting a selection of oysters fresh from Cat Island, Grand Pass, Barataria, Biloxi, and Mobile, which he served with wines, Scotch ale, and Philadelphia porter.[21]

Surveying the different types of eating establishments in New Orleans—coffeehouses, hotels, seafood houses, oyster saloons—one can note that the commercial dining scene in the 1840s bears little resemblance to what we think of today as the city's classic repertoire. We find no red beans and rice, no poor boys, and no oysters Rockefeller. Soufflé potatoes and crawfish étouffée have yet to make an appearance on restaurant bills of fare. Those now-iconic dishes emerged considerably later, as the city's restaurants began to absorb more of the flavors and styles of local home kitchens and merge them with the evolving cuisine of French restaurant kitchens. At this stage New Orleans was a young, ambitious, and growing city, and it took its culinary cues from elsewhere—from the great restaurants of Paris, the oyster cellars of New York, and the eating houses of Baltimore and Washington. The one distinctively local dish that does appear on the city's menus—and a dish rarely seen in restaurants outside of New Orleans in this period—is gumbo, an African preparation brought to the city in the eighteenth century by its enslaved residents.[22]

Fans of New Orleans dining may notice that one name has so far been absent in this discussion of early Crescent City dining. Where is Antoine's, the famous French restaurant on St. Louis Street, the one that today has a lighted sign hanging above the front announcing "Founded in 1840" and, inside, an elaborate "1840 Room" with rich red walls and old portraits in oil? The answer is simple: Antoine's wasn't much of a player on the New Orleans dining scene in the 1840s. In fact, it wasn't a player at all, for Antoine Alciatore had yet to open the doors of his now-famous restaurant. We'll get to Antoine's in due time.

➤✳︎— Heading Upriver

Once diners left New Orleans and traveled into what was then called the "Old Southwest," their options became more spartan, for the region's cities were small and still emerging from their frontier roots. We can take as an example Louisville, Kentucky, which had just over four thousand residents in 1820. British surgeon Henry Bradshaw Fearon visited the city in 1818 and captured his experiences in *Sketches of America*. "Having been twice at Louisville," he wrote, "I boarded at both the hotels—Allen's [sic] Washington Hall and Gwathmey's Indian Queen. . . . These hotels are conducted differently than those with which you are acquainted." Both were large in scale, with Washington Hall hosting an average of 80 boarders per day and the Indian Queen 140. Most of the guests slept not in private quarters but in shared "sleeping rooms" with four to eight beds in each, and no curtains for privacy. During the day, guests occupied themselves by pacing up and down in the newspaper room and smoking cigars—a pastime, Fearon noted, that was "practiced by all without exception at all hours." Unlike in the common rooms of British hotels, most guests in Louisville kept to themselves and engaged only sparingly in conversation.[23]

Perhaps most strange to Fearon were the dining arrangements. Breakfast or supper could be had for one shilling eight pence, while the larger mid-day dinner cost two shillings three pence. (Fearon converted the prices to British currency for his English readers.) Guests wanting a bed along with all their meals paid six shillings nine pence. At seven thirty each morning a warning bell sounded to alert boarders to prepare for breakfast. A second bell rang promptly at eight, and the doors to the dining room were thrown open. "A general rush commences," Fearon noted, "and some activity, as well as dexterity, is necessary to obtain a seat at the table." That mad rush was similar to the practice at another Indian Queen—Brown's famed hotel in Washington—but the fare that awaited in Louisville was somewhat different. Breakfast consisted of "a profuse supply of fish, flesh, and fowl, which is consumed with a rapidity truly extraordinary; often before I had finished my first cup of tea, the room, which when I had commenced was crowded to suffocation, had become nearly empty." The scene was repeated six hours later for dinner: a warning bell sounded at half past one and the dinner bell at two, and the race to the table commenced. "A tea or what is here called supper" was served at six, and it usually consisted of the same dishes as breakfast.[24]

Louisville was strategically positioned at the fall line of the Ohio River, and it was just starting to emerge as a center of commerce. Its population eclipsed ten thousand residents by 1830 and doubled again over the next decade. Residents and travelers alike were given new dining options in the late 1820s when several coffeehouses and eating saloons opened their doors, though the dishes still leaned toward the simple and hearty instead of what one might call fine dining. A guest in 1830 could visit Henry Hyman's Western Coffee House and enjoy "pickled, stewed, or fried tripe; soused sturgeon; cold beef; cold ham; oyster soup; &c." The restaurant Our Friend's House promised "every delicacy of the season." Those delicacies, its ads revealed, consisted of beefsteaks, mutton chops, veal cutlets, beef soup, mutton soup, tripe, pig's feet, and eggs. Only one item on the menu—turtle soup—would likely have been considered a delicacy by East Coast epicures. That would change considerably in the decades to come.[25]

 CHAPTER 4

Fine Dining on the Brink
of the Civil War

The decade just before the Civil War was an era of elaborate public dining in the South. Building upon the foundation set by their predecessors and instructors, a new generation of cooks and caterers elevated commercial cooking to a high art—and they did it not in the kitchens of white-columned plantation houses but rather in the hotels and restaurants of the South's largest cities. Men like Henry Jakes in Baltimore and Nat Fuller in Charleston catered the banquets and feasts of their cities' most prominent social clubs and civic associations, earning fame and wealth in the process.

The broad repertoire of these cooks was hardly what we would consider traditional southern fare today. Jakes was famed for stewed terrapin, canvasback duck, ham, crab, oysters, and fritters. Nat Fuller's menus featured roasted meats and game, lobster salad, pâté de foie gras, oysters vol-au-vent, and green turtle soup, and he was particularly noted for his *pièces montées*—elaborate edible sculptures made of sugar paste, nougat, fruits, almonds, and meringues and shaped to represent ornate figures like a ship upon the ocean. A highly ritualized and standardized form of American fine dining emerged during the 1850s, and that mode was defined to a large extent by the South's cooks and provisioners. Increasingly, the region's great chefs were doing more than just replicating the culinary modes and fashions of Europe. They took the techniques and methods of the great kitchens of Europe and applied them to the ingredients to be found in the fields, woods, and waters of the American South. In the process, they created a new and distinctive culinary style.

This style was shaped by multiple economic, technological, and demographic trends that intersected during this period. The continued arrival of new immigrants who had formerly been professional cooks in Europe brought the latest techniques and fashions from Continental capitals and noble households. Advances in transportation and commerce not only expanded the palette of ingredients that chefs and caterers could incorporate into their repertoires but also delivered new customers in the form of commercial travelers. The latter brought with them not just cash and hearty appetites but a set of established tastes and preferred dishes that they wanted to enjoy when visiting distant cities.

This new commercial cuisine evolved within the context of a slaveholding society, but it did not emerge from rice and cotton plantations out in the countryside. Contrary to myths that would be promulgated in later depictions of antebellum southern cuisine, the driving force behind southern restaurants wasn't "old mammies" who cooked by mystical instinct under the tutelage of white mistresses. That cuisine instead was created by a remarkable cast of talented and determined men and women who navigated a complex web of social conventions and legal restrictions to achieve commercial success as professional cooks and caterers. Some even got rich doing it.

⇒)⚹(← A Grand Commercial Hotel

Though it had been America's wealthiest city during the colonial era, Charleston's economy sagged during the early nineteenth century. By the 1830s the city was at a turning point. The Lowcountry's best rice and cotton lands were already under cultivation, and the city's once-lucrative import and export trade was being siphoned away to the rising ports of Baltimore and New Orleans. Charleston's economy had long been dominated by planters and merchants, and those elites staunchly resisted the arrival of manufacturing and other industry. The city's leaders refused to allow steam-powered mills to be built within the city proper and forced railroad lines to terminate at the city boundary—decisions that proved significant barriers to economic growth. The old-money elites clashed frequently with the city's younger, more ambitious residents, many of whom had been born elsewhere. The latter wanted to transform Charleston into a regional distribution center, and they became the founders and directors of the city's nascent railroad companies, six of which were launched between 1820 and 1860. These railroads brought cotton in from the backcountry for export and helped breathe new life into the city's flagging economy, as the trade grew from thirty-five thousand bales in 1835 to almost two hundred thousand just a decade later.[1]

By the mid-1830s, local merchants concluded that Charleston needed a grand new hotel of its own, one that would, as one newspaper put it, "sustain the large drafts upon her hospitality, which the extension of our intercourse abroad, require at her hands." The Charleston Hotel Company was chartered in 1836, with Alexander Black as president and many prominent local businessmen as stockholders. They engaged Charles F. Reichardt, a German immigrant practicing in New York, as architect and Colonel Jacob Small of Baltimore as the lead contractor, and crews broke ground in February 1837. Just over one year and $200,000 in capital later, the Charleston Hotel opened on Meeting Street between Pinckney and Pearl (present-day Hayne Street), a block north of the Public Market. A four-story edifice in grand Greek Revival style, the building featured an iron-railed piazza on the second floor beneath a colonnade of fourteen Corinthian columns.[2]

As was standard practice at the time, the company owned the building itself but leased the premises to a proprietor who operated the business. The Charleston Hotel's operator was James H. Page, who formerly had managed the Exchange Hotel in Baltimore. From the start, he emphasized the hotel's "splendid saloon" and its haute cuisine. On March 26, just before the hotel opened to the public, the stockholders and their guests gathered for a convivial dinner staged by Mr. Page. Though the reporter for the *Charleston Courier* dutifully transcribed the numerous toasts delivered following the meal, he neglected to record the menu, noting only that "the viands were of the choicest description, the cooking worthy of the immortal Ude himself"—a reference to Louis-Eustache Ude, *chef de cuisine* at the fashionable Crockford's gentlemen's club in London and the most famous French chef operating in England. Mr. Page, the reporter added, "has thus proved himself a most successful and excellent caterer."[3]

It was a promising start, but Page's fortunes quickly turned. On the night of April 27, just a month after the hotel opened, a fire broke out behind a fruit store on King Street. Charleston was in the middle of a drought, and sparks borne by a dry wind quickly carried the fire to the north and east. Hampered by a lack of water, the fire companies were unable to control the blaze, and the city engineer was forced to blow up buildings to contain the conflagration. By morning some 560 buildings, including all of the Ansonborough neighborhood, were destroyed. The whole of the Public Market from Meeting to Queen Streets was decimated, and the city's new hotel lay in ruins. The hotel's stockholders voted unanimously to rebuild, however, and quickly solicited bids for builders to reconstruct the building

The Charleston Hotel in 1865. (Library of Congress,
Prints and Photographs Division)

on the old foundations using the original design. On October 15, 1839, the Charleston Hotel reopened for business, and the city finally had a modern commercial hotel.[4]

The Charleston Hotel was built during a period of great culinary ferment in the South. In city after city, new restaurants were upping the quality of their fare and eclipsing the plain meals previously found at coffeehouses and early hotels. The older Planter's Hotel had already renovated its kitchen, installing Dr. Nott's Patent Portable Baker and Boiler in 1834. The handiwork of Dr. Eliphalet Nott, the president of Union College in Schenectady, New York, and a noted orator, minister, and inventor, it was one of the first practical stoves that could burn hard anthracite coal. Just two years previously, in 1832, Nott had patented his stove, which featured a brick-lined firebox and rotary grate that helped the anthracite burn evenly by causing ashes to fall to the rear of the stove. Patent stoves like Nott's allowed cooks to boil, bake, and roast at the same time, and their coal fires were more consistent and easier to regulate than those with wood. Other inventors soon brought improvements to the market, and over the course of the next two decades coal-burning stoves would become the standard in commercial kitchens.[5]

Banquets and public dinners had been an essential part of the city's social life since colonial days, and they only increased in size and grandeur as the city grew and more charitable societies and social organizations were formed. In 1841 the Hibernian Society, which had long been holding meetings and banquets in various hotel dining rooms and coffeehouses, completed construction of Hibernian Hall, a grand two-story Greek Revival structure with a brick exterior clad in white-painted stucco and fronted by six tall Ionic columns and a footed pediment. The St. Cecilia Society, which had originally been established as a music society but quickly shed its artistic mission to serve a primarily social one, began holding its exclusive balls there, and Hibernian Hall became one of the main venues served by the city's caterers.[6]

Charleston gained another commercial hotel in 1840 when the Victoria opened on King Street. Visitors to Charleston, whether planters and their families coming in for the social season or commercial travelers engaged in the city's slowly but steadily increasing wholesale trade, could now choose to stay at the grand Charleston Hotel on Meeting Street, the new but smaller Victoria on King, or the older but still respected Planter's Hotel or Jones' Hotel. They could eat well in any of those establishments' dining rooms, or they could stroll over to King Street and visit one of several confectioneries for bonbons or pastries or, if the weather was warm, dishes of freshly made ice cream. Gentlemen seeking something a little more earthy could duck into a coffeehouse for an afternoon dinner or partake of shellfish and rare beefsteaks at their choice of a half dozen oyster houses. At the New-York Oyster House the roasted, stewed, or raw oysters they enjoyed would have been freshly harvested from local waters off Sullivan's Island.

⇒)∦⊂ From Pastry to Catering to Hotel Keeping

Jehu and Abigail Jones, Charleston's pioneering African American hoteliers, never regained their earlier success after their legal struggles in the wake of the Denmark Vesey revolt. Abigail Jones remained exiled in the north with her daughter and, despite her husband's appeals, was refused permission to return to South Carolina. She died in New York City in the early 1830s, and Jehu Jones died soon after in 1833. He left his entire estate to be divided equally among his stepdaughter, Ann Deas, and three of his sons. That estate included Jones' Hotel on Broad Street along with five enslaved persons: an elderly woman named Sylvia, a boy named Henry, a "young wench" named Martha, and her two small children, Allen and Lewis.[7]

In October 1833, Ann Deas and Eliza A. Johnson announced that they had purchased the Jones sons' share of the property and would resume keeping the Broad Street establishment as "a respectable boarding house." Ann Deas, left alone and nearly destitute in New York after her mother died, had returned to South Carolina illegally, but "many respectable ladies of Charleston" petitioned Governor George McDuffie on her behalf, testifying to her "exemplary good character," and he granted her a pardon in 1835. She and Johnson operated their boardinghouse or hotel (calling it by each name at different times) for more than a decade.[8]

Guests of Deas and Johnson during this period included the famous British actress Fanny Kemble and the Irish actor Tyrone Power, who occupied what he described as "comfortable summer quarters in an out-building." Like Sally Seymour and Eliza Lee, Eliza Johnson also served as an instructor of cooks for Charleston's slaveholders. An 1843 advertisement in the *Charleston Courier* offered for sale "A negro girl, aged about 20 years" who was "apprenticed to Mrs. Johnson, of Jones' hotel, to be learned meat and pastry cooking for 3 years." Three years later a similar ad offered a "likely colored girl, 20 years of age, brought up by Mrs. Johnson, (keeper of

Jones' Hotel)," noting that she was being sold because "her owner lives at the North and does not wish to keep her to work out."[9]

John and Eliza Lee, meanwhile, were looking to expand their operations. In 1835 they purchased Dewar House at 78 Tradd (now 92 Tradd), near the intersection with King Street. John Lee continued to work as a tailor for some time, while Eliza maintained her pastry business, selling pastries, cakes, and savory pies to the public from their home on Tradd Street. The couple began developing a thriving catering business, too. In 1838 John Lee was paid $34.75 on two occasions for providing "refreshments" for the German Fusiliers, a local militia unit, and the Citizens Guard. It is safe to assume that Eliza Lee and her team of enslaved and apprenticed cooks prepared the actual meals.[10]

The fortunes of the Lees rose while those of the Joneses fell, and the two families ended up trading places quite literally. The quality of accommodations at Jones' Hotel seems to have sagged under Mrs. Johnson's watch. When Fanny Kemble stayed there in 1838, just after fire had leveled the newly constructed Charleston Hotel, she called Jones's old establishment "the best at present in the city." That was faint praise at best, for she recorded being appalled by the rude manners of the hotel staff and the state of the furnishings, which she described as "old, and very infirm—the tables all peach with one or other leg,—the chairs are most of them minus one or two bars." Business declined further in the years that followed, and in 1846 the Protestant Episcopal Society brought suit against Johnson for the debts she owed the organization. The hotel was ordered sold by the master of chancery, and the building was bought for $7,900 by Edward Gamage.[11]

Gamage promptly turned around and rented the hotel to none other than John and Eliza Lee, who announced in September 1847 that they had made "many important improvements," including installing "neat and genteel" furniture and "bedding in complete order." For the moment, the Lees were riding high—the most in-demand caterers for the city's increasingly crowded slate of banquets, balls, weddings, and other public celebrations. But the couple's fortunes stumbled just a few years later as they, too, fell victim to what would prove one of the biggest risks to the South's culinary entrepreneurs: debt. Eliza Lee's kitchen remained the training ground for many of the Lowcountry's best cooks, both in commercial settings and in private households, but she and John seem to have overextended their credit. In 1850 the Lees put Jones' Hotel up for sale along with their entire stock of furniture, bedding, glassware, china, and kitchen utensils. The following year, James Paine engaged John Lee for the summer season to oversee the kitchens at the Moultrie House, a newly opened hotel on Sullivan's Island. Lee's health was failing, though, and he died before the year was out.[12]

To satisfy her late husband's debts, Eliza Lee ended up selling much of the property that had been placed in trust for her. Her brother William Seymour, who had helped run Jones' Hotel, departed for Georgia, where he signed on to oversee the kitchen at a resort called Madison Springs. Now living independently as a free woman of color, Eliza Lee was required by law to have a white trustee supervise her affairs, and in 1853 the wealthy Charleston merchant Henry Gourdin was appointed to that role. Eliza Lee got back on her feet the best she could. By 1856, styling herself "Eliza Lee, Pastry Cook," she was operating out of her residence at 18 Beaufain Street, where she sold cakes, pies, jellies, and other pastries, hosted private parties, and served a daily lunch that included oysters.[13]

Eliza Lee still catered for many of her old clients, including the Charleston Ancient Artillery Society and the South Carolina Jockey Club, but finances were a constant struggle. In 1856 she wrote to Gourdin and entreated him to help her with repairs on one of the rental houses she owned. "I have expended every dollar in my possession and even now the repairs are not completed," she wrote, estimating she needed $350 more to complete the work. "I am in a very bad way and unable to do any thing for the want of means."[14]

As Lee struggled, new figures were appearing on Charleston's commercial dining scene. Recent European immigrants, including confectioners Rémy and Théonie Mignot, were already playing an influential role in the city's culinary life, and these newcomers' ties to family and friends back in Europe drew even more immigrants to the city. The influx surged after 1848, when a wave of revolutions destabilized Europe amid rising nationalism and a pent-up demand for democratic reforms. The monarchy in France collapsed in February, and revolutionary fervor spread quickly across the Continent, including in the Austrian Empire, Italy, Denmark, and the various Germanic states. Few Germans and Austrians had been involved in southern culinary businesses before 1848, but afterward they began to play increasingly prominent roles. That same year, a potato blight struck Ireland, prompting many Irish to look overseas for better prospects, too.

This influx of immigrants had an outsized influence on the commercial dining culture in the South, for many of those seeking greener pastures in America had previously made their living serving European nobility and elites. Their influence was fundamentally French, though many of the immigrants were not themselves from France. They had been born in Italy, Germany, Greece, the Netherlands, Switzerland, and elsewhere, but all had been steeped in formal French culinary techniques. Many had gone to Paris for culinary training and then cooked in the homes of European nobility before being displaced by the disturbances of 1848.

One such displaced cook was Adolphus Johannes Rutjes, who had family connections to Rémy and Théonie Mignot. Born in the Netherlands, Rutjes was a confectioner, and his brother, T. A. Rutjes, was a musician. Both had moved to Paris to pursue their fortunes, arriving, in a stroke of poor timing, just months before the 1848 revolution. T. A. Rutjes decided to try his luck next in Charleston, announcing in February 1848 that he had arrived in the city and, in addition to performing piano concerts at Hibernian Hall, was "happy to give instructions on the Piano Forte." Soon after, he was joined in the city by his brother Adolphus Johannes, who in his newly adopted country was frequently called Adolph John.[15]

A few months after the Rutjes brothers arrived, Rémy Mignot died, leaving Théonie a widow. In January 1850 she and Adolph Rutjes married, and he joined his bride in her pastry and candy business on King Street, which they renamed the Cheap Confectionery. To his wife's repertoire of ice cream and frozen confections, Rutjes added fancy cakes, "many of them his own, or the latest inventions of Paris." He also introduced Charleston to a long-running French passion, "pyramids"—displays of cream puffs, fruits, or similar treats arranged into large pyramids, a legacy of the Egyptomania that had enthralled Paris in the wake of Napoleon's conquest of Egypt.

In 1851 Adolph and Théonie Rutjes purchased the property adjacent to their shop and launched a "ladies restaurant"—that is, a dining room reserved for women dining alone or in mixed-gender parties. The restaurant stayed open until 11:00 p.m. to accommodate guests returning from the theatre, and the bill of fare blended American favorites with a few French flourishes. These included *filet de boeuf, galantine de capon*, and *ris de veau piqué aux petits pois verts* (spiced sweetbreads with green peas), served alongside ham and eggs, wild ducks, woodcocks, and "oysters of every description." In the spring of 1852 the Rutjeses converted the empty lot between their confectionery and their restaurant into the Mount Vernon Ice Cream Garden, which they operated during the summer seasons. The garden was fitted out with gas lighting so that on warm evenings Charlestonians could enjoy their ice cream well into the night, often accompanied by the music of the German Brass Band.[16]

Adolph John Rutjes,

174 KING STREET, CHARLESTON, S. C.

WHOLSALE AND RETAIL

CONFECTIONER,

Importer and Dealer in

German and French

TOYS,

Baskets, Fire-Works, &c.

SYRUPS

AND

CORDIALS,

of all kinds constantly on hand.

DINNERS, BALLS,

Parties and Suppers

served on the most reasonable terms and at the shortest notice.

Orders from the Country thankfully received and promptly attended to.

Advertisement for Adolph John Rutjes's confectionery store, in *Directory of the City of Charleston, for the Year 1852* (Charleston, S.C.: J. H. Bagget, 1851).

This new influx of European confectionery helped diversify the city's banquet and restaurant menus. Those menus were also being expanded by the increased availability and variety of venison, game birds, and seafood, the result of a growing national trade enabled by advances in transportation. Early railroads had connected the interior to eastern ports, but their lines were built in a patchwork fashion, with many short, independent stretches that didn't connect with each other. In 1840 there was no way to ship a package directly from New York City to Detroit, for no single carrier traveled between the two cities. "Express shipping" companies arose to address this problem, functioning as agents who would coordinate and oversee shipments across a complex series of hops.

One of the pioneers of express service was Henry Wells, who later founded the firm Wells Fargo. In 1841 he partnered with George Pomeroy to create the Albany & Buffalo Express. In the early years, Wells carried the parcels himself in a carpetbag and trunk, and his route from Albany to Buffalo was anything but direct. He first took a train from Albany to Auburn, New York, then made a twenty-five-mile stagecoach ride to Geneva, where he caught the still-unfinished Auburn & Rochester Railroad to Rochester. In Rochester he switched to the Tonawanda Railroad, took their cars to Batavia, and made the final forty-mile leg to Buffalo via yet another stagecoach. From there his parcels could be sent on to Detroit and other western cities by steamboat. That journey—about three hundred miles as the crow flies—took Wells three full days in 1841, but that time shrunk as more railroad lines were completed.[17]

Some of the earliest commodities to be shipped westbound by express freight were perishable luxury foods that were previously unavailable in the West—shad, lobsters, fruit, and oysters. For the return trip east, agents brought back to New York something the western states had in great abundance: wild game. These railroad and express networks in New York State were a thousand miles away from Charleston, but the innovations had a direct impact on the southern city's menus. Much of the game carried over the rails from western prairies to Manhattan next made its way southward, for New York was developing into the central hub of a national game trade.

An early "steam packet" service between New York and Charleston, which carried passengers and freight on new side-wheeled steamships instead of slower sailing ships, had been established in the mid-1830s, but it was abandoned after a series of disasters, most notably the death of around a hundred persons when the *Home* sank off Cape Hatteras in 1837. Almost a

The *Southerner* began steam packet service between Charleston and New York in 1846, providing the city access to New York's large game market. (Library of Congress, Prints and Photographs Division)

decade later, a group of Charleston businessmen incorporated a new company to resume the service. The company's *Southerner* was the first American steamship designed specifically for ocean travel. It departed New York on its maiden voyage on September 12, 1846, arriving in Charleston a mere fifty-seven hours later. The *Southerner* and its sister ship, predictably named the *Northerner*, were soon operating on a regular schedule between the two cities, one ship leaving each port each week. They routinely made the trip in under sixty hours—roughly half the time of a sailing ship.[18]

On September 15, Thomas E. Baker and William Beard of the Exchange Cafe advertised that they had "just received from New York, per Steamer Southerner" a shipment that included fresh New York oysters, codfish, lobsters, halibut, English snipes, woodcocks, and rails. Baker and Beard soon were supplying Charleston's families with "all the delicacies of the New York market," including wild pigeon, pheasant, canvasback duck, eels, and smelts.[19]

The combination of express rail and steam packets now directly connected Charleston to the lush fields of Wisconsin and Michigan, and the game trade boomed in the 1850s. Baker and Beard dissolved their partnership in October 1848, but Baker continued on solo. In the fall of 1852, W. C. Rising, operating out of the Pavilion Hotel, also began selling game received via the New York steamers. But the most unlikely entrant into this new market—a shipping network spanning thousands of miles and supplying the most elegant tables in Charleston with animals shot on the western prairies just days before—was not a wealthy Charleston merchant with deep commercial connections, nor an established restaurateur. His name was Nathaniel Fuller, more commonly shortened to Nat, and he was one of the many enslaved African American cooks who had been trained by Eliza Seymour Lee.

Fuller was born in 1812 on a plantation in St. Andrews Parish, across the Ashley River from Charleston. Around the time he reached adulthood, he was purchased by Colonel Daniel Stevens, who in turn sold him to a man named Robert Dorrill. Those two slaveholders fell into a dispute over the terms of the sale, and the resulting lawsuit ended with Fuller's being put up for public auction in 1827. He was purchased by William C. Gatewood, an ambitious young man from Virginia who had just arrived in Charleston as the agent of a lottery company.[20]

Gatewood was not a typical Charleston slaveholder. Entrepreneurial and socially ambitious, he became involved in railways and other transport ventures, and he also purchased the Charleston Theater. As his business interests prospered, his social capital rose. He was invited to join the 17th Regiment of the Sumter Guards, one of the city's elite militia units, as well as the Grand Lodge of the Freemasons. In 1843 he built a large house on Legare Street, and Nat Fuller was one of the ten adult slaves whom Gatewood owned by 1850. Shortly after purchasing Fuller, Gatewood apprenticed him to Eliza Lee to learn the art of cookery. After Fuller finished his years of tutelage, he spent a decade overseeing the kitchen in Gatewood's Charleston town home. In the late 1840s Fuller married Diana Stobel, one of Eliza Lee's enslaved pastry cooks, and together they set out to make a career for themselves not as domestic servants but as culinary entrepreneurs.[21]

Around 1852 Fuller reached an arrangement with Gatewood to live separately and operate his own business selling game. The details of this arrangement are not known, but we can assume that Fuller shared some portion of the proceeds with his owner. Perhaps not coincidentally, Gatewood was one of the ten founding partners of the Charleston and New York Steam Packets company, and his connections may have helped Fuller establish relationships in the broad, geographically dispersed network of suppliers.[22]

Initially, Fuller sold his game from a stall in the Public Market, a series of long, low buildings stretching from Market Hall on Meeting Street all the way to the waterfront on East Bay. That same stretch is occupied today by sellers of sweetgrass baskets and tourist knickknacks, but in the nineteenth century the market's sheds housed the meat, vegetable, and fish vendors who supplied the city's homes with most of their food. In January 1854, Fuller advertised that he had just received from New York and Baltimore "fine turkeys, pheasants, grouse and capons," which he would sell in the market from seven to ten in the morning. His selection in later months included venison and wild ducks, including the prized canvasbacks, as well as New York mutton and several lots of green sea turtles. In March 1856 Fuller offered fresh Atlantic salmon, which he billed as "the first in the market this season."[23]

Fuller must have maintained a good relationship with his former teacher Eliza Lee, for in 1855 he began advertising his game for sale at 78 Tradd, the site of Lee's pastry shop and catering business. By the fall he had secured his own place at 68 King Street, likely with the assistance of William Gatewood, since an enslaved man could neither buy nor lease property. At 68 King, Fuller built an icehouse that served as cold storage for his game, and the location became the base of operations for a new line of business: catering. That December, Fuller staged the anniversary dinner for the South Carolina Medical Society, hosting it at T. C. Hubbell's auction hall at 33 Broad Street. It is probable, as David Shields has surmised, that Fuller, being newly established in the business, borrowed the necessary equipment—which would have included china, flatware, serving dishes and utensils, tables, and linens—from Eliza Lee.[24]

Fuller soon was competing with his former teacher and also with A. J. Rutjes to furnish the city's grandest banquets and dinners. In 1857, with five years of the game business under his belt and two in the catering trade, Nat Fuller was ready to take his next big step. "Nat's fame is already pretty well extended," he announced in the third person in a *Charleston Courier* advertisement, "but encouraged by past favors, he is not resting on his laurels." Fuller had just imported from Europe "a supply of china-ware (sufficient for the use of the largest balls) and table ornaments, such as candelabras (plated and gilded), fancy skewers, punch bowls, &c., &c." He had amassed a large supply of silverware, too, which he offered to rent to families hosting parties so they wouldn't have to borrow forks and spoons from the neighbors, and he continued to keep on hand a large stock of New York game and vegetables in his icehouse. Nat Fuller was ready to cater the largest and most elaborate functions "amply and elegantly."[25]

Over the next several years, Fuller secured a list of clients that included the city's most prestigious clubs, societies, and militia companies. He supplied the banquets and dinners for the St. Cecilia Society, the Jockey Club, the Aetna Fire Engine Company, the Washington Light Infantry, and the Charleston Light Dragoons. In his private rooms on King Street he hosted dinner meetings for the Society of the Cincinnati, the Chamber of Commerce, and the Medical Society. His wife, Diana, appears to have been an active partner in the business, managing the pastry side of the operation. In 1859 she began running her own advertisements under the signature "Diana Fuller, Pastry Chef," offering made-to-order mince pies, tarts, puddings, and "cakes of every description" from their storefront at 68 King Street.[26]

In January 1856 the caterer and confectioner A. J. Rutjes, perhaps in response to Fuller's horning in on his catering turf, decided to try his hand at the game business. Rutjes didn't get very far before running into financial troubles. As he would several more times over the course of his career, Rutjes appears to have gotten overextended in debt—likely from investing in real estate or buying too many supplies on credit—and he ended up selling his King Street restaurant and equipment. His wife Théonie left Charleston in September and sailed to Amsterdam, but Rutjes stayed on in the city for several more months, supplying confectionery for a few catered balls and dinners. In April 1857 he too boarded a steamer bound for Europe, but within a year the Rutjeses were back in Charleston. In May 1858 A. J. Rutjes was selling cigars at a stand on State Street, and before the end of the year the couple had resumed occupancy of their old digs on King Street and relaunched the Mount Vernon Restaurant and Shops.[27]

The store once again featured French toys, games, and dolls along with a range of cakes, candies, and confections. On the cooking front, Rutjes set his sights on the same growing market from which Nat Fuller and Eliza Lee earned their income. Rutjes had fitted up a "splendid hall," he announced, "for the purpose of furnishing suppers and dinners to Military and Fire Companies, Societies, Clubs, &c." But A. J. Rutjes abruptly left Charleston again in June 1860, authorizing his wife Théonie to act as his attorney in his absence. His departure was announced as temporary and attributed to his declining health, but the actual cause was likely the caterer's ongoing financial woes. Just a few weeks after Rutjes announced he was leaving town, the three-story brick building on King Street housing his Mount Vernon establishment was auctioned off to satisfy a lawsuit brought by Robert Minniss. Additional suits for unpaid debts were brought against Rutjes after he left the state. Where he departed for is unknown.[28]

Théonie Rutjes remained in Charleston, and she promptly leased back part of their old building and kept the confectionery business running, though now under her own name, "T. M. Rutjes." She specialized in pies, cakes, and a range of confectionery, and she advertised that, having on staff "an experienced French cook," she could host suppers or dinners for up to fifty persons. When the holidays arrived in December, Madame Rutjes was once again selling bonbon boxes and French toys for Christmas and New Year's gifts.[29]

Other new faces appeared on Charleston's culinary scene in the 1850s. Nat Fuller took on as an apprentice or protégé a young man named Thomas R. Tully, a free person of color born in 1827 on Edisto Island, just down the coast from Charleston. While still a boy, Tully made his way to Charleston, where, as one later account put it, "he picked up such an education as could be obtained by free persons of color." By 1850, at the age of twenty-two, he was making a living as a baker, and he next learned the art of catering working for Nat Fuller, whose star was still on the rise.[30]

Toward the end of the 1850s, Tully left his mentor and struck out on his own. In 1859 he partnered with Martha Vanderhorst, a free African American pastry chef, to open Vanderhorst & Tully's on King Street, a combination confectionery and catering hall where they offered rooms "for the accommodation of gentlemen's suppers, dinners, meetings, &c.," and from which they would cater weddings and public dinners. Cakes and tarts were baked fresh for the public every morning.[31]

All this time, Nat Fuller's business had been growing. In 1860 he reached an unusual arrangement with his owner, William C. Gatewood, who purchased a building on his behalf. As an enslaved man, Fuller was not "sui juris," meaning he did not enjoy the full rights of citizenship and could not own property. Fuller gave $1,000 in cash to Gatewood, who, acting as Fuller's trustee, used it to make the initial installment on a lot and building on Church Street. Gatewood secured four loans of $1,000 each for the remainder of the purchase price, which Fuller agreed to pay off with interest.[32]

Located on the northwest corner of Church Street and St. Michael's Alley, the four-story building was a fitting site for Fuller to establish a retail store and restaurant, and it also served as the base for catering operations.

The former location of Nat Fuller's Bachelor's Retreat, northwest corner of Church Street and St. Michael's Alley, Charleston. (Photograph by the author)

Two large rooms on the ground floor housed Fuller's pastry and game shops, while the two floors above were split into several large rooms for private parties and meetings. A finished attic at the top of the building was presumably used for storage and work space. Behind the main building was a yard with a large cistern, a well, and a two-story kitchen building that had cooking and washrooms on the first floor and four sleeping apartments for Fuller's live-in employees. As had Eliza Lee and Eliza Johnson, Nat Fuller staffed his kitchen at least in part with enslaved workers who had been sent to be apprenticed in the culinary arts. One of these men, a twenty-year-old named John, ran away in 1862, and his owner offered a fifty-dollar reward for his return, noting that John "has been apprenticed to Nat Fuller, in Charleston, for two years."[33]

On October 8, 1860, Nat Fuller announced to the city that his new establishment was open for business, including "neat and comfortable Chambers, Parlors, and Sitting Rooms, Dinner and Supper Halls" that could accommodate up to a hundred guests. Fresh pastries and cakes were available each day in the ground-floor shops, and his kitchens were prepared to furnish weddings, dinners, balls, and parties. Though initially he called his business simply Nat Fuller's House, he soon bestowed upon it the grander name Bachelor's Retreat. By December the Charleston Chamber of Commerce had made Fuller's the home of its regular meetings. The Medical Society of South Carolina, the Society of the Cincinnati, and the Fellowship Society all held meetings there. Though still enslaved, Nat Fuller had established himself as the city's leading caterer and restaurateur. He was an entrepreneur on the rise.[34]

On the culinary front, Fuller was performing at the top of the caterer's art. David Shields has performed the painstaking work of combing through old newspaper accounts of Charleston banquets and collating the bills of fare that can be found there to reconstruct Nat Fuller's repertoire. And what a repertoire it is. His full reach was perhaps best captured in the menu for the Jubilee of Southern Union dinner in May 1857. The event celebrated the completion of the Memphis and Charleston Railroad, which created the first uninterrupted route from the Atlantic to the Mississippi River. Guests from both cities, six hundred in total, dined at six long parallel tables running the length of Charleston's Military Hall, with a head table running crosswise at one end. The walls were lined with barrels of rice and bales of cotton, and a live palmetto tree served as the centerpiece.

Fuller's menu for the occasion is notable for its sheer variety, with ingredients sourced from the entire East Coast and prepared in a blend of classic English and French techniques—features that had emerged as the primary southern fine dining mode. Turtle featured prominently in the form of green turtle soup in the opening course and turtle steaks and fins in Madeira sauce among the meats. The fish course included boiled salmon, cod, and bass along with fried whiting and halibut. French flourishes—fricandeau of veal, capons stuffed with truffles—mingled with American wild turkey, duck, and venison. Fuller's far-reaching network of suppliers was on full display in plates of Westphalia ham, Philadelphia asparagus, and New York goose and corned beef. Most elaborate was the parade of pastry and confectionery staged for the dessert courses. These totaled more than two dozen items, including exotic fruits, macaroons, charlotte russe, blancmange, and nougat cornucopias and baskets filled with glacé fruit. The crowning creation was a splendid *pièce montée*, a grand ornament in sugar paste of "a train of cars crossing the bridge from Memphis to Charleston," accompanied by a pyramid of rice barrels and cotton bales molded from nougat. The *Charleston Mercury* characterized the dinner as "of the sumptuous character," adding that it "did great credit to the caterer, Nat Fuller." That seems something of an understatement.[35]

⇒)⋇– Up in Richmond

For Nat Fuller to achieve success as a caterer and restaurateur while being enslaved was a remarkable feat, but he was not the only person to pull it off. Other southern cities also witnessed the emergence of enslaved persons as their leading caterers on the eve of the Civil War. Richmond, Virginia, in fact, saw the emergence of three. As had been the case in Charleston, they entered a thriving commercial dining market in which free persons of color and European immigrants played an instrumental role.

After Virginia moved its capital from Williamsburg to Richmond in 1779, the city had steadily evolved into a transportation hub and the commercial and manufacturing center for most of the state. Virginia's economy, long dominated by tobacco, was starting to diversify, and wheat and corn flowed into Richmond from the surrounding countryside. Five railroad lines converged in the city, and it was the terminus of the James River and Kanawha Canal, which connected Richmond with the rich grain-growing regions to the west. Thanks to its position on the fall line of the James River, a valuable source of water power, the city soon developed one of the largest milling industries in the United States, converting the wheat and corn received from the west into flour and meal. The mills supported a range of subsidiary trades, like foundries to make milling equipment, cooperages to produce barrels, and tanneries to process leather for wagon harnesses. Richmond was also home to the Tredegar Iron Works, the largest foundry in the South, which produced railroad engines, railroad spikes, and any number of other iron products.

By the 1850s, a growing Richmond was ringed by new suburbs. Tobacco still remained an essential part of Virginia's economy, and as production shifted from the Tidewater region to the Tobacco Belt of the Piedmont, more than fifty factories sprang up in Richmond to process raw leaf into chewing tobacco and cigars. Over the course of the 1850s, the number of workers employed in the city's tobacco factories rose to over thirty-four hundred. The vast majority of these were enslaved, some owned by the factory companies but many more hired out to the factories by their owners.[36]

Richmond was a magnet for inbound migrants, too, many of them arriving from the surrounding countryside as well as from the counties further east in the Tidewater. The city's population grew from 20,153 in 1840 to 27,570 in 1850. By 1860 it stood at 37,910. In addition, Richmond had many transient residents. Country merchants arrived regularly to restock at the city's dry goods wholesalers, and farmers would visit twice a year to sell crops to commission merchants and purchase supplies for the upcoming season—and to stay in the city's growing hotels and eat and drink in its restaurants and saloons.

As was the case in Charleston, the leading caterer in Richmond before the Civil War was a person of color. Thomas Griffin was born in Williamsburg around 1791 and came to Richmond sometime in the early part of the nineteenth century. By 1850 he had purchased his freedom and was operating the American Saloon on Main Street. He also created an outpost called Griffin's Spring near Rocketts Landing on the James River, about two miles southeast of the city, where he had a house with a kitchen where he prepared dinners for local clubs and social organizations. Griffin raised pigs and fowls at the spring, which he presumably served at outdoor barbecues as well as in town at the American Saloon.[37]

Griffin's Spring was a favorite haunt of Richmond's elite militia companies, including the Richmond Blues, the Light Dragoons, and the Eagle Infantry. These troops regularly held celebratory dinners there as well as target shooting competitions and other entertainments. The Masonic Fraternity and the students of the Sunday School at Trinity Church often held picnics there. In June 1855 a group of young church scholars made the two-mile trip in William Wright's new omnibus *Reliance*, drawn by six sorrel horses and able to hold thirty passengers.[38]

Thomas Griffin's repertoire was broad, encompassing fancy banquet fare as well as more everyday dishes. The advertisements for the American Saloon regularly offered green turtle soup, terrapin, and oysters—the foundations of saloon dining in southern cities—and plenty of game birds, too, including canvasback ducks, partridges, and woodcocks. An 1853 ad promised veal cutlets, roast beef, roast duck, and roast turkey for dinner each day. Served alongside these was a long list of less elegant fare, like ham and cabbage, corned beef and turnips, fried fish, and fried tripe. Perhaps most interesting were Griffin's barbecued shoat, barbecued squirrel, and stewed squirrel.[39]

As they still do today, oyster connoisseurs in Griffin's era prized the distinct flavors that the bivalves absorb from the minerals in the particular waters in which they are raised. Griffin received regular shipments from Norfolk, and it was his practice to list their source rivers, which included the York, the Severn, and the Back, all estuarial rivers on the Chesapeake Bay. When he received a particularly large supply, as he did in February 1857 when fifty gallons of "fine York River oysters" arrived, Griffin would pickle the leftovers and keep them for sale at his bar. He featured other products of the Chesapeake, too, announcing in June 1855 that he had made arrangements to receive fresh soft-shell crabs by express shipment every other day, and he would be serving them "in every style" for $1.25 a dozen.[40]

To prosper in the culinary trade in a slaveholding society, an African American had to be determined and strong-willed. Not surprisingly, many of those who achieved success, including Tom Griffin, were also quite hot-tempered, a characteristic that sometimes got them into trouble with whites who expected deference. In April 1854 the *Richmond Dispatch* reported that Tom Griffin—now in his sixties—had been "soundly drubbed" a few days before "for giving impertinence to some gentlemen who had been patronizing his house." Several months later Griffin got into another quarrel with a white man, this time over a stolen watch. It all started when Griffin, while preparing a club dinner at his spring, removed his silver watch and hung it up in the kitchen. Jesse Josephs, a Portuguese-born man who worked for Griffin and lived in the house at the spring, found the watch and pawned it for five dollars. It ended up in the possession of a white man named Nathaniel W. Thompson, and when Griffin confronted Thompson about it, Thompson flew into a rage. He declared that Griffin was "a d——n n—— son of a b——h." Griffin shot right back, saying that if Thompson "was up town he should not have called him a n—— with impunity."

Thompson had Griffin arrested on the charge of "abuse and insolence to a white man." The caterer was brought before the mayor for a hearing, but the evidence was conflicting and the charge was dismissed. For stealing and pawning his employer's watch, Jesse Josephs was let off with a warning. He must have smoothed things over with Tom Griffin, for he was still living in the house at Griffin's Spring in December.[41]

Though Griffin was the favorite caterer for Richmond's elite, he was by no means their only option. R. W. Allen of the Alhambra offered fare very similar to Griffin's, including fresh venison, ducks, terrapin, and oysters. Born in New York, Allen spent his early years working in restaurants first in New York City and then in Washington, D.C. He moved south to Richmond in 1844 at the age of thirty-three and opened the Alhambra on 14th Street, five doors down from Main Street and on the approach to Mayo's Bridge over the James River. Allen's daily offering was generally heartier and plainer than what one might find at elegant catered banquets. An 1845 list of the Alhambra's "principal dishes" for breakfast includes beef and pork steaks, ham and eggs, fried liver, and venison. For dinners, roasted meats of all varieties led the bill, along with beef and mutton soups, boiled ham, and five preparations of oysters. Allen advertised that at his establishment "country people"—that is, planters and merchants visiting from the surrounding counties—"can obtain Breakfast, Dinner, or Supper, at ten minutes notice."[42]

For reasons unknown, R. W. Allen sold the Alhambra sometime around 1850, but in January 1852 he opened a new establishment called the Arbour at the corner of Main and 12th Streets. There he promised to "furnish elegant oyster and game suppers in the same style as he did while proprietor of the Alhambra for six years." A few months later he introduced Richmonders to a new service model, announcing that he had added "an eating room with a steam table" and would open "upon the New York Plan"—what we today might call a cafeteria model. In the 1850s that meant a broad menu where each item was priced separately, cooked in advance, and held on steam tables, ready to be served whenever a customer ordered. Declaring that "Business Men can get a snack without being detained a moment," Allen offered a selection of sixteen dishes that included fried and stewed oysters, beefsteak, lamb chops, fricassee chicken, and ham and eggs for 9 cents along with pickled oysters, pigs' feet, and "domestic pie" for 4 cents. Over the next two years he added two billiard tables and a bowling saloon to attract more patrons, and in 1854 he established his own "pleasure retreat in the country, a short distance from the corporate limits" and offered to host dinners for military companies and clubs—and presumably to compete with Thomas Griffin.[43]

Not long after, a new figure emerged to challenge Griffin and Allen for the title of Richmond's top caterer. A native of Greece, Spiro Zetelle was born to Italian parents on the island of Corfu around 1815. He studied cookery in France and became a chef first for a wealthy French family and then for the French ambassador to Athens. Zetelle came to the United

States sometime in the late 1840s, likely fleeing the same revolutionary tur-moil that drove so many other cooks to America. He wound up in Virginia, where he took posts in various hotel kitchens, including at the Norvell House in Lynchburg. In the autumn of 1856 this "Napoleon of cooks" was hired to take over the kitchen at the newly opened Ballard House in Richmond. In newspaper ads announcing the move, the hotel's manager laid it on thick, declaring Zetelle to be "so famous among epicures of the present generation, as perfectly *au fait* in all matters of the *cuisine*."[44]

The Ballard House and its sister establishment, the Exchange Hotel, were both operated by John P. Ballard. A native of Albemarle County, Virginia, Ballard progressed from running a country store to operating a hotel in Palmyra, then moved to Richmond in 1847 to take over the Powhatan

The Ballard House (left) and Exchange Hotel, connected by a bridge over Franklin Street, in the late 1860s. (Library of Congress, Prints and Photographs Division)

Complimentary Dinner
BILL OF FARE.

SOUP.
OYSTER.

FISH.
Boiled Sea-Bass, Anchovy Sauce   Rock, Egg Sauce

OYSTERS.
Fried   Escaloped   Pickled and Raw

Cold Ornamented Dishes.
Westphalia Ham   Round of Beef spiced
Saddle Mutton South-Down   Turkey

BOILED.
Ham and Cabbage   Corned Beef and Turnips
Pullet, Egg sauce,   Buffalo Tongue
Leg of Mutton, Caper sauce

ROAST.
Sirloin Beef, Yorkshire Pudding   Turkey, Oyster sauce
Saddle of Mutton, Cranberry sauce   Roaster, Apple sauce
Fillet of Veal Stuffed   Ham, Champagne sauce

GAME—Saddle of Venison with Jelly
Canvas Back Duck, Currant Jelly Sauce

VEGETABLES.
Irish Potatoes   Sweet Potatoes   Celery   Boiled Onions
Boiled Rice   Hominy   Salsifi   Beets

Spainsh Olives   Assorted Pickles

PASTRY.
Prune Pie   Green Apple Pie   Mulberry Pie
Cranberry Tarts   Peach Puffs

Ornamental Confectionery.
Grotto of Macaroons with Silver Web
Castle of Italien Maringo with Golden Web
Cocoanut Pyramid garnished with French Kisses
Temple of French Confectionery garnished with Mottoes
Pyramid of Cocoanut tipped with Buchanan & Breckinridge Flag
Temple of New York Kisses garnished with Confectionery
Pyramid of New York Kisses Transparent
Pyramid of Egg Kisses, Harlequin style
Pagoda of Cocoanut, Golden Web
French Nougat Pyramid

CREAMS & JELLIES.
Vanilla Ice Cream   Lemon Ice Cream
Madeira Jelly   Blanc Mange with Peaches   Port Wine Jelly

CONFECTIONERY & CAKE.
New York Kisses—Cocoanut Cake—Citron Cake—Frosted Pound Cake
Jelly Cake—French Mottoes—Spanish Macaroons
Crescent Cake garn'd with Jelly—Fruit Cake Frosted—Lafayette Cake.

FRUITS & NUTS.
Raisins, Apples, Figs, Almonds, Filberts, Pecan Nuts, Eng. Walnuts.

Crackers & Cheese   Coffee a la Francaise.

Menu for the Complimentary Dinner to the Democratic Electors of Virginia, hosted by John P. Ballard at the Exchange Hotel, December 3, 1856, where Spiro Zetelle was the chef. (Courtesy of the Library of Virginia)

House. In 1851 he leased the Exchange Hotel, then the city's newest and most fashionable, at the corner of 14th and Franklin Streets. Four years later he built an even more modern four-story brick building on the opposite side of Franklin Street and connected them with a second-floor bridge that spanned the street below. On December 3, just shortly after assuming his post as Ballard's caterer, Spiro Zetelle prepared the bill of fare for a celebratory banquet for the Democratic Electors of Virginia at the Exchange Hotel. Notably absent from the menu's multiple courses were any French flourishes. The meal began with oyster soup, followed by a round of fish and oyster preparations, then proceeded to cold and boiled meats, six different roasts with sauces, and a game course featuring saddle of venison and canvasback duck accompanied by a half dozen vegetables and assorted olives and pickles. Almost half of the menu was given over to the desserts that rounded out the meal, with an elaborate array of ornamental confectionery, creams, cakes, and fruits. (See menu, page 85.)[45]

Zetelle didn't stay at the Ballard House for long. By February 1857 he had opened his own establishment, which he called variously the New French Eating House, Zetelle's Eating Saloon, and the Rendezvous. Located next door to the Exchange Bank on Main Street, Zetelle's became a Richmond institution. Following Allen's lead, his restaurant was "arranged on the New York plan" and offered breakfast from 6:00 a.m. to noon, dinners from noon until 6:00 p.m., and suppers until 10:00 p.m. Snacks, ranging in price from 12½ to 50 cents, were served at any hour. Upstairs Zetelle had two private dining rooms that could seat up to eighty diners. His advertised specialties, like the banquet menu he had served at the Exchange Hotel, hewed closely to the standard fine-dining fare of the era: oysters "in every style," fish, game, beef, and mutton.[46]

As Zetelle's star was rising, Thomas Griffin stumbled. In September 1857, unable to pay his creditors, he was forced to give up the American Saloon. Out at Griffin's Spring, the constable auctioned off the pigs and chickens along with a cart and harness to satisfy the debt Griffin owed R. O. Haskins, a Richmond ship chandler and member of the city council. The American Saloon was taken over by two men named Heard and Heyward and re-named the Dime House. Though his resort had long been called Griffin's Spring, Griffin didn't actually own the eleven-acre tract of land, and he had to vacate the property.[47]

Griffin bounced back quickly, though. By August of the following year, S. Benjamin of the Office Restaurant was advertising that he had engaged the "far famed caterer, Tom Griffin," who was preparing "all the delicacies of the seasons." In May 1859, Griffin secured a space on the second floor of E. D. Keeling's Clothing Store on Main Street, which he christened Tom Griffin's Restaurant. Within a year he had moved it to a building next door to Purcell, Ladd & Co., just two doors down from where his original American Saloon had been.[48]

Griffin found a replacement for his picnic and shooting grounds, too. In August 1860 he announced in the *Richmond Dispatch* that he had taken possession of Vauxhall Island, a two-acre plot in the James River immediately south of downtown Richmond. Before 1821 it had been known as Buzzard's Island, but it got its more elegant name from London's famed eighteenth-century pleasure gardens. Patrons could walk over to Griffin's island on a small ramp off Mayo's Bridge, which extended across the channel from the larger Mayo Island. There on Vauxhall Island, Griffin maintained a bar furnished with good wines, liquors, cigars, and chewing tobacco, ready for the patronage of Richmond's sporting set.[49]

➤❋← Cooks and Bartenders for Hire

After Spiro Zetelle left the Ballard House to open his own restaurant, his place at Ballard's was filled by a trio of African American men: John Dabney and two brothers, Jim and Fields Cook. Each of them had been born into slavery, and they each made their way from the countryside to the city of Richmond, where they found success in the culinary trades.

The son of London and Eliza Dabney, John Dabney was born in 1824 on the farm of Cora Williamson DeJarnette in Hanover County, Virginia, just north of Richmond. His mother was a cook and maid for the DeJarnette family, and his father was a driver on a neighboring farm. Young Dabney was originally trained in domestic duties alongside his mother, but while he was still a boy, Mrs. DeJarnette decided to hire him out to one of her relatives, William Williamson, to be trained as a jockey. According to Dabney's son Wendell, who in the early twentieth century wrote an autobiographical sketch filled with memories of his father, Dabney got sent away because "his superiors learned more than was pleasant concerning his unruly temper and fighting propensities." After he grew too big to ride racehorses, Dabney switched to working as a waiter, making his way eventually to Gordonsville and working his way up by the young age of eighteen to the headwaiter position at the hotel adjacent to the railroad station.[50]

Photograph of John Dabney
from the late nineteenth
century. (The Valentine
Museum, Richmond, Virginia)

Dabney obtained these positions through the practice of slave hiring or renting, under which control of an enslaved person was transferred temporarily from the owner to someone else. The practice was pervasive in urban and rural areas alike, especially in the older slaveholding states like Virginia where the economy was diversifying and was no longer dominated by large-scale monoculture. It was applied to men and women, young and old, and it involved not just the owners and employers but a wide range of whites who interacted with hired slaves. By 1860 around twenty-five thousand enslaved Virginians—10 percent of the state's enslaved population—were hired out. Those numbers included more than half of Richmond's thirty-four hundred enslaved tobacco factory workers, who had been hired out to the factories by their owners.[51]

The living experience of most hired slaves was not significantly different from that of the nonhired, for it amounted largely to a transfer of control. Women tended to be hired out as house servants or agricultural workers, and that included pregnant women and those with young children, who all too often were viewed by their owners as little more than unproductive overhead. Hiring out frequently separated families, as husbands were sent away to work at other farms or in factories and mothers were separated from their children. It was common to hire out children once they reached a working age, which might be as young as ten years old, and often the same child might be hired out to a different employer each year.

A small minority of enslaved southerners found a scrap of opportunity in being hired out. These tended to be younger males, especially single men, who were hired into urban environments. The opportunity presented was by no means easy or uniform, for the experiences of most hired slaves, even males in urban areas, were quite horrific. But being hired out could bring a small amount of personal income as well as increased mobility and the chance to live more autonomously for those hired to work in a town or city. Frederick Douglass wrote in his *Autobiography* that "a city slave is almost a freeman compared with a slave on a plantation," for the lines between bondage and freedom blurred, especially when the worker enjoyed some degree of free movement and was able to earn a personal income.[52]

In a manufacturing environment, a hired-out slave could earn a small income from "over-work"—that is, for performing more than the assigned number of tasks. For those in the culinary trades, extra income was earned in the form of tips. A select few—including John Dabney—were able to accumulate savings from this income. "From Gordonsville to Richmond was but a step," Dabney's son later wrote. "Hotel employment offered a fine field for the tips so necessary for fattening his own purse." It's not clear when John Dabney arrived in the city, but it may have been in 1850, when William Williamson moved to Richmond and opened the City Hotel. It was certainly by 1855, for John Dabney was tending bar that year at the Columbian Hotel.[53]

Around the same time, two brothers named Fields and Jim Cook also arrived in the city. Fields, the elder, was born around 1817 in the Virginia countryside, likely on the farm of a small planter. As a boy he worked in the fields, hauled timber in an oxcart, and rode an old gray mare weekly to the mill to have the farm's corn ground. Cook later recorded his childhood experiences in a short, unpublished memoir, and he recalled that his boyhood was "different from a great many of my colore . . . for I never knew what the yoke of oppression was." He was raised in a household where "the white and black children all faired alike and grew on together highfellows." This changed dramatically as Cook neared adulthood, when the white boy with whom he had been raised almost like a brother began to act "like the peafowl in the midst of a brood of chickens" and "boast of the superiority which he had over me." It was a devastating betrayal, a misfortune that Cook ranked equal to only one other incident during his childhood: when he was horribly scalded with boiling water in a kitchen accident.[54]

Now a teenager, Fields Cook shifted his attention to courting the young women in the area. At the age of seventeen he fell madly in love with a woman from a nearby farm, and the two were engaged to be married. Through what Cook revealed only as "some circumstance which happened," they were disappointed in their "expectations." He asked that his owners allow him to move to Richmond, and they granted his request. We can assume that Cook was either hired out to someone in the city or made arrangements for himself through the practice of self-hire, under which enslaved persons would find employment and negotiate the terms, sharing a portion of their earnings with their owners.

At a holiday gathering in Richmond on Christmas Day 1835, Cook met a woman named Mary, and he fell in love at first sight. After several months of courtship, they were engaged to be married, and soon after, as Cook put it, he "had to go to the Virginia springs to stay the season." The springs in question were the resorts at the western mineral springs, which were quickly becoming another prime venue for Virginia's aspiring caterers. Just as wealthy white Charlestonians and New Orleanians headed to the beach islands or the lakeside resorts to escape the sweltering summer heat, Richmonders boarded trains and headed west to the natural springs at the edge of the Appalachian Mountains. By the 1830s such resorts dotted the countryside in the mountains of western Virginia as well as down into Georgia and Alabama—anywhere there was a natural hot spring with waters infused with sulfur and other minerals.[55]

At first the springs were visited primarily by those with various ailments and disabilities, for "taking the waters," which is to say bathing in them, was considered a therapeutic cure-all. But resort springs also appealed to those in perfect health, for they generally were found in mountainous areas that were much drier and cooler in summer than the coastal plain. Wealthy planter and merchant families soon began making their way to the springs as a more general summer retreat, and what were initially fairly spartan changing rooms and cottages evolved into elaborate resorts complete with gazebos, walking paths, gardens, and large wood-framed hotels to house the guests. A well-appointed dining room and a generously stocked bar were two prominent features, and a "hailstorm julep"—a blend of spirits, sugar, and mint served in a large cup brimming with crushed ice—was such a perfect cooling treat on a warm summer evening that it quickly became a star of the resort bar.[56]

It is safe to assume that Fields Cook headed to the Virginia springs to work in the kitchen or dining room of one of the resort hotels, not to relax in the hot mineral baths, for Richmond's cooks, bartenders, and waiters followed their customers west each summer in pursuit of lucrative tips. After the season was over, Cook returned to Richmond, and he and Mary were married later that year.

Within a decade of arriving in the city, Cook had saved enough money to purchase his freedom and to go into business on his own. The 1850 census lists him as a free mulatto engaged in the trade of "leech doctor," a practice still common at the time and closely associated with barbering. By 1854 Cook, whom the editors of the *Richmond Dispatch* described as "a very respectable colored man," had taken over the space on Franklin Street formerly occupied by a hotel and opened "a tonsorial emporium" or barbershop that included a bathing room where customers could treat themselves to clean, hot baths. As did barbers in other cities, Cook soon branched out into the culinary trades. The 1860 census lists him as a waiter and notes that he owned $1,500 worth of real estate. Sometime in the 1850s, Fields Cook's brother Jim joined him in Richmond and likewise found work in the hospitality business. By 1859 Jim Cook was employed alongside John Dabney behind the bar at the Ballard House, where they earned reputations as the city's two undisputed masters of green turtle soup and mint juleps.[57]

These days, the julep is often cast as the quintessential Kentucky cocktail, made with bourbon and sipped by white-clad colonels on plantation verandas or in the stands at the Kentucky Derby. Long before they were known in the Bluegrass State, though, mint juleps were the staple of high living in Virginia. "Julep" was originally a term for a syrup used to compound medicines, but by the 1780s it was being applied to a different sort of remedy. Accounts of life on Virginia plantations describe planters starting their mornings with a julep, which one observer described as "a large glass of rum sweetened with sugar." It soon became common to steep mint in the concoction, and the real innovation came once ice became more readily available to Virginia tipplers.[58]

In 1832 a lawyer from Baltimore named John H. B. Latrobe visited White Sulphur Springs and encountered, as he described it in his diary, "a hailstorm, that is to say, a mint julep made with a hailstorm around it." The

MINT JULEP.

A nineteenth-century hailstorm mint julep, from Jerry Thomas, *How to Mix Drinks, or the Bon-Vivant's Companion* (New York: Dick and Fitzgerald, 1862).

bartender filled a glass with finely chopped ice, poured over it the usual concoction of spirits, sugar, and mint, and then molded additional ice "in shape of a fillet around the outside of the tumbler" so that it formed "an external icy application to your lower lip as you drink it." This is the earliest known reference to a mint julep served over crushed ice, and it's quite likely that the "hailstorm julep" was invented at one of Virginia's summer resort springs. From its birthplace in Virginia, the julep made its way southward as far as New Orleans, and by 1840 it was being served by the legendary Orasmus Willard of the lobby bar in the City Hotel in New York City—just one of many southern-born recipes that influenced the larger national cuisine.[59]

John Dabney likely learned to mix hailstorm juleps when working at the western resorts, and he soon earned a reputation as one of the state's master julep makers. In 1856 he spent the summer working at Montgomery White Sulphur Springs. A correspondent for the *Richmond Dispatch*, reporting on a visit to the springs, noted that in the summer heat "a fellow does not feel like doing anything but sitting still in the coolest place he can find, with one of John Dabney's famous juleps convenient." Dabney, he noted, was "Judge of the Court of Enquiry, and always to be found practicing at the bar." Dabney served plenty of juleps back in Richmond, too. A newspaper description of one of his productions, made when he was bartender at the Columbian Hotel, notes that it was "surrounded by ice and capped off by a beautiful bouquet of flowers, interspersed with cuts of curious looking oranges."[60]

John Dabney and Jim Cook were by no means the only enslaved cooks and bartenders working in the restaurants and saloons of Richmond. Most of their colleagues' names have been lost to history, but a man named John Washington captured his experiences in an autobiographical narrative, and that account offers perhaps the most detailed description of the practice of self-hire in any extant slave narrative, though it is still only a brief glimpse.

Washington was born in 1838 near Fredericksburg, Virginia, the son of an enslaved mulatto woman and a white slaveholder. After spending his early childhood on a farm, he moved into town at the age of ten after his owner, a Mrs. Taliaferro, was widowed for the second time. At Christmas in 1850, Washington's mother and younger siblings were hired out to work at a girls' boarding school in western Virginia, and Washington, then just twelve years old, remained in Fredericksburg. In "Memorys of the Past," which he wrote in 1872, Washington recalls the "bitter pangs" that the separation created, which kindled a secret hatred against his oppressors and sparked a determination to run away and escape as soon as he had the opportunity.

At the age of eighteen Washington was hired out through a series of one-year contracts, first to Mrs. Taliaferro's neighbor, for whom he drove horses and tended gardens, and then to work in the Alexander & Gibbs tobacco factory. The factory operated under the task system, and the laborers were expected to twist at least 66 pounds of tobacco per day or face whipping. For each pound of tobacco beyond 100 pounds that they twisted, they were paid a small sum that they could keep for themselves. Washington found that with sufficient effort he could regularly earn three to four dollars a week. His employment came to an abrupt halt in December 1860, when South Carolina declared it was seceding from the Union and commerce froze between North and South, causing the tobacco company to close its doors.[61]

"I had long desired to go to Richmond," Washington wrote in his memoir. "I had been told by my friends that it was a good place to make money for myself." He was placed in the hands of Hay Hoomes, a hiring agent, and taken south by train. They arrived in Richmond at three o'clock, and before the end of the day Washington had been hired out to work for Spiro Zetelle, the Greek immigrant who operated an "eating saloon" on Main Street. About six months later, at the outset of the Civil War, Zetelle sold his restaurant to Caspar Wendlinger, a German-born man who had arrived in the city around 1840 and established a successful tailoring business. "Both of these men," Washington recalled, "were low, mean, and coarse. They treated their servants cruelly often whipping them their selves or sending them to the slave jail to be whipped where it was done fearfully for 50 cents." Washington himself, though, "got along unusually well" with both men, especially Wendlinger, and he stayed on at the eating house, which Wendlinger still advertised as "Zetelle's Restaurant" or "Zetelle's Saloon," through the end of the year.[62]

John Washington doesn't record how much tip money he made working for Zetelle and Wendlinger, but his colleague John Dabney earned a significant sum from his talents behind the bar—and from his facility for engaging with and pleasing customers. Dabney married Elizabeth Foster in 1856, and their first son, Clarence, was born the following year. Around the same time, he struck a deal with his owner, Cora DeJarnette, and began paying in installments toward purchasing his eventual freedom. Soon, however, Elizabeth Dabney's owners, who were facing mounting debts and were unhappy that she was paying more attention to her new family than to theirs, decided to put her up for sale. John Dabney went to Mrs. DeJarnette and asked her if he could suspend the payments he owed her. She agreed, and Dabney arranged for some white friends to purchase his wife on his behalf, postponing his own freedom to preserve his family.[63]

As 1860 approached, John Dabney and the Cook brothers were prospering, and they showed a facility for public relations equal to their skills behind the bar and in the kitchen. Dabney's and Jim Cook's names appeared regularly in the local newspapers, thanks to the turtle soup feasts they staged at the Ballard House, and they were soon vying for Zetelle's title as "the Napoleon of cooks" in Richmond. In June 1859, Jim Cook was able to procure a four-hundred-pound sea turtle, one of the largest ever seen in Richmond, which he transformed into 140 gallons of "smoking, savory, and delicious" turtle soup in "an immense cauldron, mixed with spices and other ingredients." The soup was served free to all comers at the Ballard House barroom. As was his habit, Cook dispatched a waiter with a few bowls of soup and some accompanying mint juleps to the newsroom at the *Richmond Whig*. The editors returned the favor in the form of publicity, declaring, "Jim has 'immortalized' himself as the Napoleon of cooks, and deserves a coat of arms with a turtle as the chief emblem upon his escutcheon."[64]

Like Tom Griffin before them, Jim Cook and John Dabney were driven men with fierce tempers, and that often got them in trouble when dealing with white customers. In November 1859 the police raided a "low groggery" owned by a free person of color named John Moore, seizing cards, dice, and other gambling paraphernalia. Moore was a close friend of Jim Cook's, and when members of the watch later retired to the Ballard House bar for a drink, Cook gave them an earful for disrupting his friend's business. The officers, the local newspapers reported, warned Cook to watch his tongue or face a lashing, and Cook immediately shot back "that no one should whip him, and that they (the watchmen) were only fit to perform such work, and that the business of 'licking n———s' had brought the state of Virginia to her present condition." Cook wound up getting arrested, hauled before the mayor, and sentenced to receive forty lashes. It wasn't his last run-in with the law in Virginia.[65]

➤❇← Washington, D.C.

While John Dabney and the Cooks were establishing their reputations in Richmond, new faces were appearing on the scene in Washington, D.C. Gadsby's and Brown's remained the city's principal hotels through the 1850s, but they gained an able competitor in a young Vermonter named Henry Willard. Willard arrived in the city in 1847 and leased a two-story-and-attic town house at the corner of 14th Street and Pennsylvania Avenue, which he converted into a small hotel. Willard's brother Joseph soon joined him in the venture, and in 1853 the brothers purchased the building along with the five houses adjoining it and began combining them into a single hotel structure. In 1858 the Willards expanded around the corner, buying an old mansion on the southwest corner of 14th and F Streets, demolishing it, and replacing it with a six-story addition to their hotel. The combined structure contained 150 rooms and eventually spanned the entire block on 14th between Pennsylvania Avenue and F Street. Henry Willard himself directly oversaw the kitchens and larder, rising early to go to Center Market to procure the day's supply of meat, and later personally supervised the slicing of the roasts. He kept gardens in nearby lots that produced fresh lettuce, spring onions, beans, radishes, and asparagus for his tables.[66]

President Franklin Pierce leaving Willard's Hotel during his inauguration, from the *Illustrated News*, March 12, 1853. (Library of Congress, Prints and Photographs Division)

A visitor in the early 1850s making the mile-and-a-half ride along Pennsylvania Avenue from the U.S. Capitol to the White House would pass by hotels, restaurants, shops, and elegant town houses, many of them newly constructed or remodeled. "A person absent from the city for a twelve-month," the *Republic* wrote in March 1853, "would be surprised by the increase of beautiful stores, within that brief period, on the line of the principal thoroughfare."[67]

A block west of his original shop, Charles Gautier constructed an elaborate new restaurant and confectionery, with a mind to filling what the *Daily National Intelligencer* called "a deficiency that has long been felt here." The oyster saloons and eating houses of Washington had always been exclusively male spaces. Women visiting the city from nearby towns or the countryside to do their shopping had few options for getting a bite to eat short of going to a hotel or "imposing themselves, perhaps inconveniently, on acquaintances." Gautier aimed to remedy that with a restaurant that catered first and foremost to a female clientele.

Completed at a cost of $60,000, the three-story building was the most elegant restaurant the city had yet seen. Guests entered from Pennsylvania Avenue into a confectionery store with white marble counters, checkered floors, and elaborately embellished walls and ceilings. On the far side of the shop, up a few steps, they could enter the main dining saloon with marble-topped tables, rich carpets, and beautifully papered walls. Here female visitors or parties of ladies and gentlemen—but no gentlemen dining without ladies—could enjoy a meal or a sweet confection. For men alone, there was the Gentlemen's Restaurant, described by one newspaper as "a plainer but more comfortable room," along with five rooms for private parties. The basement held Gautier's facilities for making his famed ice creams and confectionery along with his kitchens, which were fitted up with the latest ovens and gas-powered equipment. The establishment opened its doors to the public on November 1, 1853.[68]

Among Gautier's many catering engagements in the 1850s were the inaugural balls for Presidents Franklin Pierce in 1853 and James Buchanan in 1857. The bill of fare for the Buchanan dinner shows Gautier's blending of French and American dishes and a particular focus on ice cream and confectionery. It includes saddles of mutton and *filets de boeuf en belle vue* followed by *marrons glacés, bavaroises,* and ice creams in fancy molds. (See illustration, page 98.) These delicacies were served in truly massive quantities: 60 saddles of mutton and 4 of venison, 74 hams, some 400 gallons of oysters, and 1,200 quarts of ice cream.[69]

Inaugural balls were special occasions, but more ordinary dining in Washington was serious business, too, particularly among the southern contingent. James A. Gray, who worked as a private steward and caterer in Washington in the 1850s, recalled that when it came to their private parties, Senator Jefferson Davis of Mississippi and his fellow southerner politicians "were lavish, and carte blanche was the rule." A typical catered dinner was served to sixteen or twenty guests, who were seated at a long table with the host at one end and the hostess at the other. The ladies sat to the host's right and the gentlemen to the left. It was the host's duty to ladle out the soup and carve the roast onto plates, which would then be passed by the attending waiters to each diner. The hostess played a similar

BILL OF FARE.

Paté Truffle.
Saddles of Venison and of Mutton.
Boar's Head, stuffed and decorated.
Boned and roasted Turkeys.
Spiced Rounds of Beef.
Filets de Bœuf en Belle Vue.
Boned and roasted Pheasants.
Tongues and Hams, decorated.
Aspic de Volaille.
Lobster, Chicken and Russian Salad.
Terrapins and Oysters.
Cream and Water Ices, in fancy moulds.
Marons Glacés.
Charlotte Russe.
Meringues, Plombières, Bavaroises.
Jellies and Puddings.
Fancy Cakes, Preserved Fruits, Confectionery.
Roman Punch, Apple Toddy.
Wines, Liquors and Cordials.

An idea of the quantity of these delicacies may be formed from the fact that Mons. Gautier among other things provided $300 worth of wine; 400 gallons of oysters; 500 quarts of chicken salad; 1,200 quarts of ice cream; 500 quarts of jellies; 60 saddles of mutton; 4 of venison; 8 rounds of beef; 75 hams; 125 tongues, besides patés of various kinds. At the head of the table was a pyramid of cake four feet high, with a flag of each State and Territory.

Charles Gautier's bill of fare for the Inauguration Ball for President James Buchanan, from *Frank Leslie's Illustrated Newspaper*, March 21, 1857.

role for the dessert course, and at the end of the evening the guests retired to the parlor for coffee and cordials. For those who didn't care to host such events in their homes, Joseph Boulanger's restaurant on G Street, just northwest of the White House, remained a popular destination for private entertainments.[70]

Four blocks east of Gautier's on Pennsylvania Avenue, Absalom Shadd continued operating the National Eating House, which since the 1840s had set the standard for fresh game and seafood procured from across the Mid-Atlantic region. Shadd had entered into a partnership with William Walker in 1849 and took over the operations shortly thereafter, as Walker announced his intention of leaving the city. Operating under the name Walker & Shadd, Absalom Shadd advertised to local hunters that he would pay the highest prices in the city for woodcock and that he needed fifty brace per day. During the warmer months, the National Eating House regularly served turtle from the West Indies, soft- and hard-shell crabs from Annapolis and Baltimore, and fish and oysters from Norfolk.[71]

Almost two decades had passed since Walker's original business partner, Beverly Snow, was run out of the city, but restaurateurs of color still faced daunting challenges, and these only heightened as sectionalist tensions and abolition fears increased. As part of the Compromise of 1850, which instituted a strict Fugitive Slave Law and admitted California to the Union as a free state, the slave trade was outlawed in the District of Columbia, but slavery itself remained legal. By 1860 only 5 percent of the city's population of sixty-one thousand were enslaved, while 15 percent—close to ten thousand residents—were free people of color. A large proportion of those male persons of color made their living as carriage and wagon drivers, while women worked primarily as domestic servants—cooking, sewing, washing, child care.[72]

In terms of demographics and political sympathies, white Washingtonians were decidedly southern. Some 90 percent of the white population had been born either in the South or in Washington to southern parents. The city government was controlled by Democratic mayors, and the police department was riddled with corruption and actively hostile to the city's African American residents, harshly enforcing the slave codes as well as the Black Codes that governed free persons of color. The mayor and local courts were notorious for imposing arbitrary fines and fees on African American citizens.

In 1851 the firm of Walker & Shadd fell afoul of the Corporation of the City of Washington, as the city government was known, when a magistrate declined to issue it a liquor license, asserting that persons of color were not entitled to such a privilege under the law. Shadd continued selling liquor while he appealed the decision—and was fined twenty dollars for it on at least one occasion—but in October 1853 the Circuit Court affirmed "the right of the corporation to discriminate between white and colored persons to keep taverns and ordinaries."[73]

The decision was a death blow for Shadd's business, for liquor sales were essential for any eating house of the period. Soon after, he sold the restaurant's equipment and lease to a white man named David G. Fuller, who continued operating under the National Eating House name. By the end of the year Shadd and his family had moved to Chatham, Ontario, just across Lake St. Clair from Detroit, where he farmed for four years and died in 1857. The National Eating House changed hands several more times over the next few years, staying in business for another decade, but it never regained the culinary reputation it had enjoyed under William Walker and Absalom Shadd.[74]

At the same time that Shadd floundered, William Wormley's brother James was on the rise. Rather than aligning with abolitionists, he put himself in a position to interact with Washington's wealthiest and most powerful white men. In 1853 Wormley was named the steward of the newly founded Washington Club, which established its rooms in the old Rodgers Mansion overlooking Lafayette Square just north of the White House. Its members included dozens of army and navy officers, wealthy local businessmen like bankers William W. Corcoran and George Riggs, and plenty of members of Congress, including Senators John J. Crittenden of Kentucky, Edward Everett of Massachusetts, and Hamilton Fish of New York. Good eating was a core function of the club, whose stated purpose was to "promote social intercourse, and to afford the advantages of a Reading Room, Library and well appointed Refectories." The club facilities also included a billiard room and card room for the use of members and their out-of-town guests. In addition to furnishing meals and refreshments, the steward was responsible for managing members' accounts and taking their payments.[75]

Wormley remained at the Washington Club until 1857, when he signed on to be the steward of the steamship *Maryland*, an excursion boat that made regular trips down the Potomac and the Chesapeake Bay to Norfolk and the resort at Old Point Comfort. As 1858 opened, Wormley made a big move, securing a location at 314 I Street between 15th and 16th Streets and opening what he called Wormley's Club House. It was a prime location two blocks north of the White House and the War Department, in the heart of the city's political and social life. It was on the same block where his sister had operated her schoolhouse two decades before. Wormley promised customers "every delicacy which can be procured, either North or South." In February, at a time when the fields around D.C. were fallow, he advertised that he was receiving "new vegetables weekly from Charleston and Savannah, regardless of cost." When the marsh hunting season opened in August, Wormley announced that he would be receiving fresh ortolan and reed birds every afternoon.[76]

Wormley maintained the influential relationships he had cultivated while serving as steward of the Washington Club. In fact, when the members gave up their facilities and dissolved the club in the fall of 1859, they met in rooms at Wormley's Club House to plan how to pay off the organization's remaining debts. By early 1860, when General Winfield Scott boarded in his rooms, Wormley had established himself as an independent restaurateur, living on I Street with his wife and four children. At least four persons in his employ also lived in the Club House facilities: two waiters, William Murrey and Douglass Smith, an oyster shucker named Wesley Harris, and a cook named Julia Robertson, all of whom were African Americans and had been born in the District of Columbia. Wormley was already worth $8,000 in real estate and assets, and he was well positioned to accumulate more.[77]

➤)※- Baltimore

What does one do with Baltimore? Is it a southern city or a Mid-Atlantic one? That question has been the subject of quite a bit of debate, for Baltimore straddles the blurry line between North and South. Geographically it is at the northern edge of even the most expansive definition of the South, roughly at the same latitude as Indianapolis and Columbus, Ohio. But it is a mere forty miles north of Washington, so if you consider Washington a southern city—and in the 1850s it undoubtedly was, both in demographics and character—then it's hard not to categorize Baltimore as southern, too. Maryland did not join the Confederacy, but it was a slaveholding state, and like Washington and Richmond it is linked by rivers to the Chesapeake Bay and its splendid bounty of fish and game.

Regardless of how we classify it geographically, Baltimore had an unde-niable influence on what people throughout the South ate in restaurants, hotels, oyster saloons, and coffeehouses in the middle decades of the nine-teenth century. The cuisine of the Mid-Atlantic—the food of Washington, Richmond, and Baltimore—had evolved into a distinctive style, and thanks to continuous improvements in transportation and communication, the region's specialties soon made their way westward to places like Louisville and New Orleans and northward to Philadelphia, New York, and Boston, helping shape fine dining menus throughout the country. It's perhaps un-surprising, given their close geographic proximity, that the hospitality and culinary trades in Washington and Baltimore were directly linked by indi-viduals who operated hotels and restaurants in both cities.

At the opening of the nineteenth century, Baltimore had only two cof-feehouses and a single cookshop, but there were around a hundred taverns and inns, many of them clustered along the water in Old Town and Fell's Point and catering to sailors. Among the taverns was the Indian Queen, which had opened way back in 1780 and was taken over by John Gadsby in 1808. That's the same John Gadsby who would later move to Washington and found the National Hotel. After Gadsby departed Baltimore, David

Barnum took over the Indian Queen and operated it for seven years before opening Barnum's City Hotel, Baltimore's first hotel in the modern sense, and one that became famous for its accommodations as well as the products of its kitchens.[78]

Charles Dickens, after departing Washington during his 1842 tour, stayed briefly at Barnum's Hotel as he passed through Baltimore. Boz recorded no comments about the food, but he was complimentary about the accommodations, writing in *American Notes* that "the most comfortable of all the hotels of which I had any experience in the United States, and they were not a few, is Barnum's in that city." He appreciated in particular the curtains on his bed and having more than enough water for washing himself. Another frequently cited British commentator, Frances Trollope, offered high praise for Barnum's as well, while simultaneously backhanding Americans' sophistication. In 1832 in *Domestic Manners of the Americans* she wrote, "Mr. Barham's [*sic*] hotel is said to be the most splendid in the Union, and it is certainly splendid enough for a people more luxurious than the citizens of the republic appear yet to be."[79]

The other great epicurean hotels of 1840s Baltimore were Guy's Monument House, which overlooked Monument Square, and the Eutaw House on the northwest corner of Baltimore and Eutaw Streets. The former was operated by John Guy, a Pennsylvania-born hotelier. The Eutaw House was an all-brick structure built specifically as a hotel, opening in 1835 under the proprietorship of Asahel Hussey. It boasted cool and airy apartments in the summer, and modern grates and fireplaces to keep it warm in winter.[80]

In May 1843 a correspondent for the *Baltimore Sun* raved about the "delicacies of the season" he found at the city's leading hotels. At Barnum's he tucked into "salmon, mackerel and lobsters, fresh from the north, and green turtle, soft crabs and green peas, fresh from the south, meeting on common ground." He enjoyed turtle soup at both Guy's Monument House and Barnum's City Hotel, diplomatically declaring Guy's "as fine a turtle soup as any epicure would desire" and Barnum's "not a whit behind the former in excellence."[81]

Turtle soup was more popular in Baltimore than anywhere else in the South. Starting each May in the 1840s, it was widely advertised at places like Thomas Sutton's Military Hall on Gay Street and Hugh Kenneday's Baltimore Tavern on Lombard. Baltimore even had a street named in honor of the dish: Turtle Soup Alley, which adjoined Eutaw and Warner Streets. Turtle soup and aldermen were, for reasons lost to history, routinely linked in jokes during this era. This example, from the *Baltimore Sun*, is typical: "'We part to meet no more,' as the turtle soup said to the platter when an alderman entered the room." Humor does not age well.[82]

During the early years, the city's leading confectioner and caterer was Alexander Butcher. Born in Pennsylvania, he arrived in Baltimore in the 1820s and by 1841 had opened a confectionery. He operated his establishment at 160 Baltimore Street for the next two decades, specializing in ice cream and water ices but also serving tea, coffee, chocolate, and meats. He also began to host private dinners and dances in the rooms on the upper floor of his confectionery and also to furnish parties, balls, and weddings as a caterer.[83]

As in the other cities we've surveyed, in the 1850s Baltimore saw a person of color emerge as its leading caterer, eclipsing his mentor in the process. Henry Jakes Jr. was born in Baltimore, the son of a free African American barber. Both Henry Jr. and his brother Frederick followed their father into the trade in the family's shop at 4 Banks Lane, just behind Barnum's Hotel. Henry Jr. drew upon the connections with white customers that he established as a barber—as well as the income he earned—to transition into the catering trade. He got started by assembling a regular crew of waiters who could be hired by the city's caterers to support their large events. In April 1858 he assisted at the assembly of the American Association for the Advancement of Science. "The banquet was prepared by the excellent caterer, Mr. Alexander Butcher," the *Baltimore Sun* reported, "and the renowned Henry Jakes, with his corp of admirable waiters, superintended the tables and promptly attended the requirements of the guests." In language, at least, the menu for this affair had plenty of French flourishes, including "Spring Chickens, *de la Francaise*" and "Sweet Breads, *aux Petits Pois*." Reflecting Butcher's primary trade as a confectioner, two-thirds of the menu was given over to desserts, which ranged from cream baskets and charlotte russe to water ices and meringues.[84]

Jakes soon began catering events on his own. In 1859 he provided the refreshments for a private excursion on the B&O Railroad, and the correspondent for the *Daily Exchange* observed, "Those who know Baltimore know 'Henry Jakes,' as those who know Fifth Avenue know 'Brown'"—a reference to Isaac Brown, the sexton of Grace Church and famed organizer of parties and dinners for New York's elite. "It was this other 'Brown,'" the correspondent added, "only more so, (in complexion) who had the charge of our rations and our refrigerator." By 1860 Jakes had amassed a large supply of equipment—silver, glassware, china, candelabras, brackets, and "epergnes," or centerpieces—that he not only used for his own engagements but also rented out for weddings, balls, and parties. He still maintained a team of cooks and waiters that he hired out, too. Operating out of his home at 121 St. Paul Street, he does not appear to have had private rooms or served meals to order, but he did take orders for game, terrapin, and oysters in season, functioning in effect as a game dealer. In the 1850 census, Jakes had listed his occupation as barber. By 1860 he identified himself as a caterer, and he had $15,000 in real estate and another $1,000 of personal estate to his name.[85]

Baltimore's most important contribution to the evolving southern cuisine was oysters, for the city became the hub of a thriving oyster packing and shipping industry with national reach. The pioneer of the field, C. S. Maltby, was a native of Connecticut who moved to Baltimore in the 1830s and got started in the raw oyster trade, founding his own packing house in 1836. As business grew, Maltby established wagon lines from Baltimore to Pittsburgh, some 225 miles inland, and began supplying western Pennsylvania with fresh oysters long before the B&O Railroad reached the region. By 1850 Baltimore's six oyster packing houses were producing 400,000 to 500,000 cans per year and selling them wholesale at $7 per case, which held a dozen cans.

Oysters could be steamed or pickled to preserve them in transport, but raw oysters brought a higher price and were consistently in demand. Workers in the packing houses shucked freshly harvested oysters and packed the meats in small airtight tin cans of about a quart capacity. The cans were arranged in rows in long wooden boxes or packed in specially made cedar kegs or barrels and topped with ice. Thus secured, the oysters could remain fresh for between a week and ten days in transit, provided the weather didn't turn unexpectedly warm. They were shipped westward via the express services or, as the industry developed, special "oyster trains" that carried nothing but packed bivalves on ice. In the matter of a few short years, raw oysters fresh from the saline waters of the Chesapeake became available to connoisseurs as far inland as Nashville and Louisville. Baltimore remained the center of the industry in the boom years that followed. By 1865 an estimated 2 million bushels of oysters were packed raw in Baltimore and another 1.4 million bushels pickled or otherwise preserved.[86]

Oysters were an essential component of what had coalesced into a distinctive mode of Mid-Atlantic dining. In 1857, when a group of aldermen from Washington visited Baltimore, they stayed at Guy's Monument House, and founder John Guy's son William prepared them an extravagant ten-course menu comprising more than a hundred dishes. Between the entrees and the vegetables, Guy added a unique "Maryland course" to showcase the state's culinary specialties. It included roast saddle of mountain mutton with currant jelly, fried soft-shell crabs with butter and parsley sauce, broiled soft-shell crabs, deviled hard-shell crabs, summer ducks with olives, green goose with applesauce, and roasted ham with Champagne sauce. The meal opened with green turtle soup—the guests were aldermen, after all—and several more local specialties were featured in the other courses, like Chesapeake Bay mackerel, "young chickens, Maryland-style," and "crab salad, Baltimore fashion."[87]

✺ The Southern Fine-Dining Menu in the 1850s

By looking across southern cities on the Atlantic Coast, we can now assemble a portrait of a typical fine-dining menu on the eve of the Civil War. That menu would be very similar whether one were dining in Baltimore, down the coast in Charleston, or even far to the south in New Orleans. Oysters and turtle soup would begin the affair, followed by fresh fish like shad and seasonal treats like soft-shell crab. The middle courses brought game birds—especially canvasback duck and sora—along with venison. The bills of fare for fancy dinners and banquets were decidedly European in their structure, with the soup followed by the fish followed by the roasts and dessert, but the dishes that composed each course were thoroughly American.

This new southern fine-dining menu resulted from the convergence of cooks with immediate roots in Europe and those born and raised in America, many of whose roots stretched back to Africa. It was the convergence as well of the best that the region's fields and seas produced, prepared by those who had apprenticed in professional kitchens and were cooking with the latest ranges, cookware, and techniques. Though their preparations were shaped by European styles and techniques—indeed, many of the immigrant chefs had trained in the finest restaurants in Paris and elite noble houses on the Continent—they were not purely French or English in style. Turtle soup was a thoroughly American preparation, as were the mint julep and canvasback duck, two of the great culinary icons of the Mid-Atlantic.[88]

One common theme can be seen in contemporary accounts of these pioneering chefs' work. Cooks weren't looked on as artists in the sense of being individualistic and inventive creators. They were expected to execute faithfully an already established repertoire of esteemed dishes. Their reputations were based upon their skill in executing those preparations, not their creativity in coming up with new ones. The chef as a romantic figure—the artist in the kitchen—came much later. What was important in this period was their ability, first and foremost, to procure the very best ingredients, especially the rarest and finest seasonal ingredients like shellfish and game, and then to prepare them with precise skill. Equally important were their talents as a host: the ability to greet, entertain, and accommodate their guests' many needs.

Surprisingly, considering the large number of African American southerners who made their livings as professional cooks and caterers, the flavors and techniques of African foodways do not appear prominently in the commercial cuisine of the era. The African influence is undeniable in the world of southern home cookery. It permeates the "receipts" captured in books from elite white writers like Sarah Rutledge, author of the 1839 *Carolina Housewife.* Okra, gumbo, benne (sesame) seeds, peanuts—so much of the southern home cooking canon is rooted in African traditions inherited by the region's enslaved domestic cooks. Considering the sheer number of African American cooks who worked in southern commercial kitchens in the nineteenth century, we might expect to see a significant influence from the foodways of Africa on the fare being served in restaurants and at elaborate banquets. That doesn't seem to be the case, at least not in the names of dishes on the bills of fare for the great balls and public dinners of the era, nor on the menus or lists of specialties of early restaurants and hotel dining rooms.

➤❋⟵ A Julep for the Prince

In the summer and fall of 1860, Edward, Prince of Wales—Queen Victoria's eldest son and the future King Edward VII—made a four-month grand tour of Canada and the United States. Cities throughout the country jockeyed for a spot on his itinerary, and crowds thronged the streets to greet him when he arrived in Detroit and Chicago. (Victoria, for her part, considered her eighteen-year-old son a ne'er-do-well and was quite happy to have him overseas and out of her sight.)

When word spread that the prince was making his way south to Richmond, hoteliers and restaurateurs started falling all over themselves to lure him to their establishments. The railroad lines between Richmond and Charleston were offered free of charge should the prince wish to visit South Carolina. The proprietors of the Spotswood House in Richmond offered their hotel for his use free of charge, sweetening the deal with the promise that "the famous cook Zetelle would be chef de cuisine during his stay."[89]

The royal party instead chose the Exchange Hotel, where they experienced firsthand the julep wizardry of John Dabney and Jim Cook. The prince and his entourage arrived the evening of Saturday, October 6, and were taken by barouche to the Exchange Hotel and Ballard House, where an immense crowd awaited in the streets. The royal party dodged them by slipping in through a side entrance, then took occupancy of the entire second floor of the Ballard House. The prince had planned to attend the opera, but he was fatigued from his journey and decided instead to retire to his "royal couch." The following morning he attended services at St. Paul's Church, then toured the Capitol, Hollywood Cemetery, and other sights west of town before retiring again to his hotel. That evening he was introduced to the handiwork of what one newspaper described as "the best compounder of cooling drinks in the world."[90]

Whether that compounder was Jim Cook or John Dabney is a bit of a mystery. Newspaper articles from the late 1860s identify the maker as Jim Cook, as does testimony from Jim's brother Fields. Later articles, however, identify John Dabney as the man who served the prince, and Dabney's own son Wendell Phillips Dabney said his father made juleps for the Prince of Wales. It may well be that both of the men, as cocktail historian David Wondrich has proposed, were involved. After all, both were working in the bar at the Ballard House, and surely both would have wanted to attend to such an esteemed guest.

In any event, the prince wasn't about to patronize the public bar at the Ballard House, so either Cook or Dabney (or perhaps both) went to him. There the julep maker mixed his "cooling ingredients" in a quart-sized tumbler, then filled an obelisk-shaped mold with thinly shaved ice and compressed it into a single cone-like mass. He fitted that pyramid into the top of the tumbler and decorated it with a bouquet of flowers before inserting several silver straws through the frosty pyramid. The masterpiece complete, he presented it to the Prince of Wales.

The prince, a contemporary account captured, took a sip and "started back in astonishment at the luscious taste of the liquid." His Royal Highness promptly finished off the first julep, then order a second and shared it with the Duke of Newcastle, the Earl of St. Germans, and Major-General Robert

Bruce. The following morning, before departing for his nine-o'clock train to Baltimore, the prince requested another julep be sent up. This one—complete with thirteen straws, one for each member of the royal party—was the largest of all, and it earned the julep maker a twenty-dollar gold coin as a tip.[91]

Whether the prince knew that the man—or men—who made his juleps were enslaved is not recorded.

CHAPTER 5

Fine Dining Heads West

From time to time, when they weren't enjoying their canvasback duck, their aspics, and their *filets de boeuf en belle vue*, connoisseurs of fine dining in New York, Richmond, and Charleston liked to poke a little fun at the less-than-sophisticated fare that was said to plague the emerging cities on the frontier. In 1854, for instance, the *Knickerbocker Magazine* published a mock bill of fare from "Barkis' Hotel," which it identified only as being "somewhere 'out west.'" It followed the standard menu format of the day, starting with Roasted, Boiled, and Baked courses followed by Cold Dishes, Pastry, and Liquors. The dishes within each course, though, were a bit more pork-centric than what one might find at the Bachelor's Retreat in Charleston or one of Gautier's balls in D.C. (See menu, page 110.)

Through the first half of the twentieth century, fresh shad, Lynnhaven oysters, and giant edible *montées* were far more likely to be found in East Coast cities than they were further west. As frontier trading towns grew into cities, though, they began offering new options for gourmands, and the delicacies of the East became more widely available as the network of rail and water transport improved.[1]

To be fair, most of these frontier cities were much younger and smaller than their eastern counterparts. Nashville, for instance, was chartered in 1806, but it wasn't until 1843, when it was named Tennessee's permanent capital, that it began to grow. The population increased from just under 7,000 in 1840 to more than 10,000 in 1850 and 17,000 by 1860. The town's commercial dining options were slim in the early days. The business directory for 1845 listed four hotels and only a single "restaurat"—H. L. Davis's Nashville Eating House, located just across the street from the

Barkis' Hotel.

BILL OF FARE.

THURSDAY, MAY 15, 1851.

ROASTED.

| Pig, | Pork, | Ham, | Hog. |

BOILED

| Ham, | Eggs, | Ham and Eggs, | Ham. |

BAKED.

| Beans, | Pork and Beans, | Bread, | Biscuit. |

COLD DISHES.

BOILED—Ham,	ROAST—Swine,
" Pork,	" Pig,
" Pig,	" Pork,
" Swine.	" Ham.
COOKED—Animals,	BAKED—Pig,
" Injun,	" Ham,
" Pies,	" Pork,
" Cake,	" Swine,
" Biscuit,	" Hog,
" Beans.	" Beans,

PASTRY, ETC.

PIE—Mince,	CAKE—Fruit,
" Berry,	" Sponge.
" Apple,	" Cymbals.

APPLES AND CHEESE.

LIQUORS

Jamaica Rum,	Pale Brandy,
Monongaheel,	Dark do.
McGuckin Gin,	Whisky Bill.

A pork-centric bill of fare from Barkis' Hotel, "somewhere 'out west,'" in the *Knickerbocker*, 1854.

Nashville Inn on Lower Market Street (today's 2nd Avenue). The following year, James Zanone opened a competing restaurant that adjoined a tobacco warehouse on Market Street, but that establishment seems to have lasted less than two years.[2]

For almost a decade, H. L. Davis had the dining market cornered in Nashville. Styling himself "Harry of the West"—a nickname borrowed from the Kentucky statesman Henry Clay—he operated at his Lower Market Street location until 1849, when he leased a building further up the street and launched "an eating and drinking saloon" called the St. Charles, a name perhaps meant to evoke the St. Charles Hotel in New Orleans. He upgraded his establishment the following year, rebranding it Davis Eating Palace and boasting that he would "keep a better eating establishment during the season, than has ever been kept in this city before." Davis catered primarily to travelers, especially "gentlemen arriving by steamboat, stages, or other conveyances" from the countryside, and lunch could be had for ten cents and dinner for twenty. The restaurateur promised to serve oysters in soups, fried, or stewed along with the best meats the market afforded, "got up in the finest French style." The fare that appeared in his advertisements was not noticeably French, though, consisting of "all kinds of fish" and "all kinds of birds," along with squirrels and wild game from the local markets. "Ham and eggs, pigs feet, fine tripe and chicken gizzards, eggs and brains" could be had at any hour of the day.[3]

As competitors to Davis arrived in the 1850s, they emphasized the western nature of their food. In the fall of 1851, John W. Bell opened Bell's Exchange on the south side of the public square, and his advertisements reached out to "transient visitors to the city," including members of the House and Senate. Bell asserted that his was "believed to be the finest house west of the Allegheny Mountains" and that he had engaged "the best cooks in the Western country" to produce "the best eating the Western country can afford." That eating included quails, partridges, rabbits, fish, venison, squirrels, and "all the rarities of the Western countries." The one exception to the explicitly western fare was oysters, which were shipped in cans from Baltimore.

Nashvillians' access to delicacies from beyond the region was hampered by the fact that no railroad connection to the city existed before the 1850s. Nashville had emerged as a regional trading hub thanks to its prime location on the Cumberland River, which snakes more than six hundred miles from its headwaters in the Kentucky Appalachians to its confluence with the Ohio River above Paducah. A thriving river trade developed early in the nineteenth century, and much of that traffic was made up of flatboats. These were flat-bottomed, box-shaped craft that averaged fifty feet in length and twelve feet in width, propelled by the current and navigated by a stern oar. They carried corn, whiskey, furs, flour, and fruits and vegetables like apples and squash from the surrounding Tennessee and Kentucky countryside all the way down to New Orleans. Upon reaching their destination, the boatmen dismantled their flats, sold the lumber, then either walked home or bought passage on a steamer. A steamer trip upriver from New Orleans to Nashville via the Mississippi, Ohio, and Cumberland took several days. Steamers regularly delivered cans of fresh oysters on ice from Baltimore, but few other perishables could survive the long journey.

"Harry of the West" seems to have lived a life of misfortune. In October 1850 his son and another boy were out shooting with bird guns on a Friday evening when they decided to amuse themselves by climbing up into trees and taking shots at each other through the branches. Though their guns were loaded only with bird shells, a single piece of shot pierced the young Davis boy's heart and killed him. This unfortunate event occurred just weeks before H. L. Davis opened his new Davis Eating Palace, which would be the last restaurant he owned.[4]

In 1852 Davis gave up his restaurant and went to work for W. R. Demonbreun at the City Arcade, where in addition to "a better dinner than at any house in the city," gentlemen from the country could enjoy the "finest Juleps, French and American Cobblers, and all other fine refreshments." Davis occasionally offered turtle soup to lure customers, and one Monday in September 1852 he upped the ante with an even bigger draw: a "mammoth Rattle Snake" which was "turned loose in the front show window for public exhibition" at precisely ten o'clock in the morning.[5]

H. L. Davis remained at the City Arcade until at least 1854, but he lost that position as he slid into dissolution. "Since we have known Harry Davis by sight," the *Tennessean* observed in 1858, "his career has been downward. From respectable proprietor he climbed down to employee. His glossy hat was exchanged for one napless and unbrushed—his flashy waistcoat gave place, like his other articles of apparel, to seedy successors." Davis enjoyed his liquor, and he apparently took more and more to the bottle as he sunk. In the summer of 1858 he set up an open-air operation on the Buena Vista road outside town, where he sold whiskey to the occasional thirsty traveler from a barrel on an impromptu counter. Living in a tent at the site, Davis soon fell ill, and he passed away in October. "Thus died a dealer in poison," the temperance-leaning *Tennessean* concluded. "May his life and death be a warning to those who are following in his trade."[6]

As Harry Davis was slipping downward, the city of Nashville—as small and remote as it was—gained European-trained caterers of its own. In December 1855 the brothers Edward and Augustus Jonnard presented the editors of the *Nashville Union and American* with a Christmas gift of a can of fresh Baltimore oysters and a bottle of "sparkling Catawba," a Champagne-like wine made from the first successful domestic wine grape, which surged in popularity in the 1850s. The Jonnards' establishment on Union Street was a combination bar, liquor store, and confectionery. They stocked imported brandy and sherry, domestic whiskey, and English ale on draft.

Over the next few years, they catered events like the Grand Ball at the Odd Fellows Hall. Though local papers referred to the Jonnards as French and even "Parisian-born," census and immigration records show they were born in Belgium. It is unknown whether that was a mistake on the part of the editors or an impression cultivated by the Jonnards. (Being French was good marketing.) Continuing in another long-running tradition for European-born restaurateurs in the South, the Jonnards managed to rack up a mountain of debt very quickly. In 1858 their shop and its contents were seized by the sheriff and put up for auction to satisfy creditors. Edward Jonnard seems to have left the city soon after, but Augustus stuck around and played a leading role in the city's culinary life for years to come.[7]

➤✳— Louisville

The same forces that shaped the menus of East Coast restaurants—especially increasing trade and improved transportation—transformed dining in cities further west as they grew from frontier outposts to large centers of commerce. Regardless of differences in climate, flora, and fauna, that transformation played out in a remarkably homogenous way across the South. Commercial travelers and local gourmands had their preferred slate of relatively standardized fine-dining dishes, and they could be increasingly confident of finding them whether they were eating in New York or Charleston—or, by the 1850s, in Louisville, Kentucky. Louisville, in fact, is a prime example of this midcentury dining transformation.

Between 1840 and 1850, Louisville's population had more than doubled, from twenty-one thousand residents to forty-three thousand, surpassing Charleston and making it the third largest city in the South, after Baltimore and New Orleans. As was the case in many other western cities, the leading figures on Louisville's emerging culinary scene were not native Kentuckians but people who had migrated there from the East.

William H. Walker was born in 1812 in Alexandria, Virginia, and arrived by the 1830s in Louisville, where he established Walker's Coffee House, which soon became a regular meeting place for the Whig Party. At first Walker didn't put much emphasis on the food side of his business. In 1836 the *Louisville Daily Journal* lauded him as "the prince of coffee-house keepers as well as of generous fellows," and implored its readers to "go and try one of his juleps." Even after Walker remodeled and enlarged his establishment, renaming it Walker's Eagle House, his definition of "every inducement to the merchant, mechanic and farmer" included his slate of liquors and wines, the sleeping rooms, and the selection of newspapers from around the country, in that order. His early ads make no mention of what might be had to eat.[8]

Soon, though, Walker began to expand his culinary repertoire, and he started with oysters. Just before Christmas in 1839 he announced that he had received a few barrels of "superior Baltimore shell oysters" along with another lot of oysters in large and small cans. By the summer of 1844 he was serving turtle soup, and a few months later he was advertising a full repertoire of "substantials and delicacies" that included venison, blue-wing duck, woodcock, partridge, and sardines. A significant portion of Walker's business was driven by Louisville's rising wholesale trade, and he promised that "country merchants and others visiting the city" could order meals at any time of the day.[9]

In 1845, his business thriving, Walker moved to a new building at the corner of Pearl and 3rd Streets. It was three stories high, with numerous outbuildings in the back. Patrons entered from 3rd Street into a large barroom that had fourteen-foot ceilings and dispensed both libations and news, for it was stocked not only with the finest spirits but also with "all the best daily journals and periodicals." Behind the bar was a large dining room, and beyond it the kitchens. The entire second floor, which was entered by a staircase from the barroom, was a single room divided by folding doors, which could be thrown open to create a public dining hall or be closed to create separate rooms for private parties. Five sleeping chambers were on the third floor, while the cellar beneath the barroom was initially used as a wine cellar, though Walker announced his intention to convert it eventually into an oyster cellar. A cistern with a pump in the back of the lot provided water not just to the restaurant and hotel but also to the building next door, which Walker had fitted up as a barbershop and bathhouse.[10]

The advertisements for Walker's New City Exchange highlighted not just the exotic foods he was serving but also their sources, giving us a clear view of how the steamship trade expanded culinary supply chains. The evening mail boat brought fresh lobsters from Boston, oysters from New York, and cans of French sardines. On November 29 the steamer *Palestine* delivered forty brace of grouse and fifty of quail, direct from the western prairies by way of St. Louis. For something to drink alongside, Walker regularly sold aged port wine, London porter and brown stout, Edinburgh ale, pale ale from Poughkeepsie and Philadelphia, and Kentucky crabapple cider. In February 1846 he offered for sale a very rare spirit: cherry brandy, described as "old and very rich, made from the wild cherry (the seed not mashed in it)." It had been imported by Walker in 1834, shortly after he arrived in Louisville, and had since aged a dozen years.[11]

Though much of Walker's game and seafood came from a thousand miles away, there was still a distinct seasonality to the fare. Canned oysters from Baltimore made their first appearance during the "r" months of September and October. Around the same time, local hunters began delivering wild ducks, quail, and pigeons. The trade in game from the distant prairies kicked up around November, once the weather got cold enough for the birds to be shot, dressed, and shipped on a multiday journey without refrigeration. Fresh "shell oysters"—that is, oysters still in the shell, not shucked in cans—began arriving toward the end of November, and they included not just Chesapeake bivalves from Baltimore but also Gulf oysters from Biloxi and New Orleans.

As the weather warmed in April, Walker's offering shifted. He began advertising "spring and summer drinks," which included both plain and fancy juleps—the latter most likely adorned with fruits and flowers in the style of the great Virginia julep makers—along with punches, cobblers, cherry brandy from Copenhagen, strawberry and pineapple lemonade, and a mysterious concoction known only as Walker's Summer Beverage. Around the same time, the first green sea turtles of the season made their appearance. These were captured in the Gulf of Mexico, shipped live up the Mississippi and Ohio, and slaughtered at Walker's restaurant. Each time a steamer delivered a fresh victim, which happened every week or two through August, Walker served turtle soup and turtle steak to the local epicures.[12]

We know little about how Walker's kitchen staff cooked those ingredients sourced from afar, but the dishes were likely quite varied. An 1846 advertisement for the City Exchange noted that "French, German, Italian, and Kentuck cooks are employed to suit all tastes." We can assume those "Kentuck cooks" were enslaved African Americans, for census records show that Walker's household included four enslaved males between the ages of 10 and 23 and one enslaved woman between 36 and 54.[13]

Walker's Exchange was Louisville's leading restaurant, but it was by no means the only place where diners could find an upscale meal. Walker's chief competitor was Samuel Hyman, a New Yorker who had migrated to Louisville in the 1830s and opened a coffeehouse. It was officially the White Hall Coffee House but was frequently referred to simply as Hyman's. In January 1837 the *Journal* observed that Hyman was "distinguishing himself by the superior elegance and taste with which his establishment is conducted." As at Walker's Exchange, the bar was the centerpiece of White Hall, and in Hyman's case it was a true showpiece. Made of beautifully variegated mahogany, it was topped with a slab of imported Italian marble which one visitor described as "as beautifully shaded and delicate in hue as the evening sky." In the center was a gigantic marble urn that cost $200, and the main counter was flanked on either side by smaller ones topped with Kentucky marble, which were regularly graced by "blooming juleps, with their ever-green heads." Sideboards were loaded with glasses, decanters, vases, and gilt bottles of every color and tint of the rainbow, and Hyman served claret from the blue, hock from the green.[14]

Over time, the reputation of Hyman's kitchen grew to match that of his bar. His cuisine blended imported luxuries with down-home staples, ranging, as the *Journal* put it, "from the fresh and tempting oyster 'direct from Baltimore' to the rich buckwheat cakes direct from 'Kaintuck'." Early on, the local newspapers praised his fish preparations, which included striped bass in butter as well as fresh haddock, turbot, codfish, and salmon. In 1839 Hyman announced that he had made arrangements in New Orleans and Philadelphia to ensure a continued supply of fresh oysters in the shell. The national game trade had not yet developed by this point, but Hyman announced that "hunters are especially employed to keep me constantly supplied with pheasants, partridges, pigeons, rabbits, squirrels, ducks, and every other variety of wild game."[15]

One fish in particular, though highly prized by southern gourmands, could not be had at White Hall: fresh shad, an article available only in the eastern cities. That didn't keep a few sharpers from trying to scratch the market itch. In 1837 the *Picayune* of New Orleans scoffed at "all the up-river papers from Baton Rouge to Louisville prating about the nice fresh Shad" that had been caught that season in the Ohio and Mississippi Rivers. "We would like to see one of these shad—once," the editors wrote, speculating that the supposedly fresh shad might be "pickled shad, caught—by hand—out of certain tubs of water where they had been placed to freshen." Indeed, the white shad beloved by diners in the coastal areas of the Atlantic was not to be found in the Mississippi Basin, which has only two smaller varieties—the gizzard shad and threadfin shad—that are forage fish for other game fish but not eaten by humans.[16]

In 1845, for reasons unknown, Samuel Hyman suddenly shut down White Hall, announcing that he was "giving up housekeeping" and putting most of his furniture and paintings up for auction. It's possible that he overextended himself with his creditors, as did so many other restaurateurs in this era of recurring financial booms and panics. Hyman remained in Louisville, however, operating a grocery store and produce stand for a few years before teaming up with a man named Daniel Hewes in 1849 and getting back into the culinary business on an even grander scale.

Hyman and Hewes christened their new establishment Marble Hall. Located on 5th Street between Market and Jefferson, it had the entirety of its hundred-foot front stuccoed to imitate Italian and Egyptian marble. Guests entered via the Julep Saloon, which had a twenty-foot ceiling decorated with medallions representing the Muses. A gallery ornamented with statuary and supported by faux-marble columns stretched across the front of the room, and the walls were covered with elaborate golden paper ornamented with fountains, designed by Le Pere of Paris at a cost of 300,000 francs. The entire chamber was lit by gas, including a gigantic gas-burning chandelier that hung from the center of the ceiling, its burners fashioned into figures of spread eagles with lions cowering beneath them. Hyman's old marble-topped bar now stretched along the back of the saloon, with gilded moldings of dolphins playing in water and a twelve-foot-high French mirror on the wall behind it. Divans, sociables, tête-à-têtes, and ottomans carved from mahogany with embroidered velvet cushions dotted the room.

"There is nothing equal to this in the country, nor in the great cities of Europe," the editors of the *Louisville Daily Courier* declared, apparently sincerely, adding that Hyman and Hewes were "determined to keep the finest table d'Hote in this country." That table was set in the rooms to the right of the Julep Saloon, which included the restaurant dining room as well as an oyster saloon. The upper floors contained rooms for private suppers and dinner parties, and the kitchen was equipped with "all the modern improvements of the culinary art," including gas ranges with the capacity to prepare dinners for more than a thousand guests. The attached larder was filled with every variety of game, which a local reporter insisted "must be seen to be appreciated, and no epicure should miss the opportunity." To top everything off with a little entertainment, Hyman and Hewes installed a "bowling saloon," which was more than a hundred feet long and had six lanes and cushioned sofas for spectators.[17]

Daniel Hewes left the partnership in 1850, and Samuel Hyman continued as the sole proprietor. To fill his impressive game larder, Hyman no longer had to depend upon local hunters but instead sourced meats via the newly launched express companies. In November 1850 he received a shipment of wild geese and ducks—canvasback, mallard, and blue-wing teal—along with twenty barrels of New York winter oysters in the shell. He bragged that "my larder is, as usual, crowded with every variety of dainties from a Pee Wee [a small bird] to a Buffalo Tongue." His offering wasn't limited to meats but included, as he pitched it in one advertisement, "all the various delicacies of this and other climes." In March 1851 he wowed his customers with an unseasonably early selection of green peas, asparagus, and cucumbers, which presumably he had shipped in from warmer parts down South. Less than a month later he was offering spring chickens and a most notable new arrival: fresh Baltimore shad filled with roe. Shipping reports from the period indicate that Hyman received much of this produce from steamers arriving downriver from Cincinnati instead of upriver from New Orleans, indicating that the goods had traveled westward over the mountains via express trains.[18]

By 1851 Samuel Hyman and William Walker were competing head-to-head to procure the most impressive array of delicacies from distant places. Over the course of three days that summer, the two men sent multiple rounds of turtle soup to the editors of the *Daily Courier*, who declared equitably that diners "can be supplied with the soup in all its richness and excellence . . . either at Marble Hall or the City Exchange." Hyman got a leg up when he delivered a tray of East Coast oysters and clams on May 28. The editors marveled at "shell oysters in Louisville at this time of year . . . something out of the usual order of things" and declared that Hyman was "pretty apt to procure everything rich and rare that tact and money can get."[19]

A growing Louisville was gaining new options in the way of sweet treats, too. Alfred Borie had operated a wholesale and retail confectionery and

Advertisements for Samuel Hyman's Marble Hall, in the *Louisville Daily Courier*, November 28, 1850, and May 24, 1852.

fruit store on Pearl Street since 1843, selling handmade candies and imported fruits like raisins and fresh Smyrna figs along with the occasional can of Baltimore oysters. In the late 1840s, Dr. James Wood opened the Eagle Confectionery and Ice Cream Saloon, where in addition to cakes, candies, and frozen treats he sold a medicated lozenge called Wahoo Candy for the cure of coughs and colds. Any southern city worth its salt needed a French confectioner or two, and Louisville secured theirs in 1849. Roemer and Specht, advertising themselves as "Late from Paris," opened a wholesale and retail confectionery on 4th Street, where they manufactured "pyramids, cakes and ornaments for weddings and parties, confectionery toys & c."[20]

By 1851 Samuel Hyman was doing so well that he opened a branch location of Marble Hall on Wall Street. He embarked on a tour through northern cities in 1851 to make arrangements "to obtain, with despatch, a regular supply of every desireable article, such as Oysters, Game, Fish &c." Starting in May 1852, he began publishing the bills of fare for the "extra lunch" served in his Julep Saloon, which varied each day and give us a good glimpse into his kitchen's repertoire. The dishes range greatly in style, and they reflect a dining culture in transition. Plenty of the items could have come straight from the kitchen of Barkis' Hotel—pork and beans, boiled beef, and "jole and cabbage"—but there are some tempting American regional specialties, too, like "gumbo fille" and stuffed crabs. These are intermingled with a few French and Italian flourishes, like "Veal Espagnole," "Grenadios of Veal, a la Toulouse," and "Maccaroni, a la Nepolitaine."[21]

Even with established suppliers and a French-inflected menu, running a restaurant remained a risky proposition. For Samuel Hyman it all collapsed in 1853, and he may have overextended himself with his second location. Hyman announced that he was "about to remove South this fall" and was putting up for sale his entire stock of wines, liquors, and cigars as well as all of the furniture in Marble Hall. He offered to either sell the building outright or rent it by the year to a prospective tenant. The United States had tumbled into another of its recurring recessions in 1853, and Hyman struggled to find a taker. By August he had closed Marble Hall and was offering to sell his liquor supply at cost. Two months later, insisting that he had to wrap up his affairs by November first and leave town, he announced the remainder of his booze was for sale "cheap, very cheap . . . less than cost." He also offered out for hire "a superior man cook, one that has cooked at Marble Hall for the past four years."[22]

Hyman never did manage to remove to the South, but he was finished as a restaurateur. Unable to sell the building, he converted Marble Hall into a concert hall and hung out his shingle as a stockbroker and real estate dealer.[23]

Hyman's fall offered an opportunity for a young German immigrant named Charles Casper Rufer. Born near Frankfurt in 1831, he emigrated to New York City at the age of eighteen and found work in a grocery store. In 1852 he headed south, intending to move to New Orleans. He stopped along the way in Louisville and found the city to his liking, so he decided to stay there instead. Rufer went to work as a bartender for W. H. Walker at the Exchange Saloon, and he spent four years learning the restaurant trade and saving enough money to set out on his own. In March 1856 he took over the former Washington Hall near the corner of 5th and Main and renamed it the St. Charles Restaurant. Soon he was rivaling his former employer as the top destination for gourmands.[24]

Rufer quickly proved himself as adept as Walker in establishing a network of suppliers and obtaining provisions from distant markets. On May 1, 1858, the steamer *Woodford* left New Orleans, and it arrived in Louisville a week later carrying, in addition to its main cargo of coffee and molasses, two splendid green sea turtles and a crate of pompano, which C. C. Rufer promptly put on the menu at his restaurant. Rufer was an early customer of the "fast freight line," a new approach for speedily moving freight across the still fragmented rail network. These companies were separate from the railroads themselves, and they paid to have their own cars carried over the lines of different railroads, with faster schedules than normal freight. Fast freight cars were often equipped with "compromise" wheels that could be adjusted to fit tracks of different gauges, since American railroads had yet to standardize their rails. One of the first of these was the Merchant's Dispatch from the American Express Company, which in 1856 began running cars from New York and Boston to various western cities, including Buffalo, Cleveland, Chicago, and Cincinnati. By July 1857 it had established a connection all the way to Louisville, making it possible for freight to be shipped from New York City to Kentucky in three days or less.[25]

Charles Rufer made liberal use of the Merchant's Dispatch services, and by 1858 he was announcing regular shipments of fresh eastern shellfish. In July the company's couriers delivered him three thousand fresh clams, which arrived from New York in just three days and were incorporated into a fine soup at the St. Charles. Two months later more than twelve hundred

BILL OF FARE.

SOUP.

Oysters.

FISH.

Baked Pike, with Oyster Sauce.
Broiled Pike, with Butter Sauce.
Baked Bass, with Lemon Sauce.
Broiled Bass, with Butter Sauce.

OYSTERS.

Raw.   Broiled.
                Fried.
Scolloped.   On Half Shell.

ROAST.

Saddle of Venison, Currant Jelly.
Roast of Venison, Sauce a la Teine.
Saddle of Lexington Mutton, Green Crab Apple Sauce.
Young Pigs, Stuff'd, with Giblet Sauce.
Turkey, a l'Anglaise.
Stagg's Hams, Braised, a la St. James.
Ducks, Giblet Sauce.
Chicken, Roubite Sauce.

COLD DISHES.

Buffalo Tongue, with Aspic Jelly.
Beef Tongue, with Aspic of Fowl.
Ducks, with Aspic of Fowl.
Turkeys, Braised, with Aspic.
Ham.
Beef, a la Mode.

ENTREES.

Westphalia Hams, Champagne Sauce.
Boned Turkey, stuffed with Trouffle, Brain Sauce.
Braised Ducks, Olive Sauce.
Croquettes of Fowl, Ravigote Sauce
Boar's Head, Braised, a la Francaise.
Fillet of Chicken, Sauce a la Slaughter.
Atkinson Ham, Baked, Hock Wine Sauce.
Broiled Rabbits, Butter Sauce.
Broiled Squirrels. Clam Sauce.
Wild Geese, Sherry Sauce.
Diamond-back Terrapin scolloped, Sauce a la St.
Charles.
Diamond-back Terrapin fricassee, Madeira Sauce.

BROILED.

Quails on Toast, Butter Sauce.
Prairie Grouse, Madeira Sauce.
Ducks, with Quince Jelly.
Ducks, with Currant Jelly.
Bear Steaks, Meringo Sauce.

RELISHES.

Pickles. Horse Radish. Mangoes. Spanish Olives.

Menu for the Grand Union Festival banquet at the Masonic Temple in Louisville, catered by Charles C. Rufer, from the *Louisville Daily Courier*, January 25, 1860.

oysters arrived from Prince's Bay on Staten Island, waters famous at the time for their top-quality shellfish. Express shipments from the West brought grouse and blue-wing ducks "direct from the prairies," too. A shipment of "the most splendid specimens of Mallard ducks that were ever seen" was sent to Rufer by C. A. Weisert of Vincennes, Indiana, in December, a fact that so excited the editor of the local *Vincennes Sun* that he predicted, "Rufer's epicurian customers can prepare their palates for the most agreeable surprise that this popular caterer ever gave them." Not yet thirty years old, Rufer had established himself as the leading caterer in Kentucky.[26]

In January 1860, as secessionist sentiments in the South were coming to a boil, the legislatures of Tennessee and Kentucky gathered at the Masonic

Temple in Louisville to "renew their earnest devotion to the Union" and enjoy a grand banquet. The walls were festooned with evergreen boughs interspersed with shields emblazoned with the national colors and the names of the country's great patriots. The tables were adorned with a form of ornate confectionery that had been introduced to East Coast cities like Charleston more than a decade before: "pyramids with names essentially French." These Louisville versions were the creation of the talented young caterer Charles C. Rufer. The menu that evening comprised fourteen courses, starting with soup, fish, and oysters and finishing with four rounds of desserts, then fruit and coffee. The four meat courses offered a sumptuous array of thirty-one dishes that spanned the full breadth of the nation's bounty, including two preparations of eastern diamondback terrapin—one scalloped in sauce *a la St. Charles,* the other fricasseed with Madeira—and a slate of dishes from out West, like buffalo tongue with aspic and prairie grouse with Madeira sauce. Local fields and pastures were well represented by saddle of Lexington mutton with green crabapple sauce and two ham dishes that—a good century and a half before it became a farm-to-table menu trope—included their purveyors in their names: Stagg's ham braised *a la St. James* and Atkinson's ham baked with hock wine sauce.

Louisville had come a long way from mutton chops and pig's feet.[27]

➤)(— New Orleans

Some twelve hundred miles down the Ohio and Mississippi Rivers from Louisville, the commercial dining scene in New Orleans continued to thrive, making it the most acclaimed culinary city in the South and, depending upon whom you asked, perhaps even the United States. Local partisans maintained that the "model French dinner" from the Martin brothers at Victor's Restaurant was "equal to the best served in Paris." One noted that fashionable Frenchmen visiting New Orleans ranked Victor's "fully equal to those of Very's, the Provencaux Freres, and other famous Parisian restaurants."[28]

In the 1850s, Moreau's Restaurant emerged as the leading rival to Victor's. Founded on Customhouse Street in the late 1830s by Jean-Baptiste Moreau, a recently arrived Frenchman, the restaurant's culinary fame came under the two men who succeeded him, F. Moulin and Charles M. Rhodes. Rhodes was born and raised in Baltimore, where he started working in restaurants in his early teens. In 1839, at the young age of seventeen, he set out for New Orleans to try his fortunes, taking a job as a waiter at Moreau's shortly after he arrived. He flourished there, rising through the ranks to become the restaurant's manager. In the early 1840s, Moreau sold the business to Moulin, his *chef de cuisine*, and Moulin later invited Charles Rhodes in as a partner. In 1850 the two men moved Moreau's Restaurant to a three-story building at 77 Canal Street in the heart of the booming commercial district. The menu appears to have been thoroughly French, for the *New Orleans Crescent* commented in 1858 that Moulin was still cooking "in a manner that might confuse Soyer himself"—a reference to the famous French chef who cooked at London's Reform Club in the 1840s.[29]

Jean-Baptiste Moreau bounced around several different kitchens after selling his eponymous restaurant. He worked for a time as the chef of the St. Louis Hotel, then in 1847 he partnered with a man named Louis Tournoi to take over the old Maison Dorée on Natchez Street and relaunch it as the Restaurant du Cardinal. Advertising their location as being "in a convenient part of the Second Municipality for men of business," they offered meals at all hours in "both American and French styles." Two years later, having ended the partnership with Tournoi, Moreau moved his restaurant two blocks over to the Commercial Exchange Building on St. Charles Street, where he operated until 1853. He ended up moving out to the lake resorts, opening Moreau's Restaurant at the end of the shell road out at Old Bayou St. John.[30]

In 1859 a commentator for the *Daily Picayune* mapped out a taxonomy of the city's restaurants, ranking them from high to low. "The Moreaus, the Victors, the Johns, Boudreau have a fame of their own," he wrote, putting them in the top tier. The "John" in question was John Strenna, a Corsican-born man who arrived in New Orleans in the 1840s, mentored under some of the city's leading caterers, and in 1853 opened the John Restaurant on Carondolet. The writer's "second class" of establishments included highly furnished saloons and restaurants that served a clientele of regular boarders, who ate "a fixed number of dishes" and were astonished if a nonregular came in and ordered a one-off fifty-cent meal. Down at the bottom was the "dingy, damp room, where customers sit on benches and eat pork and beans, or bacon and Irish potatoes."

The writer held a particular fondness for the city's many "cheap restaurants . . . where you will be astonished at everything, and to begin with, the very small amount your dinner will cost." These typically had "high-sounding" names, like the Republic, the Independence, or the Four Nations. At the

Oriental one could order "vermicelli or macaroni soup in the original Italian style, in which you can plant your spoon and leave it standing." For as little as 25 cents guests could have a tender beefsteak or "as good a piece of fried redfish as you may desire," accompanied by "a certain Catalan wine that will stir up the blood in your veins," and finish with coffee and cigars.[31]

Befitting a hub of international trade, New Orleans's restaurant fare was cosmopolitan in style and scope. In a letter written on New Year's Day in 1850, a correspondent for the *Intelligencer* of Concordia, Louisiana, captured how the city's residents greeted the new year. "In New Orleans people live well," he noted. "I wish you could be here with me to-day, to stroll through the various restaurants and coffee-houses . . . to taste the profusion of delicacies with which they are supplied. This is a general feast day, and our enterprising purveyors have taxed the whole world to gratify their customers." The bills of fare he enjoyed included whitefish from Lake Superior, pompano from Tampa Bay, and fresh salmon from Oregon, delivered by way of Panama. The requisite canvasback duck from the Chesapeake was joined by snails from France, beef from Kentucky, and buffalo tongue from Independence, Missouri. Of particular note was "Birds' nest Soup, from China," the first ever imported to the city.[32]

Despite the city's deeply entrenched culture of slaveholding, no enslaved caterers or restaurateurs appear to have attained prominence in New Orleans the way they did in Charleston and Richmond. Perhaps more surprising, considering that New Orleans had a substantial number of free persons of color, none appear to have operated a coffeehouse or restaurant of any significance during this period—or if they did, their names have not survived in newspapers, travelogues, or city directories. The city was, however, a great magnet for immigrant restaurateurs, like Fritz Huppenbauer. Born in Württemberg around 1825, Huppenbauer left Germany in the wake of the revolutionary ferment of 1848 to seek better opportunities abroad. He went first to Ireland, then sailed from Cork to New Orleans on the barque *Orion*, arriving in 1849 at the age of twenty-three. He listed himself on the ship's passenger logs as a "garcon de sale," or waiter, and he quickly found work in one of the city's many thriving restaurants.[33]

In 1852 Huppenbauer took over the Commercial Restaurant at 52 Customhouse Street, which is today known as Iberville Street. There he earned a reputation as a skilled host and caterer. Seven years later Huppenbauer saw an opportunity emerge when Pierre Leveque, one of the two founders of the United States Restaurant, passed away and his former partner, Auguste Pino, put the establishment up for sale. Huppenbauer took over the lease on the building on Common Street and purchased all of the restaurant's equipment, which included modern cooking furnaces, a complete array of copper cookware and utensils, and a fully stocked wine cellar.

Huppenbauer acquired more than just the physical location and the goodwill of the United States Restaurant's name. He also acquired, in a literal sense, many of the workers who had made the kitchen such a success. Despite being raised to adulthood not knowing slavery, Huppenbauer, like many other immigrant restaurateurs from Europe, appears to have taken to the institution quite readily once he moved to New Orleans. Leveque and Pino had purchased several slaves during the 1850s, including a man named Jake, who was twenty-two years old when the two restaurateurs bought him for $1,150. At first Huppenbauer appears to have hired these enslaved workers from Pino when he took over the United States Restaurant in 1859. In August of the following year, he purchased outright from Pino four enslaved men named Moses, Louis, Alfred, and Jake.[34]

In 1859, the same year that Huppenbauer acquired the United States Restaurant, a French immigrant named Antoine Alciator opened a small restaurant and boardinghouse at 60 St. Peter Street. Alciator had been born in 1825 in Marseilles, and he arrived in New Orleans sometime in the early 1850s. Though in the twentieth century Alciator's son Jules would begin advertising that his family's now-famous New Orleans restaurant was founded in 1840, the historical record makes clear that it was actually 1859—qualifying it as an antebellum restaurant, but only barely so. Antoine's went on, however, to become not only an influential New Orleans restaurant but also its longest lived, the only antebellum restaurant in the South that is still in operation today. Antoine Alciator died in 1877, but his wife, Julie, styling herself the Widow Alciatore, continued the business, and their son Jules took over in 1898. It was Jules who introduced what became many of Antoine's most celebrated dishes, like *tomates glacées* (chilled tomatoes filled with crabmeat), *ravioli au parmesan*, and the now-legendary oysters Rockefeller.[35]

Not all European immigrants who passed through New Orleans's commercial kitchens stayed as long as Huppenbauer and Alciator. Charles Ranhofer was born in France, the son of a restaurateur in St. Denis, and left home at age twelve to study the art of pastry making in Paris. He spent his teenage years working in the châteaux of European nobility. At the age of nineteen

Antoine's Hotel

— AND —

Restaurant,

65 and 67 St. Louis Street,

Established 1859.

FRENCH STYLE.

Board by the Day, Week or Month.

WIDOW ALCIATORE, Proprietress.

Advertisement for Antoine's Restaurant indicating its original founding date as 1859, in the *New Orleans Times-Democrat,* September 1, 1888.

he came to the United States in the service of the Russian consul to New York, but he was soon lured southward to Washington, D.C. In February 1857, G. E. D'Ivernois, the proprietor of the short-lived D'Ivernois's Hotel on Pennsylvania Avenue, announced excitedly that "he has now engaged a competent and professional French cook recently arrived from Paris, where he has gained an extensive reputation as a first rate artist at his business." This was in all likelihood Charles Ranhofer. He stayed only a short time in the nation's capital, though, making his way later that year to New Orleans, where he took a position in the kitchen of Francois Lefevre and perhaps some of the city's other restaurants. Ranhofer remained in New Orleans until 1860, when he briefly visited France and then returned to New York City. He put to good use the culinary tutelage he had gained on his southern sojourns when he was hired in 1861 as chef of the newly opened Maison Dorée in Union Square. In February 1863 he was hired away by a noted New York restaurateur named Lorenzo Delmonico. Charles Ranhofer oversaw the kitchen at Delmonico's for the next thirty-four years.[36]

CHAPTER 6

Conflict and Commerce

Catering and Bartending during Wartime

On November 9, 1860, a delegation of prominent businessmen and politicians from Savannah arrived in Charleston to celebrate the reopening of the Charleston and Savannah Railroad and to reaffirm the tight bonds between South Carolina and Georgia. They boarded the steamer *Carolina* for a harbor tour and then, escorted by the Washington Light Infantry and the Citadel Cadets, took carriages to the Mills House for a grand banquet. Just three days before, Abraham Lincoln had been elected president, and secession fever was rippling through the South. That evening word arrived from Columbia that the state senate had voted 44 to 1 to delay a secession convention until after the New Year, hoping that cooler heads would prevail.

That evening in the main dining saloon of the Mills House, two hundred guests were treated to a feast that the *Charleston Mercury* called "a spread that would have satisfied the Lord Mayor of London." The dinner was most likely prepared by George E. Johnston, an African American man employed by hotelier Thomas S. Nickerson first at the Charleston Hotel and then at the Mills House, which opened in 1853. The spread embodied the full breadth of the southern fine-dining repertoire, opening with green turtle soup and broiled whiting and ending with pyramids, meringues, and twenty-three other desserts. The entrées and roast courses featured fricassee chicken *a la financiere*, shrimp patties, turkey stuffed with chestnuts, and a saddle of venison with cranberry jelly.

After rounds of toasts and a final course of coffee and liqueurs, the leading members of the Georgia delegation were escorted to a massive rally at Institute Hall, which had been organized independently of the dinner by

The Mills House in Charleston, from *Gleason's Pictorial Drawing-Room Companion*, December 10, 1853. (Courtesy Special Collections at Addlestone Library, College of Charleston, Charleston, S.C.)

Robert Barnwell Rhett. One of the Georgians, Francis Stebbins Bartow, had until recently been a vocal Unionist, but now, his belly full and well plied with fine Madeira, he declared thunderously that if South Carolina seceded, then Georgia must follow course and join with its neighbor as a single nation. Bartow was followed by Savannah attorney Henry Rootes Jackson, who echoed Bartow's sentiments and insisted that South Carolinians must act without delay. Telegrams were immediately dispatched to Columbia informing South Carolina legislators of Georgia's pledge of solidarity. A special train was hired to whisk a delegation to Columbia in the morning so they could drum up support in the capital. By six the following evening, both branches of the legislature unanimously approved holding a secession convention on December 17.[1]

When the convention convened at the First Baptist Church in Columbia, its 169 delegates passed a unanimous resolution to secede from the Union.

They assembled two days later at Institute Hall in Charleston to draft the Ordinance of Secession. More than three thousand people gathered that evening to witness the ceremonial public signing. "The Union Is Dissolved!" the *Charleston Mercury* declared in a full-page headline. Four months later, after a tense standoff with Federal troops occupying the forts around Charleston, fifty Confederate cannons under the command of General P. G. T. Beauregard opened fire on Fort Sumter.

BILL OF FARE.

SOUP.
Green Turtle   Printeniere.

FISH.
Broiled Rock, Anchovy Sauce
Broiled Whiting, a la Maitre d'Hotel.

BOILED.
Leg of Mutton, Caper Sauce
Turkey, Oyster Sauce   Chicken, Celery Sauce
Ham   Tongue.

COLD DISHES.
Boned Turkey, garnished with Jelly
Boned Capon, garnished with Jelly
French Game Pie, Chicken Patti
Patti de Fol Gras
Lobster Salad
Chicken Salad.

ENTREES.
Broiled Lamb Chops, with Green Peas
Fricassee Chicken, a la financiere
Shrimp Pattie
Ducks, with Olives
Salme of Game, en croustard
Timball of Maccaroni
Fried Oysters
Broiled Green Turtle Steaks, Wine Sauce.

VEGETABLES.
Baked, Mashed and Boiled Potatos
Rice   Beets
Onions   Turnips, &c.

RELISHES.
Celery   French Mustard   Lettuce   Mixed Pickles
Worcestershire Sauce, &c., &c.
Currant and Cranberry Jellies.

ROAST.
Beef   Saddle of Mutton, Currant Jelly
Chickens   Turkey, Stuffed with Chesnuts
Baked Westphalia Ham, Champagne Sauce.

GAME.
Wild Turkeys   Wild Ducks
Saddle of Venison, Cranberry Jelly.

PASTRY.
Cabinet Pudding   Fruit Jelly
Apple Pies   French Biscuit
Cranberry Pies   Cakes, &c.
Cocoanut Pies   Omelette Souffle
Meringues   Ornaments
Cream Cakes   Crystallized Fruits
Kisses   Pyramids
Burgundy Jelly   Nuger Ornaments, &c.

FRUITS.
Vanilla Iced Cream
Apples   Raisins
Oranges   Almonds
Grapes   Walnuts
Bananas   Figs.

COFFEE AND LIQUERS.

Bill of fare for the banquet celebrating the reopening of the Charleston and Savannah Railroad, Mills House, Charleston, from the *Charleston Mercury*, November 10, 1860.

The Civil War disrupted the business of restaurants, hotels, and saloons, and for many in the culinary trades it proved ruinous. Others, though, found it a time of opportunity, and a few entrepreneurs even managed to prosper amid the chaos and deprivation of war.

Virginia seceded from the Union three days after the Confederates fired on Fort Sumter. "From that time forward," John Washington recalled in his autobiography, "Richmond became the seat of the Rebellion." In May 1861 it was made the capital of the Confederacy, and thousands of troops soon marched through the city on their way to attempt capturing Washington, D.C. "So many troops of all description was landed there," Washington wrote, "that it appeared to be an impossibility, to us, colored people, that they could ever be conquered."[2]

In addition to troops passing through on their way to the front, a constant stream of officers and enlisted men poured into the city on leave. In a matter of months Richmond's population effectively tripled, and housing was in short supply. Enterprising men threw open dozens of new saloons and cafés to cater to the troops swelling their city, and alongside them flourished lowlier establishments like gambling dens and cockfight pits. Soldiers drank on the streets, got into brawls, and broke into closed saloons on Sundays. One soldier smashed a plate glass window at the American Hotel with his fist to win a bet. Periodic whiskey shortages swept the town, and robberies were rampant. There were frequent fires, many of which were set intentionally. Vandals even broke into the House of Delegates, where they smashed a clock and stole furniture.[3]

Spiro Zetelle, Richmond's leading caterer and restaurateur, did what many other immigrant restaurateurs did across the South: he left town. On September 23 the Confederate steamer *Arrow* departed Norfolk, flying under a flag of truce and carrying seven paroled Union surgeons who had been captured in early battles. Also on board, the *Richmond Examiner* reported, was "Mr. Zatelle and family, who are on their way to Europe, under the protection of the English flag." Over the summer Zetelle had leased his restaurant to Caspar Wendlinger, and he left his real estate holdings in the care of Gustavus Myers, a New York attorney, and Frederick J. Cridland, the acting British consul in Richmond.[4]

Wendlinger kept the name Zetelle's Restaurant and operated it through at least 1863. John Washington, who had been hired out to Zetelle, stayed

"The Civil War in America: High Street, Richmond, Virginia," sketch by
Eyre Crowe in the *Illustrated London News*, July 26, 1862.

on and worked for Wendlinger, but he was really just biding his time, reading the newspapers and monitoring the fighting. In July 1861, after a few
encouraging victories in small battles in western Virginia, President Lincoln
ordered Union troops under Brigadier General Irvin McDowell to launch
an advance toward Richmond. On July 21, 20,000 Confederate troops re-
pulsed a larger force of 35,000 Union soldiers at the First Battle of Bull
Run, sending the Union army retreating toward Washington. The first major land battle of the war, it resulted in 3,000 Union casualties and 1,750
Confederate, and it made clear to both sides that the war was not going to
end as quickly or easily as many had believed.

"It had now become a well known fact," John Washington recalled, "that
slaves were daily making their Escape into the union lines." Washington
had formulated an escape plan of his own. It was a common practice for
hired-out workers on annual contracts to return home to visit their families
during the Christmas holidays and return to work on January first, either re-
suming a position renewed for the upcoming year or going under contract
to a new employer. Accordingly, Washington had received a pass and train
fare to return home to Fredericksburg. "I bid Mr Wendlinger and my fellow

servants good-by," he wrote. "They expected me back the 1st of January again to live with them another year."[5]

Washington had other plans. Back in Fredericksburg, he arranged a position for himself as a steward, or dining room waiter, at the Shakespeare House, which was owned by James Mazeen and George H. Peyton. He did well at the Shakespeare and was soon promoted to tending bar, for which he got paid $37 a week plus tips. But Washington had another motive for remaining in Fredericksburg instead of returning to Richmond: he wanted to stay close to the Union lines.

In April, as General McClellan's Army of the Potomac was beginning its Peninsular Campaign, Union troops advanced on Fredericksburg, and many of the city's white residents began evacuating. John Washington's employers, Mazeen and Peyton, announced they were closing the Shakespeare House. Washington was supposed to go with them to Salisbury, North Carolina, and serve as a personal servant to the two men, who had been elected officers in the 30th Virginia Infantry. On April 18, as Union troops started to appear on the far side of the river, Mazeen thrust a roll of banknotes into Washington's hand. "Pay off the hired servants and close up the Shakespeare House," Mazeen instructed his bartender, then mounted his horse and headed south.

Washington put things to rights at the hotel, then closed the doors and the shutters and called all the servants to the barroom. There, he recalled, he "treated them all around plentifull and after drinking 'the Yankees' health, I paid each one according to Orders. I told them they could go, just where they pleased but make sure the 'Yankees' have no trouble finding them." Washington then put the hotel keys in his pocket and went to pay a visit to Mrs. Taliaferro, his owner, who was hurriedly packing her silver spoons and preparing to flee to the country. "Child, you better come and go out in the country with me," she told him, with tears in her eyes. "So as to keep away from the Yankees." Washington told her that he would, but he had to deliver the hotel keys to Mrs. Mazeen first.

Washington did indeed take the keys to Mrs. Mazeen, but then he walked to the shore of the Rappahannock River and watched as Captain Wood of Harris's Light Cavalry of New York crossed over in a boat and ordered the mayor of Fredericksburg to surrender by ten the following morning. Next, Washington, along with his cousin and another African American man, walked up the river until they found a party of Yankee soldiers in a boat, who offered to take them over to the other side. Once he landed on the far shore, Washington was informed by the soldiers that Emancipation had been declared in the District of Columbia just two days before. John Washington was a free man.

That night Washington slept on a wooden bench in the town of Falmouth, but he awoke invigorated. "I felt for the first time in my life," he recalled, "that I could now claim every cent that I should work for as my own. I began now to feel that Life had a new joy awaiting me."[6]

John Washington made his way to Washington, D.C., where he found work as a waiter and remained for the duration of the war.

⇒)(⇐ Martial Juleps

Unlike Washington, John Dabney and Jim Cook stayed where they were in Richmond, and they prospered in the wartime economy. After a series of devastating battles in June and July of 1862, Union troops withdrew toward D.C., unsuccessful in their effort to take the rebel capital. Richmond remained a Confederate city for almost three more years.

Running a restaurant in wartime Richmond was a two-sided coin. On the one hand, the city was flooded with customers, and they spent money with reckless abandon. In July 1863 a correspondent from Richmond reported to the *Cincinnati Gazette* that, despite there being "200,000 Abolitionists within two days march," the city's shops were bustling, the hotels were filled, and "restaurants abound with guests. A single meal at one of these establishments—a beef steak, one dozen oysters and coffee—costs $5. A partridge, $1.25."[7]

At the same time, sumptuous meals were considered by many to be a shameful indulgence during a time of war, and as the Union blockade tightened, provisions became more difficult to procure, even for those willing to pay inflated prices. The government and military authorities did everything they could to suppress the sale of intoxicating liquors, too. On March 1, 1862, President Jefferson Davis suspended the writ of habeas corpus and declared martial law in Richmond. On the same day, the Confederate army banned the sale of "spirituous liquors, of any kind" and ordered the closure of any establishments that sold them. Jim Cook quickly ran afoul of this measure. On June 17 the *Richmond Dispatch* reported that "the celebrated toddy-mixer" had been put in Castle Godwin, the African American jail, "on suspicion of dispensing the ardent contrary to the provisions of the proclamation declaring martial law in Richmond." He was apparently released not long after.[8]

Despite such impediments, John Dabney and the Cook brothers took advantage of the war boom to launch businesses of their own. In July, Dabney left the Ballard House and teamed up with an African American man named Robert Taylor to open the Senate-House Restaurant on the second floor of a building on 8th Street, about two blocks from the capitol building. It isn't clear what legal requirements Dabney would have had to meet to open such a business, but it is likely that, like Nat Fuller in Charleston, he made an arrangement with a white trustee to lease the property on his behalf. He must have also reached an agreement with his owner, Cora DeJarnette, to share some portion of the proceeds. Taylor didn't last long in the business, and before the year was out Jim Cook had left the Ballard House and signed on as Dabney's new partner. Cook's brother Fields decided to get into the restaurant business, too. In October he announced that he and a man named J. Taylor had taken over a location at the corner of 10th and Main Streets. Calling the establishment Fields Cook & Co., they announced that they had just received a lot of "the finest oysters."[9]

On November 19, Dabney and Jim Cook were nabbed in one of the frequent raids conducted by officers from the Provost Marshal's office, who found a small amount of liquor on the premises of the Senate-House and ordered the restaurant closed. The city jail was already filled to capacity, so Dabney and Cook were locked up instead in Freeland's factory to await trial. The *Examiner* expressed skepticism that such raids would have much effect, noting that the Senate-House was just one of an estimated five hundred "drinking inlets" in operation in Richmond.[10]

By early December, Dabney and Cook were out of jail and back in operation at the Senate-House. On December 8 they delivered a "sumptuous lunch" of fresh venison steak to the editors of the *Richmond Whig*, who declared it "as tender as the frill of an Irishman's shirt." The editors made profuse declarations of guilt for "indulging in such luxuries, in times of general distress," but argued that they were obliged to fulfill "the ancient custom, by a considerate *restaurateur*," and added that "we only wish every soldier in the Confederate army could have had a ration of that same venison."[11]

Despite the efforts of the Confederate and city governments to limit alcohol sales and other forms of vice, Richmond remained wide open for most of the war. The combination of young, disaffected soldiers and alcohol was a dangerous one, and restaurateurs and saloon keepers were under the continual threat of violence. The risk was doubly severe for an African American bartender dealing with intoxicated white customers. John Dabney got into numerous fights with Confederate soldiers during the war. On one occasion, according to a story that Dabney repeatedly told his son in later years, four soldiers entered his bar and restaurant and started an altercation. The soldiers "threw everything throwable at him," Dabney's son recalled, and the julep maker caught anything that he couldn't dodge. "When the ammunition was exhausted, over the counter Pop went, and with his good oak club kept for emergencies . . . he 'laid about so lustily' that the four guardsmen fled."[12]

In April 1863 the Confederate authorities allowed Richmond's city government to resume some level of control, including issuing liquor permits in the city. Richmond's barrooms were officially back open for business. On April 29, C. C. Field and his partner J. C. Taliaferro—the first to be granted a new liquor license—announced that their Congress Hall Restaurant had "employed the celebrated caterer and bar-tender Jim Cook" and were ready to serve "the finest meats and delicacies the market affords." Even amid the wartime blockade, the market could apparently afford quite a lot. The Congress Hall had purchased "a large quantity of the finest Liquors and Wines, from Europe" and, "having secured ice enough to last through the season, Juleps, Punches, Cobblers, Sangarees & c. can always be had, mixed and prepared in the true old Virginia style." In June, Jim Cook once more could treat the editors of the local newspapers to turtle soup and "imperial" juleps. "It is not often that a 'treat' is given in these days," the *Richmond Examiner* noted, but Jim Cook repeated the same feat in July and August.[13]

➤❊— Washington, D.C.

Just a hundred miles to the north, restaurateurs in the Union capital were adapting to wartime conditions, too. Located just across the Potomac from rebel-held Virginia, Washington was under constant threat of attack for the entirety of the war. Indeed, the primary strategy of Confederate leaders was to capture the city, believing that if they did so, the Union would collapse. From the start, there was much worry of internal subversive threats from Confederate sympathizers in a city whose residents had long-running ties to the South. The Democratic mayor, James Berret, was arrested for Confederate sympathies and forced to step down, replaced by Richard Wallach of the Unconditional Union Party. Many of the police force defected and headed South to join the Confederate army. Washington was put under martial law, the writ of habeas corpus suspended, and the provost guard ordered to arrest suspected Confederate sympathizers.

Washington's population, like Richmond's, tripled over the course of the war, and not only from an influx of troops. In April 1862 the Compensated Emancipation Act freed Washington's thirty-two hundred enslaved residents, and the city became a magnet for fugitive slaves, some forty thousand of whom—including John Washington of Fredericksburg—made their way there from Virginia and Maryland in the years that followed. The city was soon transformed into a military encampment, supply depot, and massive field hospital. Seas of army tents ringed the city, and soldiers camped on the White House lawn. Many were merely passing through on their way to battlefields further south, but a standing force of fifty thousand troops was stationed in Washington to defend the capital. Railroads from the north brought arms, ammunition, provisions, horses, and mules closer to the front. The mall around the still-unfinished Washington Monument was converted into a grazing pasture for beef cattle to feed the soldiers. As the fighting intensified, more than a hundred hospitals were eventually established, staffed by volunteers from across the northern states and treating hundreds of thousands of sick and wounded men who were brought to Washington.[14]

At the outset of the war, the city remained, as Charles Dickens had observed two decades before, largely unfinished. The dome of the Capitol reached only the second tier of columns, the post office was only a third completed, and work on the Washington Monument had come to a halt with the obelisk at only a third of its anticipated height. The city lacked modern water and sewers, and epidemics of smallpox, typhoid fever, and measles swept through, creating repeated public health crises. There was perennial talk of throwing in the towel and moving the nation's capital west to St. Louis or a similar more suitable and central location. During the war years, though, the seeds were planted for the transformation of the District of Columbia into a modern city. In 1863 a twelve-mile aqueduct was completed to bring clean water from above the Great Falls in the Potomac, the first of many improvements that would reshape the landscape and living conditions in the city.[15]

The influx of soldiers pushed Washington's places of public accommodation away from sophisticated fine-dining fare and more toward the realm of boozing it up. Pennsylvania Avenue remained the center of the city's commercial and culinary life, and the stretch between 13th and 14th Streets, which before the war consisted of residential town houses, was transformed into a strip of restaurants, saloons, and gambling dens that became known as Rum Row. It would remain a notorious district for many years after the war ended. The local newspapers routinely ran lists of establishments fined or closed down by the Provost Marshal's office for having open bars and selling liquor after the mandated 9:30 p.m. closing time. Included on the list of repeat offenders in March 1863 was the National Eating House, which was now being operated by a man named Dubant and was ordered shut down for one week.[16]

The war marked a permanent shift in the city's culinary life away from the culture of banquets and public dinners and toward a more modern style of restaurants and cafés. English novelist Anthony Trollope visited Washington at Christmastime in 1861 and captured his observations in *North America*. "Everybody acknowledged," he wrote, "that society in Washington had been almost destroyed by the loss of the southern half of the usual sojourners in the city." Southern senators and government officials, he observed, had been more prone to hospitality than their northern brethren and more likely to spend lavishly while in the city.[17]

Joseph Boulanger, whose American and French Restaurant had been among D.C.'s top dining destinations in the 1850s, was now in declining health. In June 1862 the seventy-five-year-old Boulanger announced that he was putting his restaurant up for sale "on account of general debility and nervousness, superinduced by great age." Few restaurateurs in the nineteenth century got to enjoy retirement, including Joseph Boulanger. He passed away in August after a culinary career of more than thirty-seven years in the American capital. His restaurant's two buildings and all their furniture and fixtures were put up for auction.[18]

James Wormley, on the other hand, flourished during the war. His hotel hosted military and political leaders like General Winfield Scott, General George McClellan, and Senator Charles Sumner, and he received military contracts to cater dinner meetings at the War Department and to feed Confederate prisoners. His business got a boost from Anthony Trollope's visit, for a friend of Trollope's arranged for the author to stay "in the house of one Wormley, a coloured man, in I Street." The hotel, Trollope wrote in *North America*, "I can recommend [to] any Englishman who may want quarters in Washington." He admitted that Willard's, not Wormley's, was considered the city's top hotel, but he detested Willard's constant crowds and noisy corridors. Wormley had his main building on one side of the street and private rooms in houses on the opposite side, where Trollope took his lodgings, and he found the comfort and privacy to be much more to his liking.[19]

Advertisements for John Welcker's Buhler Restaurant and other competing restaurants in wartime Washington, D.C., in *Boyd's Washington and Georgetown Directory*, 1864.

138

The war brought a wave of new restaurateurs to the city. One who would be quite influential after the war ended was John Welcker, a native of Prussia, who immigrated to New York as a child. In 1861 he came to Washington and was involved in supplying provisions to the U.S. Army. By December he had entered into business with William Buhler, who owned a well-known restaurant in New York and had decided to open a branch on the second story of a Pennsylvania Avenue building between 9th and 10th Streets. The *Evening Star* called Buhler's Restaurant "the center of attraction of all here learned in the art of good living" and claimed that it surpassed even Buhler's own New York establishment. By 1862 Welcker had taken over from Buhler and was describing his restaurant's style as "*a la Maison Doree*," a reference to the famous Paris restaurant. He served breakfast from eight to noon and dinners at all hours, with an emphasis on game and oysters.[20]

The newspapers from 1863 to 1865 are filled with advertisements announcing the opening of one new restaurant after another, like the Gosling Restaurant, "formerly of New York," and V. Dengel's Rialto House at 9th and D, which featured steamed oysters "furnished at the shortest notice." Of particular note are two brothers, George Washington Harvey and Thomas Harvey, who in 1858 opened a small stand on the corner of 11th and C Streets, where they shelled out York River and other local oysters. As more and more soldiers arrived in the city, Harvey's Oyster Depot became a favorite military haunt, offering cheap steamed oysters and plenty of beer. Unlike Charleston and Richmond, where restaurateurs were cut off by the Union blockade and threatened by fire and artillery shelling, the dining business in Washington boomed, setting the city up for a very different look at the end of the war than it had at the beginning.[21]

⭐ Wartime New Orleans

On April 11, 1861, the members of the Orleans Cadets "whose good luck," as one newspaper unironically put it, "was to be chosen to go to Pensacola," packed their knapsacks at the city armory. Among their clothing and military gear they tucked caches of cigars, brandy, and other farewell gifts from friends and family. The troops marched down Camp and Chartres Streets through cheering crowds to the Pontchartrain Railroad Depot, where they boarded the three o'clock train to Milneburg. "Most of the members of this gallant company," the *Daily Picayune* noted, "were born and brought up in this city, and belong to well known families." Once the cars arrived at the end of the line, the cadets found that "all the hostelries, restaurants, and bar-rooms of that pleasant summer resort" were jammed with well-wishers who treated them to rounds of drinks and toasted their health and welfare. Miguel's Restaurant was the center of the bustle, and once his larder and cellar were depleted, the cadets boarded the steamer *Florida*—"the safest and most comfortable on the lake"—for a short voyage across Pontchartrain and then along the Gulf Coast to Pensacola. They were the first volunteer company mustered into service from the state of Louisiana. Their commander, Lieutenant Colonel Charles D. Dreux, was shot three months later by a Union scout near Newport News, Virginia, becoming the first Confederate officer to die in battle.[22]

A month after Miguel hosted the Cadets' send-off, three burglars broke into his restaurant and, when discovered by the proprietor, drew their revolvers on him. Miguel proved himself, as the *Daily Picayune* put it, "as good at a fight as in the kitchen," drawing his own revolver and wounding one of the men in the leg. The police promptly arrived and arrested the miscreants. A week later Miguel learned that his three assailants were all members of the Confederate navy. He dropped all charges, explaining that he did not want "boys so useful to the country" to be sent to the penitentiary. "Miguel," the *Times-Pic* added, "is a patriot."[23]

Miguel wasn't the only immigrant restaurateur to cast his lot with the Confederacy. In May, Fritz Huppenbauer ran an ad in the local newspapers announcing that, "in obedience to his patriotic promptings," he had changed the name of his restaurant from "that of the United States to the CONFEDERATE STATES RESTAURANT." He assured his patrons that "a cook of European education, and long experience in catering to Southern tastes," presided over his kitchen, and he welcomed "his old cash customers." He added that "those who prefer establishments where a different system prevails are not solicited, and they may go elsewhere."[24]

New Orleans's restaurateurs entered the war years with optimism, for business was booming. The Martin family—brothers Victor and Jules and their nephew George—had expanded to Baton Rouge in the fall of 1860, taking over the Gem Restaurant from its proprietor, Madame Eugène Flêche, and creating a second outpost of Victor's. They promised that each packet boat from New Orleans would deliver "fresh oysters, crabs, fish, and every delicacy that the New Orleans market can afford." The young Madame Eugène—just twenty-four years old—took the opportunity to move to New Orleans, where she took over a restaurant called Le Pellerin from Auguste

Broué, who was retiring and returning to France. In December 1860 John Galpin, formerly the chef at the Veranda Hotel, declared a secession of his own, leaving the hotel and launching "John Galpin's New Restaurant."[25]

That optimism faded quickly. The Union blockade effectively shut down New Orleans's port traffic and choked the city's economy. The value of imports plummeted from $155 million before the war to just $30 million in 1862. In April of that year the Union's West Gulf Blockading Squadron, under the command of Flag Officer David G. Farragut, fought its way past two Confederate forts about seventy miles downriver from New Orleans and steamed toward the city, which wasn't prepared to defend itself against an assault from the river. Confederate commander Major General Mansville Lovell saw no option but to evacuate. On April 29, Farragut and 250 Marines entered the city, lowered the Louisiana state flag flying over City Hall, and replaced it with the Union stars and stripes. Two days later, General Benjamin Butler and five thousand troops occupied the city without resistance.[26]

On May 2 the *New Orleans Crescent* reported that in the wake of the Confederate evacuation, the city's leading hotels had closed their doors, and so had many of the first-class restaurants. "The benighted bachelors, or poor fellows who have for so many years been enjoying the good living of the St. Charles, City, and St. James Hotels," the paper reported, "were quite astounded a few days ago, when they were notified to quit, though they had paid their bills honorably on demand." The paper painted a picture of "our bachelor and widowed friends and acquaintances, with their portemonnaies and wallets full of the best and first class shinplasters and banknotes, looking around for their gumbo, beef steaks, and choice saloons, and not an entrance to be found." After a few days, though, John Galpin, "with his usual good-humored phiz and philanthropy," opened a few of the rooms of his "recherche establishment." John's and Moreau's partially reopened, too, though with greatly restricted menus. The *Crescent* recounted the case of one "old fogy, who came from down East about forty years ago," who "innocently remarked that he would like to have a little codfish, and naively inquired if there were any expected by the vessels now coming up the river." Those vessels, for the time being at least, were bearing only Union troops.[27]

Falling early to Union forces proved fortunate for New Orleans, sparing its residents—including its coffeehouse keepers and restaurateurs—continued deprivation from the blockade and, in particular, from the physical destruction by siege that would be visited upon many southern cities.

The St. Louis Hotel remained closed for the duration of the war, serving for several years as a hospital for wounded soldiers from both the Federal and Confederate armies. But many of the city's other hotels and restaurants limped back to life. The Union blockade had previously cut off New Orleans's supply of pompano from the Gulf, but in July 1862 Boudro announced that he had just received a fresh shipment and would resume serving it at his resort out at the lake. In August 1862 the bar at the St. Charles Hotel was reopened to the public, and in December proprietor O. E. Hall reopened the entire hotel, operating again on the European plan.[28]

The flow of provisions was fully resumed by the end of 1863. In November the proprietor of Cassidy's Restaurant and Supper Rooms announced that he had just received on the steamers *Columbia* and *Yahoo* fresh mutton, venison, salmon, striped bass, codfish, shad, eels, turkey, capons, prairie chickens, Shrewsbury oysters, Little Neck clams, and a fine assortment of wine, brandies, and ale. It was still a war economy, though, and these good things came at a price. In July 1864 a correspondent signing himself "Union" protested in the *Times-Democrat* the "extortionate demands of those vampires known as restaurant keepers." Admitting that "everything in the eating and drinking way is too dear" in the current market, he maintained there was still no justification for the steep decline in the quality of those edibles sold at extraordinary prices. "Let us, then, rise en masse," he urged, "withdrawing our support from these fat, sleek-looking, *nonchalant, soi-disant* French restaurant keepers of St. Charles, Canal and Royal Streets!"[29]

The 1865 city directory lists thirty-eight restaurants in operation in New Orleans, including Victor's, Moreau's, Galpin's, and Le Pellerin. Antoine Alciatore was operating a small boardinghouse and restaurant on St. Peter, which he would move to St. Louis Street in 1867, where it is still in business today. These were augmented by fifty-five oyster saloons. Fritz Huppenbauer, now thoroughly reconstructed, was operating once again under his old banner, the United States Restaurant.[30]

One prewar caterer no longer in the city was Victor Martin. In an odd twist, he had turned the management of Victor's Restaurant over to his brother Jules and headed not northward to the front lines but south to Mexico. His destination was Bagdad, a city that no longer exists but at the time was an overnight boomtown. The Union blockade had choked off cotton exports from southern harbors, but vessels departing Mexican ports could not legally be intercepted. Confederate cotton was carried by wagon to Brownsville, Texas, then ferried across the Rio Grande to Matamoros and carted down to Bagdad at the mouth of the river, where it was loaded onto waiting ships. What was once a dusty little fishing village blossomed almost overnight into a buzzing shipping hub, its harbor jammed with vessels waiting to load and its population surging to some fifteen thousand residents, including blockade runners and desperadoes and the kind of people who catered to them.

Victor's plan, it seems, was to establish a Mexican outpost of his hotel and restaurant and cater to crowds of Confederate hustlers flush with cash instead of the impoverished loyalists lingering in New Orleans. But his luck didn't hold out. Victor died sometime in early March, and his brother Jules ended up going down to Bagdad to complete the venture. On March 17, 1865, just one week before Robert E. Lee's Army of Northern Virginia launched its final offensive with an attack on Grant's forces at Petersburg, Jules Martin announced in the New Orleans papers that he had purchased "the Restaurant and Hotel, known under the name Richelieu's Hotel in Bagdad, Mexico," where he promised "attentive service, a good restaurant, a well provided cellar, and comfortable rooms." He expressed sincere hopes that "his friends, customers, and the public in general" would extend their patronage to him down in Mexico. Few did. Less than two months later, Jules had given up the Mexican outpost of Victor's and was back in New Orleans.[31]

⇒※← The Flight of the Julep Maker

The closing years of the war proved challenging to culinary businesses throughout the South, but some proprietors found rewards of a different sort. In Richmond, Jim Cook's run at Congress Hall came to an abrupt end on September 17, 1863, when the restaurant was destroyed by fire—an act of arson suspected to have been committed by the friends of a counterfeiter who was scheduled to go on trial the next day in the Confederate States District Court, which met on the second floor above the saloon. Most of Congress Hall's ample stock of liquors was saved by rolling the barrels into the yard, but Jim Cook lost his trunk and all of his clothing in the blaze. He bounced from job to job after that, taking a position at Oak Hall on Franklin Street in December, then moving to the Chickahominy Saloon in April 1864.[32]

While at Oak Hall, Cook, "the renowned mixer of fluids and caterer," sent a letter to John Hunt Morgan, the notorious Confederate general who had led destructive cavalry raids behind Union lines in Ohio before being captured and sent to the Ohio State Penitentiary. Morgan escaped in

November 1863 and made his way to Richmond, where he took up lodging at the Ballard House in January. In his letter, Cook extended "his most profound respects" to the daring general and, having heard of his many exploits, wished him even more success in the future. "As a slave," Cook wrote, "he bids General Morgan God speed in his good and righteous works," and he sent along a small token of his appreciation. That token, the *Richmond Examiner* reported, included "dishes of viands, rare as exotics in a desert, and liquors of unsurpassed brands, forming, altogether, a feast sufficient for the General and his staff."[33]

By this point the Union and Confederate armies were gearing up for a brutal war of attrition in Virginia. In May 1864, General Ulysses S. Grant marshalled a massive force of 120,000 Union troops and began advancing toward Richmond to engage the 64,000 men in Robert E. Lee's Army of Northern Virginia. As the state braced for prolonged battle, the Virginia legislature outlawed the sale of liquor, bringing a halt to the restaurant and saloon business in Richmond. On April 30, the night before the ban took effect, John Dabney, "the cunningest compounder of beverages," treated the editors of the *Richmond Whig* to one last julep, with "pyramidal adornments and floral and fruity garniture." The law had forced Dabney from behind his counter, and he appears to have closed the doors of the Senate-House shortly after. Jim Cook, now ensconced behind the bar at the Chickahominy, was still serving turtle soup, but the *Whig* noted that going forward he "will have but little chance to exercise his skill in compounding juleps whilst this war lasts."[34]

That September, newspapers across the South reported a stunning piece of news from Richmond. Jim Cook, "the famous negro bartender," who had concocted "a grand monster mint julep" for the Prince of Wales, "has deserted old Virginia and gone over to the Yankees." He may have written letters to Confederate generals currying their favor (and tips), but Cook, it seems, had been biding his time just like John Washington. Cook reportedly had taken up residence in the District of Columbia, where he was delivering addresses to the crowds, standing atop a dry goods crate on Pennsylvania Avenue—working a different sort of crowd for tips, but this time as a free man.[35]

The Siege and Fall of Charleston

We'll end in Charleston, where it all began. From the beginning, the war turned Charleston's culinary life upside down. Some, like the famed pastry chef Eliza Lee, saw the writing on the wall early. On April 6, 1861, six days before the Confederate batteries opened fire on Fort Sumter, she left the city and sailed to New York, then made her way west to Cleveland, Ohio, where she remained for the duration of the war.[36]

Many of the city's residents, though, were thrilled by the prospect of battle. The Irish journalist William Howard Russell visited Charleston in the middle of April and described the ebullient scene. "The streets of Charleston present some such aspect as those of Paris in the last revolution," he wrote. "Crowds of armed men singing and promenading the streets . . . restaurants full, reveling in bar-rooms, club rooms crowded, orgies and carousings in tavern or private house." That confidence was boosted by the Confederate victory at the First Battle of Bull Run in July, but before the year was out, disaster struck the city.[37]

On the evening of December 11, 1861, General Robert E. Lee, then the commander of South Carolina, Georgia, and Florida, completed an inspection of the city's defenses and adjourned to dine at the Mills House around eight thirty. Just a few hours later, a campfire at the foot of Hassell Street flared out of control and ignited the walls of a sash and blind factory. The flames, fanned by gale-force winds, quickly spread southwestward to Market Street, setting ablaze a row of wooden tenements, then igniting the gasworks. The explosion sent fire sweeping down both sides of Meeting Street, destroying the Circular Congregational Church and the Institute Hall, where the Ordinance of Secession had been signed just a year before. City officials blew up fourteen houses to save the Marine and Roper Hospitals, the Medical College, and the Catholic Orphan House, and the fire finally burned itself out a little before noon the following day. The conflagration left a black scar of ruins across the peninsula, running from the front of Hassell Street to a point between Tradd and Gibbes.[38]

Among the hundreds of homes and businesses destroyed was Madame T. M. Rutjes's confectionery and restaurant at 174 King Street, as well as a house her husband owned on Horlbeck Alley. In the wake of the fire, Madame Rutjes decided to leave the city and move inland to Columbia, the state's capital. There she opened the Central House, "a first class boarding house," which catered to other southerners displaced by the war. Madame Rutjes advertised that "families giving up housekeeping can be accommodated, with or without furniture," and she operated her boardinghouse in Columbia for the remainder of the conflict. Notably, in the city that was the seat of the rebellion, the restaurateurs who stayed and kept in operation—Nat Fuller, Tom Tully, and Martha Vanderhorst—were persons of color.[39]

Conditions in Charleston took a turn for the worse in the summer of 1863, when Federal forces launched their third effort to take the city. After two infantry charges failed to dislodge Confederate forces from the north end of Morris Island, General Quincy Gilmore dug in, aiming his long-range guns at Fort Sumter in the middle of the harbor and a single 200-pound Parrott rifle at the city of Charleston. On August 22 the first Union shell was fired on the city, beginning a bombardment that lasted 587 days. The navy tightened its blockade as the shelling intensified. In the early years of the war, blockade runners had routinely slipped past the Union fleet, carrying cotton to Bermuda and Nassau and returning with dry goods, groceries, and even luxury items like European wines. Those covert ships were no longer able to enter the harbor, and farmers had stopped bringing produce into the city. Food prices soared. Beef, which had sold for 15 cents a pound at the outset of the war, was now going for $3, and a bushel of corn for $225. Affluent Charlestonians fled inland to Columbia, Camden, and the mountain resort of Flat Rock, while the ranks of the poor were swollen by maimed soldiers, widows, and orphans from the countryside. City officials struggled to feed the destitute, and they had to send agents into the country to buy or barter for rice, cornmeal, and peas in a desperate effort to prevent mass starvation.[40]

Remarkably, the city's African American restaurateurs managed to keep their businesses running despite the siege. As late as October 1863, Nat Fuller served an occasional green turtle soup at the Bachelor's Retreat on Queen Street. In August one of his advertisements declared, "Turtle Soup, as prepared by Fuller, was at any time a luxury, but in these days of blockade it is a most exquisite one." He served a daily breakfast from six until eleven and then an afternoon dinner from three to five that featured "venison and wild turkey, with appropriate sauces." The elite militia units that had once been a mainstay of Fuller's business had long since been absorbed into regular units of the Confederate army and sent to the front, but the city's great caterer still supplied periodic dinners and meetings for organizations like the Charleston Fire Company, the Burns Charitable Association (a mutual aid society for Scottish immigrants), and the concisely named Society for the Relief of the Families of Deceased and Disabled Indigent Members of the Medical Profession of the State of South Carolina.[41]

The commercial and social life in Charleston was disrupted even further in the closing months of 1863, as Union shelling forced residents to evacuate the lower part of the peninsula. The area south of Market Street—home to Charleston's famous Rainbow Row as well as Fuller's Bachelor's Retreat and Vanderhorst & Tully's restaurant—became a ghost town. Fuller shuttered his operation on Church Street and moved about a mile northward to a building on Washington Street, a half block above Calhoun. Tully and Vanderhorst did the same, transferring to new quarters on the southwest corner of Rutledge and Mills Streets, an area that is now part of the Medical University of South Carolina complex. A visitor to the city in 1864 noted that "the whole life and business of Charleston had been crammed into a few squares above Calhoun Street and along the Ashley [River]." Above Calhoun one found a "bustling, crowded scene," but going below it was "like going from life to death" as one entered an abandoned landscape of houses with shattered roofs, missing windows, and overgrown gardens, the empty streets choked with weeds and shimmering bits of broken glass.[42]

Despite such conditions, the city's culinary life continued, though in much reduced form. Tully and Vanderhorst hosted events like a collation for the 98th anniversary of the German Friendly Society in January 1864 and the 102nd anniversary celebration of the Fellowship Society in March, though that year's gathering was held as a lunch instead of the usual dinner. Perhaps as a nod to making do in hard times, Nat Fuller christened the Washington Street version of his restaurant the Accommodation Retreat. On September 21 he ran an advertisement in the *Charleston Mercury* informing the public that "rumors in the country to the contrary not withstanding," his establishment was still open. The bill of fare that day included green turtle soup, shrimp pie, and wild turkey. Where he managed to procure such ingredients remains a mystery, but we can assume he had tight relationships with the city's blockade runners and other black-market purveyors.[43]

On December 21, General William T. Sherman and his army of sixty thousand Union soldiers completed its March to the Sea and entered Savannah. It was assumed that Sherman would proceed to Charleston next, but he only feinted at taking the city, which he dismissed as a "mere desolated wreck," and marched on to Columbia instead. The Union troops occupying Morris Island continued to inch forward, and their shells began falling north of Calhoun Street. Another large Union force was massing and preparing to come ashore twenty miles to the north at Bull's Bay. The Confederate army, realizing that the city was doomed to fall, began evacuating northward across the Santee River on the night of Friday, February 17, 1865. Most of the remaining wealthy white residents fled along with them.

As they would in other cities they abandoned, like Richmond and Columbia, Confederate troops made the foolish decision to destroy goods and military assets rather than let them fall into Union hands. Naval officers blew up their remaining ironclads in the harbor, and the army set fire to stores of cotton and rice in warehouses along the Cooper River. Early the following morning, as the fires still burned, a group of small boys found a cache of gunpowder stored in the Northeastern Railroad Depot and began throwing it by the handful into a nearby cotton fire, watching it pop and sparkle as it ignited. In the process, they inadvertently created a trail of gunpowder back to the depot, and around eight o'clock a streak of fire raced to the main cache and ignited it. The entire depot was rocked by explosions, and the resulting fire killed several hundred destitute Charlestonians who had gathered there seeking food. The blaze then spread to nearby houses and buildings, destroying four blocks between Washington and Alexander Streets. Nat Fuller's restaurant on the opposite side of Charlotte Street narrowly escaped the conflagration.[44]

At ten on Saturday morning, February 18, Lieutenant Colonel A. G. Bennett, the commander of the 21st United States Colored Troops, and three officers from the 52nd Pennsylvania Volunteers and the 127th New York Volunteers, arrived by boat at South Atlantic wharf and received a note from Mayor Charles Macbeth surrendering the city. Shortly after, a detachment of soldiers, including African Americans from the 21st and the Massachusetts 54th, entered Charleston. By noon the Stars and Stripes flew above the Custom House, "waving for the first time," as the correspondent for the *New York Tribune* put it, "over free soil and a people free."[45]

The entire lower peninsula lay in near ruins from years of bombardment, and a long swath of blackened rubble still remained from the fire of 1861. Those residents left in the city were physically ruined, too. The Union troops immediately began distributing rice and grits to thousands of impoverished citizens. One resident described the crowds as "utterly destitute, undernourished, and near starvation." Some were so desperate they began eating the grain raw even as it was being poured into their bowls and bags.

Somehow, amid this deprivation, Nat Fuller had managed to maintain his supply chain. On February 22, just four days after the Union troops entered the city, his restaurant was the site of a dinner celebrating George Washington's birthday, hosted by Archibald Getty, who had just arrived from Philadelphia as an agent of a northern steamship line. The party of

The Mills House in April 1865, in a photograph by George N. Barnard.
(Library of Congress, Prints and Photographs Division)

twenty included Colonel Joseph Dana Webster, Sherman's chief of staff, several other army and navy officers, and four northern journalists, one of whom recorded that it was "held at a house of a colored man, noted . . . for being the chief of the class of caterers in Charleston." The dinner was described as "probably the best that has been eaten in this lean and empty bellied city since the blockade began." It opened with "canned fruits which had been put up in England and had run the gauntlet of the blockade." Following dinner, the guests offered toasts to George Washington, President Lincoln, and the coming of peace as well as to "Our Colored Soldiers" and the "Loyal Men of the South."[46]

For white Charlestonians, the fall of the city meant the collapse of the old social order, and they were scandalized by the sight of armed Black soldiers in the streets and the refusal of former slaves to observe old deferences, like stepping aside when a white person approached on the sidewalk. For African American residents, it was a moment of exhilaration and hope. By early March the abolitionist James Redpath, newly appointed as superintendent of schools, had opened the Morris Street School, and within two months, more than 3,100 students—most of them African American—were enrolled in classes. The city's residents staged numerous celebrations of Emancipation and the return to Union control. The largest of these was a grand parade on March 29 led by the 21st Regiment United States Colored Troops and mounted marshals in red, white, and blue sashes. A "Car of Liberty" carried 13 girls dressed all in white, and some 4,000 African American artisans and tradesmen and almost 2,000 schoolchildren processed through the city streets, carrying placards that declared "Slavery is dead" and "We know no caste or color."[47]

By the middle of March, Nat Fuller had moved back down to the lower peninsula to his old Bachelor's Retreat on Church Street and was offering lunches of "boned turkey, mock turtle soup and other delicacies." On April 6 he announced that his house was once again ready to take in "eating and sleeping boarders," and that he had on hand fine ale and porter, red drum steaks and roe, crabs, and ice cream.[48]

⇒)⊬← A Scandalous Feast

When I originally undertook the research for this book, I assumed that shortly after he reopened the Bachelor's Retreat, Nat Fuller staged his remarkable reconciliation feast, the one that Mrs. Porcher decried as "a miscegenat dinner" and that inspired the commemorative event to which I was invited a century and a half later at McCrady's Restaurant. In 2018, though, Professor Ethan Kytle of California State University, Fresno, uncovered the original manuscript version of Mrs. Porcher's letter. The relevant passage reads, "Nat Fuller provided munificently for a miscegenation dinner, at which blacks & whites sat on an equality, & gave toasts and sang songs for Lincoln and freedom." That lone sentence was not only the germ that inspired the reconstruction of the dinner but, as it turns out, the sole piece of evidence that it had even taken place. And the original letter makes it all but certain that the supposed feast never actually occurred.

Porcher's letter is dated March 29, 1865, and it was written not in Charleston but in Greenville, South Carolina, some two hundred miles to the west at the foot of the Blue Ridge Mountains. The Porcher family had taken refuge there after they, like so many other wealthy white Charlestonians, fled the city. Porcher notes that "we rarely see a paper except the Greenville Enterprise once a week, & sometimes an Augusta or Richmond Paper of old date comes along." She adds, "The Yankees' accounts of the occupation of Charleston are so sickening to me." Porcher, it turns out, was relating information that she had received second- or thirdhand from newspapers. In all likelihood, she was referring to the Washington's Birthday dinner hosted by Archibald Getty on February twenty-second at Fuller's Accommodation Retreat up the peninsula, where the guests did indeed toast Washington and Lincoln. Apart from Fuller and his serving staff, there is no indication that any African Americans were actually present for the meal. The "miscegenation" part seems to be Mrs. Porcher's own paranoid extrapolation. Nor is there any evidence of any subsequent banquet that seated white and African American guests at the same table. Such a remarkable event would surely have made it into the Yankee newspapers had it occurred, for plenty of white northerners would have found an integrated table scandalous, too.[49]

By relaunching the Bachelor's Retreat, Nat Fuller was not embarking on a new postslavery form of commercial dining that would serve an integrated clientele. His red drum steaks, boned turkey, and fine ales were reserved for well-to-do white customers only. Whether things would remain that way became a key part of the struggle for political, economic, and social control of the South in the decade that followed.

 CHAPTER 7

Reconstructing Southern Commercial Dining

In the weeks and months following Union occupation, the South's restaurateurs and caterers turned their attention to getting their businesses back up and running. Their experiences during the war had ranged from moderate disruption to downright disaster, and the path forward was by no means clear. For some, especially those in Charleston and Richmond, their restaurants had been physically destroyed—left in ruins by artillery shells or consumed by fire. Others faced legal and financial entanglements that dragged on in courts for years. The long supply chains that southern restaurateurs had developed over the course of several decades had been disrupted first by the years of blockade and then by the destruction of the southern railroad network. Their old customer base was shattered, too. A great many of the members of elite militia units and civic societies never returned from battle, and those who did faced greatly diminished fortunes. Commerce had long been the driving force behind public dining in the South, but with the region's economy in tatters, the boom years of the 1840s and 1850s were left in the past.

African American restaurateurs faced a dual task in the immediate aftermath of war and Emancipation. They needed not only to relaunch their former establishments but to adapt those businesses to a market where laws and norms were very much in flux. It was a time of daunting challenges but also great opportunity, and the former leaders of the South's culinary trade navigated them with varying degrees of success.

Around the same time that Nat Fuller moved back down the Charleston peninsula to his old Bachelor's Retreat location, his protégé Tom Tully relaunched his business, too. In April Tully announced that "he has reopened his establishment at his old stand, No. 124 King Street"—the same location he had shared with his former partner Martha Vanderhorst before Union shelling forced them to abandon it. Now operating as a sole proprietor and designating himself "Caterer," Tully reached out to his "friends and former patrons at his old stand" and encouraged their return. By June he was selling ice cream and sherbet by the glass along with fresh tarts and cakes.[1]

Eliza Seymour Lee, the city's top pastry chef before the war, also tried to get back into the game. As soon as word reached Ohio that Charleston had fallen to the Union, Lee began making preparations to return. A few days after arriving in Charleston, she learned that her trustee, Henry Gourdin, who had managed her property while she was absent from the city, had left Charleston in the closing months of the war and was not likely to return anytime soon. So Lee paid the outstanding taxes on the various properties she still owned and took up residence in her old house on Beaufain Street. When she went to another of her properties, the house at 78 Tradd, to collect rent from the tenants, she was surprised to learn that Gourdin had sold the house two years earlier. She later learned that the house she was occupying on Beaufain had also been sold and that she would have to pay rent to the new owners.

In October 1865 Lee filed suit against Gourdin, seeking to have the houses restored to her ownership. The case illustrates the double bind posed by Lee's former status as a free person of color and as a woman, which had prevented her from owning property in her own name. In 1823, shortly after she married John Lee, her husband had put a city lot and tenement that he owned into a marital trust, stipulating that Eliza should receive the rents from the property after he died. As they prospered in the catering and hotel businesses in the 1830s and 1840s, the Lees had acquired additional properties and put them into the trust as well.

Pre-Emancipation law required that this arrangement be managed by a white man, and Gourdin, a wealthy Charleston merchant, had been named Eliza Lee's trustee in 1857, after the original trustee died. In the fall of 1865, Gourdin was still in New York City, lingering ill in a hotel room and unable to return to Charleston for the court proceedings. He testified by letter that the rents from Lee's properties had plummeted after the commencement of the war and that the trust rarely had the funds necessary to pay the taxes on the properties it held. The house on Tradd Street, he claimed, "was so much out of order during the War that it was scarcely habitable." In 1863, after receiving an offer of $3,200 for the Tradd Street house and one other, he determined it best to sell, receiving in return Confederate bonds, which became worthless as soon as the war ended.[2]

The court ruled in Gourdin's favor, finding that the trustee had acted in good faith and could not be blamed for the collapse of Confederate currency. Eliza Lee was ordered to pay the court costs, and Henry Gourdin promptly requested to be relieved of the trusteeship because of her "ingratitude." Lee testified that she did not know of anyone to replace him.[3]

Eliza Lee never resumed her culinary career in Charleston. In December 1866 she appeared before the city council to declare that she was in old age and poverty and that her son had lost his reason, and she petitioned the council to have him sent to the asylum. The request was denied after the mayor testified that the City Hospital had examined the son and determined that he was not insane. Soon after, Eliza Lee sold her remaining property in the city and moved to New York, where she lived the remainder of her life with her daughter Sarah and son-in-law Edward Barquet, who worked as a janitor in Manhattan. Eliza Lee died on July 6, 1874, just shy of her seventy-fourth birthday, and was buried in Brooklyn's Greenwood Cemetery. The brief notices of her death in the New York papers made no mention that she had once been one of the most popular and influential chefs in the South, catering the grand balls and banquets of the Charleston elite and training an entire generation of cooks and restaurateurs who followed in her wake.[4]

The other grande dame of antebellum Charleston dining, Madame T. M. Rutjes, struggled to regain her footing after the war, too. In the spring of 1866 she returned to Charleston and leased the property on Broad Street that had once housed Jones' Hotel, opening it to the public in June as the Mansion House and adding an ice cream saloon in the adjoining building. Needing assistance with this side business, she advertised that she was seeking to hire a confectioner who "understands making Ice Cream and Fancy Cakes—either white or colored man." In announcing the opening of the hotel, the *Charleston Daily News* made no mention of Théonie Rutjes's absent husband, noting only that Madame Rutjes's name was "familiar to our citizens as the proprietor of an ice-cream saloon on King-street, before the war" and that, she having been burnt out twice during the conflict, first in Charleston and then in Columbia, "our people should take pride in patronizing her."[5]

Charleston's caterers and pastry cooks were intent on reviving the culinary scene that had thrived before the war, but postwar Charleston was a very different market than in the 1850s. The militia units that had been one of the pillars of their catering businesses had been decimated, and it would take two decades before the organizations resumed their old functions as social clubs for the city's elite. Elaborate weddings, society balls, and celebratory dinners were few and far between, and ambitious young men of commerce—once the prime customers for hoteliers and restaurateurs—were rare sights in the city.

Though Nat Fuller had returned to his old location, he no longer advertised it as the Bachelor's Retreat, perhaps because so few bachelors remained. Nor did he emphasize his restaurant or pastry shop. Promoting himself now as "Private and Public Caterer," Fuller offered to provide his "large airy rooms" at 77 Church Street free of charge for parties, balls, and dinners. His rooms became the regular meeting place for the Society of the Cincinnati, and he presumably resumed at least some of his previous catering business, though on a smaller scale than before. The only surviving account of a dinner Fuller furnished that year was for a harbor cruise aboard the steamer *Josephine*, staged by the local fire companies to welcome their fellow firemen visiting from Augusta. Nat Fuller, "the renowned presiding genius over many a fine dinner and supper," provided tables of "tempting viands and condiments" along with plenty of Champagne for the 150 guests to enjoy after they surveyed the ruins of the former Confederate defenses at Fort Johnson and Fort Sumter. A correspondent from the Augusta *Daily Constitutionalist* observed that Fuller "has a cunning way of fixing up water so as to take all the bad tastes out of it," noting that his formula involved ice, brandy, mint, and sugar. Fuller, it seems, like his peers John Dabney and Jim Cook up in Richmond, was skilled in the compounding of juleps.[6]

While attempting to revive his business, Fuller ran into a legal snag caused by his former status as an enslaved man—a problem faced by many other African American entrepreneurs. The effects of having once been considered not a person but property—and, therefore, not being allowed to own property—did not vanish with the Emancipation Proclamation. In Fuller's case, even though he had been the one making the mortgage payments for the property at 77 Church Street, legal ownership had been in the hands William C. Gatewood, his former master. After Gatewood died in 1861, ownership passed to the control of the Gatewood estate. African Americans did not gain property rights until the Civil Rights Act of 1866, which was passed by Congress on the ninth of April over President Andrew Johnson's veto.

Shortly after the act passed, Nat Fuller filed suit against Gatewood's widow, Madeline, and the estate's executors, seeking to secure ownership of the lot and buildings. Mrs. Gatewood seemed amenable to an arrangement, but the other executors dragged their feet. They had tried to sell the property once before in March 1864, after Fuller had decamped northward to Washington Street, but had found no buyers for a building that at the time was squarely in the path of the Union bombardment. With the city's economy limping back to life, though, the threat of sale was imminent again.

Madeline Gatewood testified in court documents that her husband had indeed purchased the building as Fuller's guardian and that Fuller, not Gatewood, had paid all of the installments. Mrs. Gatewood agreed that, once all the outstanding bonds and mortgages were paid, it would be her duty to transfer the property to Fuller, now that he could legally possess it. She even offered to loan him state and local bonds that he could use to pay off the remainder of the mortgage, but the lien holders apparently refused to accept those instruments.[7]

Nat Fuller did not live to see the case resolved. In the fall of 1866, at the age of fifty-four, he contracted typhoid fever. He died on December 16 in his family's quarters above his catering house and was buried in the African American cemetery on Heriot Street. A month later, the judge presiding over his lawsuit against the Gatewood estate ordered that the property at 77 Church be put up for sale and the proceeds used to pay off the remaining bonds. Diana Fuller and their four children moved to a house on Tradd Street, where she continued to work as a pastry chef. She apparently served only a small group of private clients, for she did not advertise in the newspapers, and no entry for her business appears in the city directories. She died on Sullivan's Island in 1884 at the age of sixty-two.[8]

Charleston's other prewar caterers fared little better. Théonie Rutjes's husband Adolph returned to the city in February 1868, but only to declare bankruptcy and discharge his remaining property. The Rutjeses had decided to try their luck further north, and Madame Rutjes announced in May that she had opened a new version of the Mansion House, this one a boardinghouse on Four-and-a-Half Street in Washington, D.C. Her reputation was apparently still strong in Charleston, for as "Madame T. M. Rutjes" she advertised in the Charleston papers that "Southerners are invited to give the Mansion House a try." The editors of the *Charleston Daily News* endorsed the idea, writing that "Charlestonians going to the capitol, cannot do better than to call at the Mansion House." This venture lasted only a matter of months. By September, Adolph Rutjes had moved to Raleigh, North Carolina, where he took a position managing the Exchange Hotel, and Théonie joined him there soon after.[9]

Tom Tully stepped into the role of the city's leading caterer after Nat Fuller's death and the departure of the Rutjeses and Eliza Lee. Charleston's many civic and benevolent societies were beginning to resume their old functions, and Tully staged anniversary dinners and celebrations for the St. Andrew's Society, the German Friendly Society, and the St. George Society. He also secured the business of many of the local fire companies, including the Stonewall Fire Company, the Phoenix Engine Company, and the Vigilant Fire Company. In addition to serving as the base for his catering operations, his shop at 124 King Street did a brisk trade in ice cream and pastries, especially during the summer months. One steamy July evening in 1867, he treated the editorial staff at the *Charleston Daily News* to a delivery of pineapple Newport, vanilla cream, "Bisquet Glace," and frozen peaches along with a selection of cakes. Each December he stocked game and poultry for local holiday dinner tables and took orders for Christmas desserts, including his famous mince pies.[10]

In the immediate wake of Union occupation, several newly freed African American Charlestonians decided to enter the restaurant business, too. In April, George E. Johnston—the former caterer at the Mills House—announced that he had opened a "first class restaurant" at 61 Hassell Street, between King and Market. His initial advertisement noted that he was "well known to the old habitués of the Charleston Hotel and Mills House" and "will be happy to again meet all his old friends." Johnston promised that his new restaurant would be "second to none in the country," and that he had engaged an experienced cook who had been "formerly employed among our oldest and wealthiest families." By May he was serving free turtle soup to draw in customers.[11]

In August another newly freed man, Archibald Wigg, opened an eating house on Market Street. Wigg's life prior to becoming a restaurateur had been quite remarkable. His father was William H. Wigg, a white planter who owned six hundred acres of land in St. Helena Parish near Beaufort

GEORGE'S RESTAURANT,
61 HASEL-STREET,
NORTH SIDE.

HAVING RECENTLY MADE SEVERAL IMPORTANT Improvements, with the addition of a CULINARY DEPARTMENT, and thankful for past favors, the public are respectfully informed that MEALS will be furnished at any hour of the day, and until 10 at night. The Tables will be supplied with the best the market can afford, prepared by one of the best and most experienced Cooks and Caterers in the city. The Bill of Fare will include OYSTERS, in every style, Beef Steaks, Veal Cutlets, Mutton Chops, Pork Steaks, Ham and Eggs, Pigs Feet Broiled, Turkey and Chickens, Fish, Sardines, Eggs in every style, Omelets, Pies, Hot Muffins, Griddle Cakes, Sausages, Coffee, Tea, Chocolate, and everything to please the palate and give satisfaction to customers. The prices will be reasonable, and every effort used for the accommodation of the public.

October 18   GEO. E. JOHNSTON.

Advertisement for George's Restaurant, opened by George E. Johnston, formerly chef of the Charleston Hotel and the Mills House, in the *Charleston Courier*, October 18, 1865.

as well as a town house in Charleston. His mother presumably was one of Wigg's enslaved workers. The elder Wigg had declared his intention of freeing Archibald and his brother John upon his death, but for unknown reasons they ended up instead being inherited by their white half brother William H. Wigg Jr. Both Archibald and John had been raised in Charleston and worked on their father's sailing ship, and around 1850 their half brother hired them out to Captain Peck of the steamer *William Seabrook*, which carried passengers and cotton between Savannah and Charleston. Archy, as Wigg was then called, served as the ship's steward and John as the pilot. Peck paid William Wigg thirty dollars a month for his half brothers' services.

Chafing at being denied his promised freedom, Archy became increasingly disruptive and argumentative. In early 1854 he forged a note, supposedly from his half brother, telling Peck to pay Archy his wages directly, which Peck did for two months before William caught on. Soon after, both Archy and John went AWOL from the steamer, and their half brother offered a twenty-dollar reward for their capture. His advertisements noted that Archy was about five foot six and was "quick spoken, and dresses well; he can read and write." The two men were nabbed a few weeks later and sent to the workhouse in Charleston, but in the interim they had engaged the services of a young lawyer named Charles H. Simonton, who would later become a prominent federal judge, to help secure their freedom. Upon learning that William intended to sell John and Archy out of state, Simonton wrote a letter to the master of the workhouse, warning him that William Wigg's authority to place his clients in the workhouse was in dispute and they should not be released to anyone.[12]

Archibald and John languished in the workhouse for three years while their case made its way through the courts. In the end it was ruled that William was in fact their lawful owner. By this point, though, William had fallen into debt, and his two enslaved half brothers were seized by the sheriff and sold at auction in April 1858. Who bought them and where they spent the next few years is uncertain, but both were living in Charleston in the immediate aftermath of the war. John worked initially as a harbor pilot, and in 1870 he moved south to Beaufort, where he became the captain of Pilot Boat Number 8. Archibald Wigg stayed on in Charleston and became a restaurateur. Wigg's restaurant was located on the south side of the City Market, between Meeting and Church Streets. He initially opened it in partnership with another of his brothers, Alfred R. Wigg, who left after a few years to pursue work as a seaman and steward.[13]

The offerings at these two newly opened establishments—George's Restaurant and Wigg & Co. Restaurant—seem more aimed at everyday dining rather than grand feasts and elegant dinners. Unlike the elaborate French-accented banquet menus he once prepared at the Charleston Hotel, Johnston's advertisements highlight a sturdier bill of fare, like beefsteaks, pork and mutton chops, veal cutlets, and "eggs in every style." Wigg, for his part, offered "every variety of Dishes at the shortest notice" and promised "you will find our Terms moderate."[14]

The two restaurateurs' advertisements raise the question of whom they were targeting as clientele. Johnston advertised in the *Charleston Courier*, the journal of white, conservative Charlestonians, and he specifically addresses "The old friends of the Charleston Hotel and Mills House," which is to say the prewar white elite. Wigg's first advertisements, on the other hand, appeared in the *South Carolina Leader*, an African American–owned newspaper founded in October 1865 and a champion of Republican politics and civil rights. In May 1866 a brief article about a stolen watch in the *Charleston Daily News* refers to Wigg's Market Street business as a "colored tavern"—an indication that de facto segregation was already occurring.[15]

On September 9, 1865, a group of African American men organized a new Lodge of Free and Accepted Masons, one of three African American lodges that were formed in Charleston just after the Civil War. Among its leaders were two of the city's new restaurateurs. George E. Johnston was elected the Worshipful Master—the senior officer of the lodge—and Alfred R. Wigg was named one of the two stewards. Composed largely of businessmen and property holders, these Masonic organizations promoted fellowship among their members and engaged in a wide variety of social and charitable activities. In the latter half of the nineteenth century, they were closely associated with advancing African American businesses and entrepreneurship. George Johnston and the Wigg brothers, it seems, saw the restaurant profession as a promising path to both financial and social success.[16]

Johnston and Wigg were competing with a number of white entrepreneurs trying their luck in the postwar restaurant trade, though most of their ventures proved short lived. Of the nine other restaurants listed in the 1867 Charleston city directory, only three were still in business two years later, and all three were run by German Americans who had been involved in Charleston's culinary trade before the war. Hanover-born E. F. Torck operated a tavern on Chapel Street in the late 1850s, and after the war he opened Our House Restaurant at the corner of Queen and East Bay Streets, which remained a popular destination for green turtle soup until Torck's death in 1872. Charles Litschgi, a German immigrant who arrived in Charleston in the mid-1850s, took over Theodore Chupein's restaurant and confectionery on East Bay Street in 1860 and operated it until the Union bombardment forced him to close in 1864. He reopened in the same location in 1866. Nicholas Fehrenbach, the American-born son of German parents, had run Fehrenbach's Temperance Restaurant on Meeting Street next to Institute Hall for two years before it was destroyed in the great fire of December 1861. By 1867 he had launched a new restaurant on Broad Street, and in 1868 he branched out and opened a billiard saloon across from the Mills House at the corner of Meeting and Queen.[17]

⇥✳⇤ New Orleans

The restaurant market in New Orleans rebounded much earlier and more quickly than in Charleston, since New Orleans fell to the Union without a prolonged bombardment and survived the war relatively unscathed. The city was also much larger, and once the shipping trade resumed, the economy cranked back up and New Orleans continued to grow. The population increased at a rate of between 12 and 18 percent each decade for the remainder of the nineteenth century. (Charleston, by comparison, limped along in the single digits.)

But New Orleans's restaurateurs still faced their share of challenges. The summer resorts on Lake Pontchartrain and Bayou St. John had largely shut down during the war years. In June 1865, just as their proprietors were reopening for their first real season in years, a great fire swept through Milneburg. It started in the Mobile Oyster Saloon, just across the street from the Washington Hotel, and quickly spread to twenty nearby buildings. Among those destroyed were Boudro's hotel, the Hope House, and—in a touch of irony, considering the name—Miguel's Phoenix Restaurant.[18]

Many of the old New Orleans hotels had closed after traffic fell off during the war, and they were slow to get back on their feet once commerce resumed. In November 1865 one resident complained in a letter to the editor of the *New Orleans Times* about the lack of accommodations in the city. "The hotels are full—in the private boarding houses the people are packed like sardines together." But still, he noted, "every arrival from sea and the upper country brings fresh hundreds to our over-loaded city—some in search of health, some to make money, some to escape justice at home." O. E. Hall, however, was working to address that. Having once more secured ownership of both the St. Charles and the shuttered St. Louis, he focused his energies first on the St. Charles. He closed it down for several months for top-to-bottom renovations, painting and repapering the walls, thoroughly cleaning, varnishing, and reupholstering the furniture—"very much needed improvements," his ads admitted. He next turned his attention to the St. Louis Hotel and put it through a similar overhaul.[19]

The St. Louis reopened in 1866 after being closed for four years, and it quickly regained its rank alongside the St. Charles. Rooms at each cost five dollars per day, and both houses kept the old practice of serving a table d'hôte. That year, *Appleton's Hand-book of American Travel* declared that Victor's and the Maison Dorée on Canal Street and the Restaurant Moreau on Canal "have no superiors in the South." It praised Galpin's on Royal for its steaks and chops and two oyster saloons, Pino's on St. Charles and Rivas on Dryades, for the quality of their shellfish. Life at the resorts along Lake Pontchartrain was soon back in full swing, too. Miguel had rebuilt his restaurant at Milneburg and was ready to open for the summer season. F. Moulin, Charley Rhodes's partner at Moreau's Restaurant, decided that

The St. Charles Hotel in 1869, with Pino's Restaurant visible in the foreground. (Library of Congress, Prints and Photographs Division)

he had earned a sufficient fortune and was ready to go home to France to retire, but Rhodes, now forty-six years old, kept Moreau's operating at the same high level as a sole proprietor. In New Orleans, at least, most of the same names and faces that had led the hospitality and dining scene before the war were back in place and ready to lead the way forward.[20]

→)⦂(← Richmond

In the former Confederate capital, daily life looked very different than it had in the 1850s or even in the days before Union troops occupied the city. The closing days of the war played out in Richmond very much as they had in Charleston. In early April 1865, Confederate troops were ordered to withdraw from Richmond, and Confederate government clerks and white residents frantically followed them, loading whatever possessions they could carry into hacks and onto wagons. After Confederate troops set fire to the tobacco and cotton warehouses, embers blown by a strong wind ignited roofs in the business district, and a powder magazine on the north end of town ignited and exploded, killing eleven paupers in the nearby almshouse. A few hours later the first Union troops entered the city, and it took until noon the next day before the blaze was extinguished. More than eleven hundred buildings were destroyed, including much of Richmond's commercial district in an area extending from the river northward almost to the Capitol building. The half mile of Main Street between 9th and 14th, where many of Richmond's restaurants and saloons had stood, was left a smoldering ruin. It's not clear whether John Dabney and/or Caspar Wendlinger were still operating their restaurants at this time, but if they had been, the buildings housing their establishments would have been destroyed. The Ballard House and Exchange Hotel, lying just to the east of the burned district, were narrowly spared.[21]

On April 4, 1865, just two days after the Confederate evacuation, President Abraham Lincoln and his son Tad arrived on the gunboat USS *Malvern* to tour the former rebel capital. "As far as the eye could see," Admiral David D. Porter recalled, "the streets were alive with negroes and poor whites rushing in our direction, and the crowd increased so fast that I had to surround the President with the sailors with fixed bayonets to keep them off." Lincoln made his way to the former Confederate White House, where the Federal troops had established their headquarters, then toured the city by carriage before retiring to the warship for the night.

Five days later, General Robert E. Lee surrendered at Appomattox Court House.[22]

The occupying Union troops were welcomed joyously by Richmond's African American residents. They were no longer required to step off the sidewalks and yield to white pedestrians, and they could now frequent Capitol Square in the heart of the city, a public space from which they had previously been barred. One of the first courses of action for Richmond's African American communities was to open new schools for their children, and they were assisted in the effort by white northern schoolteachers who came southward to contribute in their own way to reunification. One of these teachers, Sarah Chase, noted that, despite their education formerly being illegal, "nearly every colored family in Richmond has one or more members who can read" and that many of their children already knew the alphabet, and some could read and write with proficiency.[23]

Just nine days after President Lincoln toured newly liberated Richmond, he was shot by John Wilkes Booth at Ford's Theatre in Washington and died early the following morning. When word of the assassination reached Richmond, city officials feared that Confederate prisoners in the jails and partisans in the community at large would riot in celebration. A paroled Confederate officer dining at the Ballard House exclaimed that he was "damned glad that Lincoln was dead," and he was set upon by the restaurant's African American waiters and tossed into the street.[24]

To many African Americans in Richmond, it seemed that the message of hope that Lincoln had delivered on April 4 might well have died along with him. Within weeks it was clear that the occupying Union troops had no plans to ensure equal protection under the law. Needy white Richmonders had only to swear an oath of loyalty to receive rations from the army, but able-bodied African Americans had to report to the quartermaster and take work assignments to receive aid. This disparity reflected the two primary concerns among federal authorities when it came to dealing with the residents of the occupied southern states: to ensure that whites would be loyal and that Blacks would not be idle. Freedmen were encouraged to return to their former places of captivity and negotiate with their former masters for wages, and Union pickets began turning back African Americans seeking to enter Richmond from the countryside and required Black city residents to carry a pass from their employers or face arrest. Editors of the *Richmond Times* commended the military authorities for their policy "to let no idle negroes loaf around the city, but to put them to work, and to make them earn their own living."[25]

In antebellum days, caterers and restaurateurs had been among the leaders of the city's African American community, and they were among those who emerged as leaders in the fight for civil rights as the city entered Reconstruction. On June 8, members of the Black community selected Fields Cook to chair a committee to investigate the mistreatment that local residents had experienced at the hands of Union soldiers. Cook had operated his own restaurant on Main Street during the early 1860s, but he had been forced to give up that business in 1864 as the city's social and economic life disintegrated. Since February 1865 he had contracted as the caterer for the Ballard House Restaurant, which John Ballard had reopened after many months of closure.

Cook and his fellow committee members conducted hearings and compiled depositions from local residents, and they documented incidents ranging from insults and disrespect to outright violence. Workers reported being taken from their places of employment and arrested for not having passes. Two men were hanged by their thumbs for resisting the attack of a drunken white man. Most outrageous was the treatment of Ned Scott, who got into an altercation first with two former Confederate soldiers who had assaulted his wife and then with Union troops who tried to arrest him. As punishment, Scott was bucked and paddled for an hour, then paraded through the streets and forced to lie in public in a coffin, his face coated with flour and exposed through a hole cut in the lid. (The *Richmond Enquirer* celebrated Scott's treatment, sneering that "this fellow will know how to behave himself in the future.")[26]

On June 10, Cook's committee reported their findings at a mass meeting at the First African Baptist Church. Having been frustrated in their efforts to engage local authorities, the attendees voted to send the committee to Washington to appeal directly to the president of the United States. The delegation was received by Andrew Johnson six days later, and they read him a prepared address enumerating their sufferings. Cook and his colleagues emphasized that they were hardworking, gainfully employed citizens, ranging in wealth "from two hundred to twenty thousand dollars," and that they had remained loyal to the Union, serving as scouts and guides to Federal troops. The old "negro laws" were still being applied in Virginia, they told the president. Free people of color were still required to carry passes on their persons, and Black churches had to be led by white ministers and have their property owned by white trustees. Now that former masters no longer had a financial interest in their physical welfare, they argued, "the position of the colored people is worse than it was when they were slaves."

President Johnson's response was cool at best. "While you are in this transition state," he told the men, "there will be a great many things we would all prefer to have different, that must for the present be submitted as they are." He referred the delegation to General O. O. Howard at the Freedmen's Bureau, scrawled a brief note of introduction, and ended the interview. Fields Cook and his companions left the White House and made their way to the Freedmen's Bureau offices on I Street. On the way, a reporter recorded, they "emphatically stated that Mr. Johnson was 'not like Uncle Abe.' Whether they admired him for what they found different in him they did not say."[27]

But Virginia's African Americans citizens were not content to submit to things as they were. In the first week of August, the State Convention of Colored Men convened at the Lyceum Building in Alexandria. On the floor of the convention, one of the delegates read a letter that had just been received, postmarked Washington, D.C., and addressed to "Fields Cook and others of the Colored Convention at Alexandria." It opened: "Beware! Beware! Beware! Fields Cook! You and other negroes will die before the autumn leaves fall upon the unavenged graves of the many Southerners who are buried through our land." Cook took the platform briefly and declared that "His life was but of little importance" and that such letters could not intimidate him from discharging his duty. After declaring that the letter was unworthy of further consideration, the delegates proceeded to pass resolutions urging the franchise for African American men and creating a committee to work with the Freedmen's Bureau to establish common schools throughout Virginia.[28]

By autumn Richmond's commercial district was beginning to recover from the devastating fire and, despite ongoing tension between military leaders and white citizens, the business of hospitality was beginning to resume. Fields Cook's brother Jim returned to the city by August, signing on at the Franklin Hotel and promising to "dispense turtle to the bon vivants of Richmond" once again. Though well into his seventies, Thomas Griffin went back to work, too, though not at his former resort on Griffin Island. He set up shop in a new saloon on Governor Street, just east of the Capitol, and resumed procuring fish and game from his long-established network of suppliers. In September the *Richmond Whig* reported that sora had appeared earlier than expected, and though they weren't yet generally available in the local markets, Griffin was serving them in his saloon. A few weeks later, Griffin announced another first of the fall culinary season: fresh York River oysters.[29]

By September, Spiro Zetelle had returned from his hiatus in Europe and was back to serving "oysters in every style" at a new establishment that he christened S. Zetelle's European House. That same month, John Dabney opened a new restaurant as well. Dabney's House was located on the south side of Franklin Street near 14th Street, directly across from his old place of employment at the Ballard House. "The proprietor," the *Richmond Whig* noted, "is celebrated for his skill in compounding juleps and 'sich.'" Dabney demonstrated his skill by delivering to the newspaper offices "a mammoth tumbler filled with the fragrant fluid" and decorated with flowers. Though the players were largely the same, their relative prominence and reputations changed after the war. In his autobiographical sketch, Dabney's son Wendell remembered Spiro Zetelle, whom he called "a famous French restaurateur and caterer," and noted that after the war Zetelle "went down, as Pop climbed up. At first great rivals, afterwards fairly friendly."[30]

Zetelle's return was hampered by legal and financial difficulties. As soon as he arrived back in the city, he went to Gustavus Myers to retrieve the funds he had left in the lawyer's care. Myers handed him a stack of Confederate bonds with a face value of $19,000 and a market value of zero. Myers and Frederick Cridland, it turned out, had sold all of Zetelle's property and invested the profits in Confederate securities. To make matters worse, they had taken a $6,000 bond that Zetelle held, which was payable in gold and had been scheduled to mature in 1865, and sold it early, sinking the proceeds into now-worthless Confederate bonds, too. Zetelle filed suit against Myers and Cridland, accusing them of negligence. The case was originally decided in the restaurateur's favor but was overturned on appeal. The Appeals Court, echoing the logic applied in Eliza Lee's suits in Charleston, ruled that wartime transactions involving Confederate currency were valid and that during "a period of such remarkable political events" trustees could not be held negligent as long as they had acted in good faith. The former "Napoleon of cooks" had to start over from scratch.[31]

⟫✳︎⟨ Washington, D.C.

Conditions were quite different in the Union capital than they were in the former Confederate one. A tremendous number of hotels and restaurants were in operation in Washington, D.C., at the close of the war. A few of these—like Gautier's, Hancock's, and the National Eating House—had been around for years. It was in a private room at Gautier's that, on March 15, 1865, John Wilkes Booth had met with six men for a dinner party that lasted until five o'clock the next morning. The conspirators had argued heatedly over the soundness of Booth's proposal to abduct Abraham Lincoln from a theatre—a plot that Booth later abandoned in favor of assassination.[32]

In 1865 the sons of Jesse Brown sold the old Brown's Hotel, and the new owners discarded the outdated "Indian Queen" moniker and renamed it the Metropolitan Hotel, under which name it operated for another six decades. Hancock's Restaurant evolved, too, becoming less a saloon and more a dining destination. Andrew Hancock's son John had taken over after the elder Hancock passed away, but he kept his father's eccentric knickknacks and even added to them, acquiring a wanted poster for John Wilkes Booth and framed photos of the assassin's and his coconspirators' hangings. Dick Francis still bent the ears of congressmen while mixing their fancy drinks, stationed in front of a portrait of the notorious English burglar and jailbreaker Jack Sheppard. Fried chicken "a la Maryland," generously dressed in a rich cream gravy, became the specialty of the house. In 1867 Harvey's Oyster Depot, whose cheap bivalves had become a favorite of Union soldiers during the war, moved to a newly remodeled building with a stylish cast iron front at the corner of 11th and Pennsylvania Avenue, where it would continue to thrive through the rest of the century and beyond.[33]

"Dining in Washington is a great element in politics," the journalist George Alfred Townsend wrote during this era. "The lobby man dines the Representative; the Representative dines the Senator; the Senator dines the charming widow, and the charming widow dines her coming man." He singled out Welcker's Restaurant as the best in the city, saying "there is no dinner like Welcker's." As for the city's various specialties: "For reed birds the politician consults Hancock, on the avenue; for oysters, Harvey; and for an ice or a quiet supper, Wormly [sic] or Page."[34]

As in Richmond, many of the leading civil rights figures in postwar Washington were drawn from the ranks of culinary professionals. In Washington's case, it was two nationally known African American caterers, though their business careers and their political lives took very different paths. One was a native of the city, the other a recent arrival. One was politically cautious, the other outspoken and daring. Both were instrumental in shaping how civil rights unfolded in the nation's capital and the country at large.

James Wormley, Washington's leading caterer and hotelier, first became involved in political matters shortly after the end of the war. Along with

Hancock's Restaurant and Harvey's Restaurant remained in operation in Washington, D.C., until the early twentieth century. (Library of Congress, Prints and Photographs Division)

the influential African American minister John F. Cook, Wormley was a member of the board of managers for what the newspapers described as a "Great Mass Meeting of Colored People" held on the Fourth of July, 1865, in Lafayette Park, just a block from Wormley's hotel. A crowd of thousands gathered to hear speeches from luminaries like Senator Henry Wilson of Massachusetts and Representative Thaddeus Stevens of Pennsylvania, who had been a fierce opponent of slavery before the war and was emerging along with Charles Sumner as one of the leaders of the radical faction of the Republican Party. Following prayers and a reading of the Declaration of Independence, Senator Wilson took the podium. "Let every rebel in the country," he thundered, "from the Potomac to the Rio Grande, understand it, that their power, their authority over the black man of this continent has passed away forever!" Wilson announced that he was prepared, on the first day of the upcoming congressional session, to introduce a bill banishing the Black Codes and ensuring the personal liberty of all Americans.[35]

Wormley was soon joined in Washington by another prominent African American caterer who advocated for civil rights. This leader had southern family roots, though he had never traveled south of the Mason-Dixon Line. He built his career not by serving wealthy planters and merchants in the slaveholding states but rather by catering to the emerging capitalist elites in the Northeast. His name was George T. Downing, and by the time he moved to Washington in January 1866, he had already earned a national reputation as a caterer and restaurateur, following in the footstep of his father, Thomas Downing.

The elder Downing had been born free in Virginia in 1791 and made his way north to New York City in 1819, where he established a thriving oyster business. At Downing's Oyster House on Broad Street, workers roasted pound after pound of bivalves on a large gridiron over oak shavings, and diners shucked their own with English oyster knives and dressed them, still hot in the shell, with lumps of sweet butter and other seasonings. The elder Downing had helped found the United Anti-Slavery Society of the City of New York, and he was an active proponent for Black education, helping launch several elementary schools and New York's first African American high school. He was also a founding member of the Committee of Thirteen which, after the passage of the Fugitive Slave Law in 1850, assisted free Blacks who were at risk of being kidnapped and sold south into slavery.

George Downing inherited his father's culinary skills as well as his political leanings. Born in Manhattan in 1819, he attended the Mulberry Street School in New York and earned a degree from Hamilton College. He then returned to New York and established himself as "George T. Downing, Confectioner & Caterer" at 600 Broadway. The younger Downing built a loyal following among the Astors, the LeRoys, and other fashionable New York families. As so many caterers in the South had done, Downing began following his high-society clientele to their summer resorts, which in Downing's case was Newport, Rhode Island. There he operated a series of leased establishments before building the Sea Girt Hotel in 1854, which became famous for its woodcock suppers with crisp "Vauxhall sliced" potatoes—shaved paper thin and fried crisp and brown.[36]

Early in his career, Downing had become active in political causes. He was a leader in the Anti-Slavery Society in New York, and he served on his father's Committee of Thirteen in protest of the Fugitive Slave Act. Just before the Civil War the younger Downing became embroiled in the debate over the African Civilization Society, which had been founded two years

George T. Downing, engraving by Vogt Bros. of New York, 1880s. (Schomburg Center for Research in Black Culture, Photographs and Prints Division, New York Public Library)

before to encourage African Americans to emigrate to Africa. Downing believed the society's aims were deplorable, and he accused the Republican Party of wanting to "ship off the negro" to deflect charges that they were "negro-worshippers" instead of taking the necessary steps to improve the condition of African Americans in their own country.[37]

The blowback from this and other controversial stances seems to have temporarily blunted Downing's appetite for politics. In August 1860 "the famous colored restaurateur of Newport" announced his intention of retiring from social activism. He declined to attend a fete in Newport celebrating the anniversary of the Haitian Revolution, explaining in a letter, "I feel that I am working for the people with whom I am identified in oppression, in securing a business name; I shall strive for my and their elevation, but it will be by a strict and undivided attention to business."[38]

Downing remained focused on his business through the war years, but in the wake of Appomattox, his political passions were rekindled by the early efforts of Congress to reconstruct the politics and social order of the South. In December 1865 the Convention of Colored People of New England voted to send a delegation to Washington, D.C., for the congressional session. Its purpose, as captured in a resolution, was "to endeavor to influence the legislation of Congress so that in its action it may not give color to the idea that 'black men have no right which white men are bound to respect'"—echoing the language of Chief Justice Roger Taney's reviled Dred Scott opinion. The New England convention appointed George T. Downing as its delegate and appropriated $10,000 to support him while in Washington. Similar conventions in other states voted to send their own representatives, including New York, which appointed Frederick Douglass.[39]

On December 27 Downing announced that he had given up his old stand on Broad Street in Manhattan, though he retained his summer properties in Newport. By January 23 he had arrived with the rest of the delegation in the nation's capital, and at their first meeting Downing was elected their president. Among the delegation's first actions was to meet with General O. O. Howard, the head of the Freedmen's Bureau, and lay out the group's positions concerning Reconstruction policy. The delegation unanimously opposed any colonization or mass relocation of African American citizens, whether in the United States or abroad. They insisted upon the unqualified and universal right to vote for all male citizens, regardless of color, and they endorsed the recent decision by the 39th Congress to refuse to seat members from the former Confederate states. Downing and his fellow delegates declared they harbored no resentment against the states that were recently in rebellion, but the delegation remained firmly opposed to those states' being allowed to return representatives to Congress until they had abolished any legislation privileging whites.[40]

The delegation attended an even more eventful meeting on February 7, when they were received at the White House for an interview with President Andrew Johnson. Each man shook hands with the president, and then George T. Downing spoke, expressing the group's spirit of friendship toward the president and requesting legislation to enforce the abolition of slavery and recognize that African Americans "should be protected in their rights as citizens and equal before the law." Frederick Douglass next made a brief statement, then President Johnson took over the discussion. He proceeded to lecture the delegation in a manner even more haughty and dismissive than when he had received Fields Cook and the Richmond committee the previous summer.

Johnson insisted that the feelings of his own heart "have been for the colored man." In an awkward effort to support this point, he offered that "I have owned slaves and bought slaves, but I never sold one." Practically speaking, he added, "I have been their slave instead of their being mine." The president went on to insist that he would adopt no policy that created "a contest between the races," and he claimed that Black men had already gained plenty by being freed from bondage. Forcing southern states to give them the vote would "commence a war of races." After Johnson finished his lecture, both

Downing and Douglass respectfully tried to respond to his assertions, but the president shut them down, insisting that he only wanted to "indicate my views in reply to your address and not enter into any general controversy."

"The President sends us to the people," Douglass said to his delegation as they rose to leave, "and we will have to go and get the people right."[41]

Once the men had exited the room, Johnson offered his own interpretation of the meeting, in comments recorded by one of his private secretaries: "Those d——d sons of b——s thought they had me in a trap!" the president exclaimed. "I know that d——d Douglass; he's just like any n——, and he would sooner cut a white man's throat than not."[42]

In the space of less than a year, Johnson had received two separate groups led by African American caterers—Fields Cook in June 1865 and George T. Downing in February 1866. The outcome of each was indicative of his overall approach during the period now known as Presidential Reconstruction. Johnson rejected the expectations that had been created by the Union army and the Freedmen's Bureau and refused to endorse taking land from white owners and giving it to freedmen, denying those newly freed from enslavement a means of earning an income in the predominantly agricultural South. Equally frustrating to George T. Downing was Johnson's refusal to compel the rebellious states to recognize African American citizens' right to vote. In February 1866, Downing's was the first name on the delegation's petition to the Senate encouraging that body to refuse any constitutional amendment that would allow any state to disenfranchise any class of citizens based upon race or color. Downing had come to Washington with high hopes that he could get close to the seat of power and influence the course of Reconstruction policy. The first year following Emancipation, though, offered a bracing lesson: neither the Union army nor the president of the United States—nor anyone else, for that matter—was going to simply grant equal rights to African Americans. They would have to be fought for and won not on the field of battle but at the ballot box and in the halls of government.[43]

⇒)⊱⊰— Choosing Sides

As the first anniversary of the fall of Richmond approached, white Richmonders were shocked to learn that a group of African Americans were organizing a grand celebration to take place on April 3, the day Union troops had entered the city the year before. The *Examiner* urged Black residents to abandon their plans for celebrating a day that had "crushed the people of Richmond to the dust." An ensuing propaganda campaign blamed the event on "a few white fanaticks of the North," claiming that the organizers planned to drag a Confederate flag through the mud on Main Street and burn Robert E. Lee and Stonewall Jackson in effigy, and it warned of pending bloodshed in the streets. The organizers were undeterred. On April 2 they distributed a broadside notice signed by a committee of five prominent African American residents stating that "the coloured people of the city of Richmond" were planning to celebrate not the failure of the southern Confederacy but rather "the day on which God was pleased to liberate their long-oppressed race." The celebration went off as planned the following day, with some seven thousand freedmen marching from the western suburbs through the main streets of downtown, bearing banners and singing songs of celebration. "Those prophets of woe," the *Philadelphia Inquirer* noted, "the Richmond journals which predicted blood, slaughter and extermination . . . have been proven to be false counsellors and blind guides."[44]

For Richmond's caterers and restaurateurs, the controversy surrounding the event laid bare a hard truth about business in the Reconstruction era: they were going to have to choose sides in the unfolding political battle. The fortunes of the elite white community had been greatly diminished, but they still held most of the wealth, and they were determined to reestablish the old social order. When two representatives of the Freedmen's Bureau visited Richmond to interview former governor and Confederate general Henry A. Wise, he assured them that white Virginians had everything under control and urged them to redirect cases from military to local civil courts. Virginia's Black citizens would always need "superintendence," Wise maintained, "but why not [by] men that understand the negro and the country better than any stranger possibly can?" The former governor insisted that "hardly a respectable darkey" had engaged in the recent Third of April celebration. Instead, the crowd had been composed mostly of ignorant miscreants from the countryside, lured into town by white agitators. "I have respect for an intelligent negro," Wise said, and he singled out a restaurateur as an example. "Old Tom Griffin" had just asked Wise "to take a Brunswick stew with him" on the following Saturday. "I shan't fail to do so," Wise said. "And do you suppose that I will not be treated like a gentleman? If you do you are wrong."[45]

It's unsurprising that Griffin would treat Wise "like a gentleman," since treating customers with deference and hospitality was essential for a professional caterer. In the closing years of his career, Griffin seems to have placed his bets on the opposite side of the civil rights debate from his colleague Fields Cook. On May 10 Griffin was one of only a handful of African American men among the hundreds of white attendees at the anniversary gathering of the Richmond Blues, the elite militia organization that had long been one of Griffin's best catering customers. General Wise was also in attendance, and when he addressed the assembled troops, he saluted Griffin and his companions for refusing "to insult their best friends" and for bowing out of the Third of April celebrations. "The freedmen will always be protected by their former masters," Wise promised, and he urged the members of the Blues "always to guard them from wrong."[46]

The path John Dabney decided to take was more ambiguous. Professionally, Dabney had long lived on the margin between the Black and white communities, and in 1866 he and his family began living on that margin in a very literal sense. That November he purchased a house at 1414 East Broad Street, securing, as his son Wendell later put it, "a foothold on Broad Street." In the years that followed, "a few high class and very exclusive colored citizens" moved into the area, but it remained an overwhelmingly white neighborhood. The house Dabney purchased, formerly a women's seminary, was a three-story frame building with broad porches, a large lawn, plentiful shade trees, and a flower garden. It was located on the large hill in downtown Richmond that overlooks "the Valley" and the old Medical College—now the Virginia Commonwealth University School of Medicine. A block up Broad Street from their house was the Monumental Church and also the new First Baptist Church, and beyond that the state Capitol building. All of the neighborhood except the district below Mayo Street and Jail Alley was white.[47]

In September 1866 the *Richmond Enquirer* published a curious story about "the celebrated colored restaurateur of our city." During the war, as Confederate currency was rapidly deflating, John Dabney had stopped paying the installments toward his own freedom at the request of his owner, Mrs. DeJarnette. At the end of the war, the outstanding balance stood at around two hundred dollars. Dabney's friends advised him that there was no reason for him to pay the remainder because that he was now a free man. "No," Dabney replied, according to the *Enquirer*. "I owe the money honestly, and I intend to pay it." He went to visit his former mistress and "despite the hard times . . . discharged the obligation in full."

This story would be repeated in multiple variations over the years that followed, with each narrator elaborating upon it and drawing his or her own lesson from the tale. In the earliest version, the *Enquirer* explicitly linked Dabney's story to the politics of the moment—and to the conservative white view of the proper course for "reconstructing" southern society. "John belongs to that numerous and respectable portion of our colored population," the paper observed, who "attend to their own business, pay their debts, and . . . rely for their support upon their old masters who will, they know . . . prove themselves in the future as they have ever done in the past, their best and truest friends." Other observers drew very different lessons. The *Weekly Freedman's Press*, an African American newspaper in Austin, Texas, retold the story, adding this moral: "It is only another proof that a man of honor will act honorably, whether his skin is bleached or tanned."[48]

How John Dabney felt about the matter was not reported. These were by no means the last times that the story of his discharging his debt would be retold in the press.

 CHAPTER 8

Positions Lucrative, Commanding Respect

A Political Interlude

June 1866 was a rough public-relations month for George T. Downing. He succeeded in getting his name into newspapers all over the country thanks to a "card"—the nineteenth-century version of a letter to the editor—that he sent to a Washington newspaper, expressing his opinions on a recent congressional report. Dozens of newspapers picked up Downing's missive and quoted it, but not every editor framed his opinions in the most positive light. One paper ran a summary under the short heading "Negro Impudence." Another introduced Downing as a "stuck up specimen of the negro race" who had been "taught by the radical Congressmen with whom he has associated to regard himself as better than any poor white man." The paper noted that Downing would often "dine and wine" with Thaddeus Stevens and Charles Sumner, and it warned "'Old Thad's' colored housekeeper" to "see to it that he stands up to his work, and that he does not turn his back on his favorite color."[1]

One might assume that these sentiments came from unreconstructed editors at Deep South newspapers, but that was not the case. They appeared in two newspapers in Pennsylvania, the *Harrisburg Patriot* and the *Lancaster Intelligencer*. The road ahead was going to be rocky, and not just for George T. Downing. The events that unfolded in the years that followed dramatically altered the character of the southern commercial dining market by determining who would be allowed to participate in it and—just as significantly—who would not. The political battles that took place in Washington, D.C., between 1866 and 1876 established the terms and parameters of post–Civil War society, and the city's great caterers and restaurateurs were on hand not just to witness the debates but to play an active role in them.

Downing had written his card in response to the first draft report from Congress's Joint Committee on Reconstruction, which recommended that no rebellious state be allowed to seat congressional representatives until it passed a new state constitution that guaranteed equal protections under the law and the right of all men to vote, regardless of color. Downing thought the plan didn't go nearly far enough and insisted that Congress should impose universal voting rights on the South instead of using congressional seats as an inducement. Congress, nevertheless, was finally starting to assert itself and implement more aggressive Reconstruction measures than President Johnson had. That fall, with most of the former Confederate states still denied representation, the Republicans swept the congressional races, gaining a 75 percent majority in the House and a whopping 85 percent in the Senate. Just two days before the newly elected Congress convened in March, the outgoing 39th Congress overrode Johnson's veto and approved what came to be known as the First Reconstruction Act, bringing to a close the period of Presidential Reconstruction. The act directed the federal government, backed by the force of the army, to take a more direct hand in governing the southern states. To be readmitted to the Union, a state had to ratify the Fourteenth Amendment and guarantee universal male suffrage and equal rights for all citizens. Those rights, notably, included access to places of public accommodation, like hotels and restaurants.[2]

The prospect of gaining the vote thrust African American southerners onto the political stage, and politically involved caterers and restaurateurs like Fields Cook played prominent roles in the mobilization of African American voters and in formal party politics. Now that Virginia's churches were no longer required by law to be led by white ministers, Cook accepted the pastorate at the Baptist church near the Midlothian coal mines southwest of Richmond. Outside the pulpit, he poured his energies into advocating for equal rights. In the tense politics of the day, newspapers made no pretense of impartiality and showed little compunction about distorting the news or even manufacturing controversy from whole cloth. Like George Downing, Cook quickly found himself lambasted in the press. He was accused by several Virginia newspapers of leading a conspiracy "to patch up a party of black and white mosaic work." The alleged purpose of this "mongrel party" was to create a coalition of conservative Blacks and liberal whites in Richmond and divide the white electorate in the upcoming vote on a new constitution. Once the schemers secured political power, the rumors claimed, they planned to kick the whites out of the coalition and impose Black rule on Virginia.[3]

Cook's leadership in the Republican ranks was soon challenged by white politicians, who had suddenly become very interested in courting Black votes. Foremost among these was James W. Hunnicutt, an opportunistic Baptist minister and newspaper editor. In the years that followed, Cook became increasingly frustrated with the dominance of Hunnicutt and other white political leaders, whom he saw as not always acting in the best interest of African Americans. The Republican Party split into factions in April 1869, when radical-leaning Republicans nominated Charles H. Porter, a white man recently arrived from New York, as their candidate for Congress. Calling themselves True Republicans, the moderate faction ran Hunnicutt on an alternate ticket. A disgusted Cook announced that he was running for the seat as an independent. "The one hundred and five thousand colored votes in the State," he declared, "could not be controlled by the twenty-five thousand white men that belonged to the party, and if the twenty-five thousand attempted it, the one hundred and five thousand would make it 'mighty hot' for them." The majority of white Virginians—most of them old Whigs or Democrats whose parties were not allowed to participate—lined up behind Hunnicutt as the more conservative choice. "The political situation in Virginia is becoming very interesting," the *New York Herald* wrote in May, noting that it was very likely that two African Americans—Dr. Bayne from Norfolk and Fields Cook from Richmond—could be elected to Congress for the first time in American history.[4]

The outcome of the election, though, offered a lesson in party trumping principle. Despite the rosy odds given him by the *Herald*, Cook got clobbered, receiving just 228 votes, and Porter edged out Hunnicutt 6,121 to 5,705 to take the congressional seat. In the wake of his defeat, Fields Cook turned his back on electoral politics and on the culinary business, too. In a card to the *Richmond Whig*, he vented his frustration at the Republican Party for not taking the high ground, arguing that their strategy of pitting Blacks against whites had only made the rival Conservative Party stronger and more of a threat. "I therefore cut loose from all party ties," he wrote, "and shall act the freeman as I feel right to do, and will do all I can to convince others to do likewise." When the pastorate of the Princess Colored Baptist Church in Alexandria came open in February 1870, Cook accepted the position and moved to Alexandria, where he lived for the rest of his life.[5]

Cook's brother Jim took a different path in the years just after the Civil War, for he eschewed politics and remained in the culinary trade. He returned to Richmond from Washington in August 1865 and took a position bartending at the Franklin House. Just one month later Cook was arrested and charged with stealing money from his employer, Augustus F. Boyle. At the arraignment, Boyle's son and several other witnesses testified to Cook's good character, and he was released. The *Whig* predicted that Jim Cook would "doubtless live to make a good many more juleps," but those juleps would not be served in Richmond. He left the city before the end of the year, and only a few scraps survive about his life after that.[6]

➤❋ Two Washington Restaurateurs

After several frustrating months in Washington, George T. Downing might understandably have taken the path of Fields Cook and decided to retire from party politics. He still had thriving catering, hotel, and real estate ventures in Newport, but he stayed on in the nation's capital to continue the fight, becoming involved in a long series of advocacy efforts that included agitating for equal treatment for African Americans on railroads and in other places of public accommodation. Downing was convinced that African Americans needed to gain access and influence with those already in power, and he knew that one of the most practical ways of doing that was by hosting them in his own establishment and plying them with food and drink.

In February 1868 the Congressional Committee on Public Buildings turned out the old restaurant keeper in the basement of the Capitol and installed George T. Downing in his place. Such a move did not come without professional and personal risks. Two months after moving into the House restaurant, Downing received a note in the mail purporting to be from "Ku Klux Klan, Provisional Dept'mt Potomac, Washington." Marked with figures of coffins, daggers, and skulls, it read: "Downing, beware . . . stick to your oysters and let politics alone." After listing several of Downing's recent political actions, the writer warned: "If you are in Washington ten days after this reaches you it will be as a corpse." Ten days later Downing was still in Washington, catering the Knights Templar Levee at Carner's Hall. The *San Francisco Elevator*, an African American newspaper, concluded the letter was probably a hoax intended to frighten the caterer, "but they may as well try to frighten the devil. . . . They would find him an ugly customer, for he is strong as an ox, as brave as a lion, as nimble as a squirrel, an expert marksman, and is a match for any two ordinary men."[7]

Congressmen lunching with friends at George T. Downing's restaurant beneath the House of Representatives chambers, from John B. Ellis, *Sights and Secrets of the National Capital* (Chicago: Jones, Junkin, 1869).

Unfortunately, no detailed description of Downing's restaurant beneath the south wing of the Capitol survives. One brief account from 1869 notes that it occupied two rooms next to the luxurious congressional bathing rooms and that it was "handsomely fitted up." As for the food, the author notes only that Downing's dishes "are served in a style that would not shame Delmonico himself." We can surmise that Downing's bill of fare was similar to his predecessors', for his advertisements promise "all the delicacies of the season" and are decorated with images of turtles and sora. Downing's counterpart on the north end of the building was Samuel Proctor, who operated the Senate Saloon immediately beneath the Senate chambers. The Maryland-born Proctor was also a person of color, and he advertised "oysters, game, and all the luxuries of the season." Despite Joint Rule 19, which prohibited the sale or keeping of spirituous liquors or wines within the Capitol, alcohol was an important part of both men's offering. "The restaurants in both wings kept wines, liquors and cigars unmolested," the *New York Daily Herald* reported in 1870. "Nobody objected, and Senator This and

Representative That experienced no difficulty in getting gloriously elevated without leaving the capital. . . . Oysters and ale were to be had at any time, and stronger beverages were obtainable when called for under the designation of 'strong coffee.'"[8]

The elections of 1868 brought a new Congress to Washington and a new presidential administration, too. Ulysses S. Grant won in an Electoral College landslide, and as he was preparing to take office in March 1869, newspapers began reporting that "there is a struggle to get into Gen. Grant's kitchen cabinet as well as his into his political." Three "masters of the art of the cooking"—all of them African American—were vying for the post of White House steward, the role that Joseph Boulanger had played for Andrew Jackson in the 1830s. The three aspirants were William H. Smith, the steward for Vice President–elect Schuyler Colfax's household, Henry Johnson, who played a similar role for Representative Samuel Hooper, and George T. Downing, the famed Newport caterer and House restaurateur.[9]

The newspapers focused on the position's generous $2,000 annual salary, suggesting the men were primarily angling for a high-paying sinecure. Downing made a different case in a card he sent to the *New York Tribune*. He argued that he could "with some propriety claim some position under that Administration" because "at the risk of life and property," he had been an early advocate of "the sentiment that elected the incoming Administration." Grant won the popular vote by a margin of three hundred thousand, and he owed his victory to the half million African Americans who cast ballots in a presidential election for the first time. "Up to the present time," Downing noted, "colored men have been shut out from positions lucrative that carry with them commanding respect." Downing was already a prosperous businessman. His seeking of a White House position was not about lining his pockets through patronage. It was about getting closer to political power and advancing the causes he had been fighting for during his three years in Washington.[10]

Downing lost his bid, as did the other two African American applicants. Grant selected as his steward Valentino Melah, a "silver-voiced Italian" who had been the steward at the Stetson at Long Branch, New Jersey, where Grant and his family spent their summers. Downing took the setback in stride, remaining deeply involved in Republican politics and the push for civil rights. He helped secure the nomination of Ebenezer Don Carlos Bassett as minister to Haiti, the first African American to serve as a United States diplomat. He led a delegation that met with President Grant in the

White House and urged him to appoint African Americans not only to fill federal offices in the South but in the North as well. In November he wrote a series of letters to national newspapers protesting his own treatment on the Baltimore & Ohio Railroad, which sold him a reserved seat in the passenger coaches from New Jersey to Washington and then refused to seat him. He served as chairman of the National Negro Labor Convention and as president of its National Executive Committee, which was founded "to urge legislation looking to the educational, material, and political interests of the colored people of the nation."[11]

As Downing became more prominent on the national stage, his opponents began to use his background in the culinary trades as a brush to tar him with. When the *New York Herald* reported a rumor that Downing was about to be appointed collector of customs at Newport, it headlined the piece "Half a Dozen on the Half Shell" and concluded with the statement "One fancy roast, hurry up!" When Downing weighed in publicly in early 1870 on "the Georgia question"—that is, whether to admit the Georgia delegation to Congress—the *Macon Weekly Telegraph* lambasted him as "a mulatto, who dispenses coffee, fish balls, and 'cold tea' in the basement of the Capitol" and lamented the thought of "a negro bartender meddling in the affairs of a State whose record is lustrous with the names of dead and living statesmen!" When Downing dared to send a letter to the *New York Times* arguing that it was too soon to grant general amnesty to former Confederate leaders, the *Missouri Republican* disparaged his opinion as that of "a self-appointed committee of one" and suggested there was no need for amnesty to wait "until the wrathful soul of the vindictive vendor of oysters is appeased."[12]

As Downing immersed himself deeper into politics, James Wormley doubled down on business. In August 1868, at the age of forty-nine, he traveled to England with Reverdy Johnson, the newly appointed minister to the United Kingdom. When the *Washington Chronicle* reported that the caterer was accompanying Johnson "as his servant," Wormley dashed off a curt third-person correction, clarifying that "he only goes to England to arrange Mr. Johnson's house, secure him servants, &c. Mr. Wormley then contemplates leaving for Paris upon matters connected with himself, returning subsequently to this country." Wormley took with him on the voyage a cargo of live terrapins and introduced Britons to the glories of *terrapin à la Maryland* before continuing on to France.[13]

Wormley returned home in mid-September and promptly set about expanding his facilities on I Street. In December he purchased an additional lot and brick building and added it to his growing complex, announcing in January the reopening of his "celebrated dining rooms." Wormley added, "He purchased while in Paris a superb Dinner Set, which cannot be equaled in this country." He had also brought back a mechanical novelty: a pair of taxidermied birds mounted on a stand, each with a windup device inside that produced lifelike birdsongs. Wormley by this point had secured his reputation as Washington's premier caterer. When Robert Todd Lincoln, the late president's son, was married in September 1868, the wedding supper was held in the caterer's dining rooms on I Street. In December, when Secretary of State William H. Seward invited the British and French ministers to his home in Auburn, New York, he engaged "Mr. Wormley, our best caterer, to get up a Christmas dinner for them."[14]

Wormley did miss the opportunity to entertain one famous visitor, Charles Dickens, who returned to Washington in February 1868 during his second American tour. Dickens took his lodging in the rooms over John Welcker's restaurant on 15th Street. Contrary to the stories repeated by modern-day Delmonico's partisans, the New York restaurant was not the only public setting where Dickens dined during this return visit. Though not the guest of honor at any large banquets in Washington, he did dine with a party that included Senator Charles Sumner and Secretary of War Edward Stanton, and he took additional dinners in Welcker's highly regarded dining rooms. Dickens apparently approved of Welcker's fare, for he left the restaurateur an autographed note saying he kept the best restaurant in the world—a relic Welcker kept framed on his walls for many years after.[15]

Immigrant restaurateurs like Welcker do not seem to have become involved in partisan politics, whether in Washington or in other southern cities. When Welcker died of pneumonia at the untimely age of thirty-nine, a memorial in the *Capital* newspaper asserted, "Welcker was a genuine democrat; to him all were equal before the purse. . . . When the table was spread and the gas lit, what was said or done or sought or pursued was of no interest to John. His concerns never got beyond the viands and the wines." Some historians have claimed that James Wormley remained similarly aloof from politics, choosing instead to focus on his business interests, but that wasn't exactly the case—or at least not in the years immediately following Emancipation. Such interpretations seem based largely on accounts of Wormley's life published much later, many after his death. Wormley was by no means as outspoken as his fellow caterer Downing, but he hardly shunned involvement in political affairs.[16]

Wormley was a longtime associate of local minister and civil rights activist John F. Cook, and he was close friends with Charles Sumner of Massachusetts, the leading Senate champion for civil rights and aggressive Reconstruction, and Reverdy Johnson, the only Democrat to vote for the Reconstruction Act of 1867. Wormley was deeply involved in the cause of African American education, which progressives viewed as essential for ensuring economic success as well as political and social equality. In January 1870 he was among the notable attendees at a meeting held by the Board of Trustees of Colored Schools of Washington and Georgetown, which ended by resolving, "There should be no white or nor no black schools, but one school for all." Wormley was active in the First Ward Republican Club in the early 1870s and involved in many other civic improvement efforts.[17]

Wormley's sons were even more politically involved than their father. In June 1868, after the District of Columbia's Board of Aldermen passed an act making it unlawful "to make any distinction on account of race or color" in admitting patrons to a place of public amusement, James T. Wormley Jr. was one of three African American men who purchased dress circle tickets at the National Theatre, took their seats, and were asked to leave by an usher. The younger Wormley and his companions filed a complaint with the city, and the theatre's owner was arraigned on charges of violating the public accommodations law—an incident that made headlines across the country. At the time, Wormley Jr. was enrolled in the Medical Department at the newly founded Howard University, and in March 1870 he was awarded a Doctor of Pharmacy degree, becoming one of the first graduates from the university's Medical Department. He went to work initially for a white druggist at the corner of L Street and Connecticut Avenue, just a few blocks from his father's hotel. Within a year he had bought out his employer's stock and leased the store, becoming D.C.'s first Black pharmacist.[18]

Another of Wormley's sons, William, was directly involved in local party politics. Possessed of a fiery temper, he was once arrested for knocking a lobbyist to the ground on I Street after the man encouraged Congress to send recently emancipated slaves to Liberia. (William was fined $50 for the offense but, perhaps thanks to his father's connections, avoided jail time.) William aligned himself with Sayles J. Bowen, the city's controversial white Republican mayor from 1868 to 1870 and a fervent proponent of integrated schools. When Bowen ran for reelection in 1870, William

Wormley was on the ticket as a candidate for alderman. Bowen had been widely blamed for saddling the city government with debt, and a significant number of Republicans crossed party lines to support the Democratic candidate. Bowen was soundly defeated by Matthew Gault Emery, and Wormley lost his race for the alderman seat by a slim margin. He subsequently served on the Board of Trustees of Colored Schools and remained active in city politics in the years that followed.[19]

As the sons' political involvement rose, so did their father's commercial prospects. By 1870 the fifty-year-old James Wormley owned some $75,000 worth of real estate. The *Washington Capital* in 1871 declared him "one of the most successful colored men in this city . . . probably, at this time the wealthiest among them." His hotel complex consisted of five houses, which he owned outright, and he maintained a separate confectionery store next door. In addition to supplying weddings, balls, and parties, he had a contract to provide the meals for the Japanese legation, which was located nearby on 15th Street.[20]

But Wormley had even bigger plans in store. In April 1871, with the assistance of Representative Samuel Hooper of Massachusetts, he secured a large lot at the corner of 15th and H Streets and began constructing a massive new addition to his hotel. Completed in December, the new building boasted fifty rooms, each with hot and cold running water, as well as an improved elevator. The spacious new dining rooms featured all the delicacies of the mid-Atlantic, including oysters, terrapin soup, and—as one traveler in 1872 described it—"the celebrated canvas-back ducks, which are not considered good till they have fed upon the wild celery which grows in abundance in the lower reaches of the Potomac."[21]

Wormley may not have been as publicly engaged in politics as Downing, but he received his fair share of abuse in the press nonetheless. Wormley's long-established practice of snapping up rare wines and brandies at estate sales didn't sit well with the *Boston Journal.* "At the late sale of Sir Frederick Bruce's effects in Washington," the paper lamented in 1867, "Mr. James Wormley (colored) bought most of the expensive articles. What are we coming to?" Many whites took a zero-sum view of economic success, assuming that the prosperity of someone like Wormley must have come at their expense. The announcement that Wormley's niece was preparing to marry a white Frenchman named Paul Gerard created a national scandal. Rumors swirled for weeks that the pastor of St. Matthew's Church would refuse to perform the marriage, though the Catholic church had no prohibition against interracial unions. The couple was ultimately joined in matrimony on December 7th in the Reverend Dr. White's parlor. "What *will* become of the good old Washingtonians?" an aghast *New York Tribune* demanded. "Surely it is time the Capital were removed!"[22]

➤❋ The Unraveling

In July 1870, George T. Downing was notified by the Commissioners of Public Buildings that he had 30 days to abandon his restaurant in the basement of the Capitol. The move, the *Detroit Free Press* reported, was in retaliation for Downing's refusing to support the Republican candidate, Sayles Bowen, in the recent mayoral election. Downing's concession was handed to John T. Johnson, an African American barber and former alderman who had been defeated along with Bowen during that summer's elections. Downing was reportedly exasperated at the turn of events and began to harbor ill feelings against the Grant administration as a result.[23]

When Congress resumed session in December, Downing was still in Washington, throwing his energies into opposing a proposal by Senator Carl Schurz of Missouri that would return the right to vote to former Confederates. In early 1871 Downing took a trip to Richmond, the first time in his life he had traveled further south than Washington, D.C. He dispiritedly observed that among white southerners "rancor and hatred, to some extent concealed, but cropping out on all sides, exist." In a letter to the *New York Times* he wrote presciently, "I fear the South is only whipped," and noted that the "despicable proscriptions on all sides"—in the legislature, on railroads, among shopkeepers, and in schools and churches—did not bode well for equality relations in the future. He urged Republicans to "encourage the spirit of enterprise and industry" among African Americans in the South, including extending loans to Black entrepreneurs on the same terms as those given to whites.[24]

Downing was at the peak of his prominence on the national stage, his influence rivaling and even eclipsing Frederick Douglass's, according to some contemporary observers. In April 1871 the *New York Herald* declared that "no other Moses is now recognized by the colored race. True, Fred Douglass played Moses for a while, but played it badly." But Downing was becoming just as frustrated with the Republican Party as Fields Cook had been in Richmond. In a public letter he warned that white Republicans were "not treating the negro as a man and as a brother," and that if they didn't change their ways, Democrats could start luring Black votes away. Downing's charges got him crossways with his old ally Douglass, and in the summer of 1871 the two men engaged in an acerbic debate in the pages of the *New National Era* over the position of African Americans within the Republican Party. The exchange caused many to speculate that Downing was about to switch sides and become a Democrat, an idea he quickly squelched in a series of letters to various newspapers. "While I demand of the Republican party greater consistency in its relation to the colored man," he wrote in the *New York Tribune* in October, "I intend to stand by it, and work for the same, *within the party*." Downing saw no reason to align himself with the Democratic Party, which "murders ruthlessly, brutally, our best educated, our most promising young men."[25]

The rift between Downing and Douglass was emblematic of a larger factionalism that was increasingly dividing Republicans. The scandals that plagued the Grant administration prompted reform-minded Republicans to abandon the sitting president and support Horace Greeley in the election of 1872, creating a splinter party called the Liberal Republicans. In hopes of defeating Grant, the Democratic Party canceled its convention and threw its support behind Greeley. This new factionalism fractured old alignments, especially among the leading proponents of civil rights. Charles Sumner bitterly opposed Grant's reelection and threw his voice behind Greeley, as did James Wormley. Downing, though, came out in support of Grant, arguing that Greeley was too erratic and faulting him for making overtures to Jefferson Davis. That fall Downing hit the campaign trail, speaking in support of Grant at various Republican rallies in Rhode Island, Connecticut, New York, and New Jersey.[26]

Grant handily beat his challenger in November, winning 55.6 percent of the popular vote, and Greeley died before the Electoral College convened. Charles Sumner's support for Greeley greatly diminished his stature in Republican circles, and the Massachusetts senator declined both in political power and physical health over the two years that followed. On the evening of March 19, 1874, Sumner suffered a heart attack in his rooms in Washington. James Wormley was summoned to help comfort his old friend and political ally, but Sumner, who in recent months had been occupied with completing his memoirs, was fading. He stirred periodically to lament, "My book! My book! I should not regret this had I finished my book!" Several of the senator's old friends, including Representative Samuel Hooper and George T. Downing, were called to the bedside the following morning. At ten minutes before three o'clock that afternoon, Charles Sumner passed away, his doctor grasping one of his hands and Downing the other. Among his last words, Sumner implored the attending dignitaries, including Senator Schurz and Representative Hoar, "the civil rights bill—don't let it be lost."[27]

Later that year, when the contents of Sumner's Washington estate were put up for sale, James Wormley bought a divan and many of Sumner's other furnishings, which he used to fit up "Sumner's Dining Room" in his hotel—a sort of shrine to his friend and political ally. Sumner's Reconstruction causes, though, were collapsing, and the tensions and resentments that Downing had sensed in Richmond finally burst into violence. In September 1874 the White League, a paramilitary organization, began mobilizing in Louisiana. Similar groups were active across the South, including the so-called Red Shirts in South Carolina and Mississippi. Aiming to turn Republicans out of office once and for all, these loosely organized groups of armed whites staged rallies and undertook a range of atrocities to intimidate freedmen from voting.

A Democratic landslide in the 1874 midterm elections stripped Republicans of their control of the House and reduced their majority in the Senate. Before surrendering their seats, the radical Republicans of the 43rd Congress made a last-ditch effort to pass Sumner's civil rights bill. To make the measure more palatable to moderates, Benjamin Butler dropped a provision mandating integrated public schools, and he used a series of complex parliamentary maneuvers to navigate the bill to passage just before the 43rd Congress adjourned. The act affirmed the "equality of all men before the law" and guaranteed African Americans equal treatment in public transport and public accommodations, including restaurants. President Grant signed the bill into law on March 1, 1875, but conditions in the South continued to deteriorate. As new rounds of violence erupted in the run-up to local elections in 1875, George T. Downing wrote an impassioned letter to the *Boston Pilot.* "We are being deserted," he exclaimed. "Our rights of citizenship are practically nullified in nearly every Southern state, and those who call themselves statesmen look upon the outrage with complacent indifference."[28]

Congressional Reconstruction in the South was finished, and its fate may well have been sealed in a private room at James Wormley's Washington hotel. In the 1876 presidential election, Democrat Samuel Tilden outpolled Republican Rutherford B. Hayes by some 250,000 popular votes, but

Hayes held a one-point margin in the Electoral College, with the votes from Louisiana and South Carolina remaining uncounted. The elections in those two states had ended in dispute, and each had dual legislatures and two governors attempting to take their seats. Amid much legal and political wrangling, it fell to the Electoral Commission and the House of Representatives in Washington to recertify the votes and determine the winner.

Two of the commission's lawyers, William Evarts and Stanley Matthews, took rooms at Wormley's Hotel, which became a hub of Republican activity. On the night of February 26, Evarts's rooms were the site of a meeting between a delegation of Democrats from Louisiana and five Hayes associates from Ohio. What happened during this meeting, which became known as the Wormley Conference, remains the subject of much dispute. Some attendees insisted that there was no bargain of any kind, but others told the press that the parties had pledged not to divulge anything they discussed—suggesting some sort of deal may have been struck. Three days later the House of Representatives reconvened, and at four the following morning, after eighteen hours in session, the Speaker of the House declared that Rutherford B. Hayes had won the presidency by a majority of a single electoral vote.[29]

Among Hayes's first acts in office was to order the withdrawal of Federal troops from the statehouses of South Carolina and Louisiana, forcing the two Republican gubernatorial claimants to step aside and let their Democratic rivals be seated. The two new governors, Wade Hampton in South Carolina and Francis T. Nicholls in Louisiana, had both been generals in the Confederate army during the Civil War. "Home rule"—which is to say, white conservative rule—had been returned to the last of the southern states formerly in rebellion, and Reconstruction had come to an end. Whether those late February meetings at Wormley's Hotel actually produced the bargain that swung the election to Hayes will likely never be known. Wormley's biographer Carol Gelderman suggests a more useful conclusion. "Instead of blaming the electoral crisis for causing the abandonment of Reconstruction," she wrote in her account of the Wormley Conference, "it would be more accurate to argue that the abandonment of Reconstruction caused the crisis of 1876–1877." Both Wormley and George T. Downing had seen that abandonment coming for quite some time.[30]

Wormley remained in the hotel business in Washington, withdrawing further from political battles while extending his establishment's reputation as the capital's leading place of accommodation through the Hayes, Garfield, and Arthur administrations. His boarders included Senator Roscoe Conkling of New York and Representatives John L. Blake of New Jersey, William W. Crapo of Massachusetts, Frank H. Hurd of Ohio, and Hiester Clymer of Pennsylvania, as well as Yoshida Kiyonari, the secretary of the Japanese Legation. In 1883 the *People's Advocate*, an African American newspaper in Alexandria, published an editorial titled "Let Politics Alone." It included James Wormley among its list of "useful and wealthy colored men" who "do not dabble in politics, but who pursue a strict line of business."[31]

George T. Downing pulled back from politics, too, at least on a national level. After the 45th Congress adjourned in mid-March, Downing—as had been his practice in previous years—returned to Newport to spend the summer season, catering to groups like the Light Infantry, for whom he staged a dinner at the Ocean House in late May. When Congress reconvened in October, Downing decided not to return to Washington, ending his decadelong fight in the nation's capital. Downing split his time between Newport and New York, throwing himself into state politics in Rhode Island and petitioning the legislature to repeal the state's ban on interracial marriage. In October 1878 he went back into the oyster business in Manhattan, opening a new branch on Broad Street, just three doors away from where his father operated his old stand a half century before.[32]

 CHAPTER 9

Augusta, Georgia

A Commercial Dining Case Study

Around 9:00 p.m. on March 8, 1875, ten men entered Lexius Henson's saloon in Augusta, Georgia, and ordered drinks. All ten were African American. "This is a white man's bar," Henson told the group. "You ought not try to injure my business this way." But the men were insistent. Just a week earlier President Grant had signed the Civil Rights Bill into law, guaranteeing—on paper, at least—that all people, regardless of color, would have equal access to theatres, hotels, and restaurants. Henson tried a different tack, telling his would-be customers that beer now cost $1 per glass, a shot of whiskey was $2.50, and brandy $5—about ten times the market rate. The men left the saloon and stood on the street corner discussing the matter, then decided to call Henson's bluff. They pooled their money, and two of them went back inside. Each put a dollar on the bar and asked for a beer. This time, Henson refused to serve them outright, and the men departed for good.[1]

Lexius Henson had made his choice. Faced with the alternatives of putting his business at risk by accommodating African American customers or refusing to serve them and preserving his lucrative white clientele, Henson took the route that would not injure his business. It was a calculation that many restaurateurs and hoteliers had to make in the 1870s. What was different about this incident was that Henson himself was a person of color.

Lexius Henson entered the saloon and restaurant business in the tumultuous days of Reconstruction, when the culinary trade was transitioning from its antebellum mode of banquets and public dinners to the more modern conventions of restaurant dining. At the close of the war, stand-alone restaurants were rare in midsized southern cities like Augusta, for proprietors needed more than just a slate of food to attract customers. Some operated within hotels or at summer resorts, feeding travelers who were on the road and away from their regular sources of meals. Others depended upon the sale of wine and spirits, either as an on-premise saloon or as a retailer, while still others catered private events. The most successful of the South's culinary professionals performed all of these functions.

Selling food and drink offered a promising line of work for those seeking a foothold in the slowly recovering economy, be they African Americans recently emancipated from slavery, immigrants who continued to arrive from Europe, or American-born whites looking for a more lucrative trade. Most started with little or no capital, so they depended instead on establishing connections with people who could help jump-start their endeavors. Those relationships and the proprietors' interpersonal skills were as important to ensuring success as their talents in the kitchen or behind the bar. Caterers and restaurateurs were the hosts for large parties and banquets, which required hospitality and showmanship, the ability to wow a crowd. Their customers were often "patrons" in the older sense of the word—wealthy benefactors who provided financial support to a restaurant, which often created unbalanced power relationships.

Initially, African Americans and European immigrants competed head-to-head with native-born whites as proprietors of saloons and restaurants, just as they had before the war. But what were at first promising fields of enterprise for all three groups took on very different shadings as the South moved from Reconstruction into the Jim Crow era. These commercial dramas unfolded in the rising cities of the New South, which were navigating an uncertain course from an agrarian, slaveholding economy to the slowly emerging industrial and commercial future. Some 150 miles to the west of Augusta, Atlanta was just beginning its phoenixlike rebirth from wartime devastation to becoming the South's leading commercial center, but the speed and scale of its boom made it an outlier. We will focus instead on the example of Augusta, a medium-sized but steadily growing city, for it offers a representative case study of the market and societal dynamics at work in the postwar South, dynamics that played out in similar ways in cities throughout the region.

➤❋⟵ Commercial Dining in Postwar Augusta

Augusta's economic destiny was shaped by two important assets. The first was the Georgia Railroad, which linked the city to Atlanta and, from there, to Chattanooga and the Tennessee River, giving Augusta shipping access all the way to the Mississippi River. In 1847 the thirteen-mile Augusta Canal was completed. One of the few successful canal projects in the South, it allowed flatboats from the upcountry to bypass the falls above Augusta and reach the city. It also provided power that could drive mills, and hydro-power transformed Augusta into a producer of gunpowder and textiles, making it one of the few manufacturing centers in the antebellum South. Between 1840 and 1860, Augusta's population doubled to almost 12,500 residents, making it the second largest city in Georgia behind Savannah. Of those, 3,700 were enslaved African Americans and close to 400 were free persons of color.[2]

Both physically and financially, Augusta fared far better during the Civil War than Atlanta or Charleston. Augusta was home to the Confederate Powder Works and was an important center for producing war materiel, but Sherman bypassed it, expecting it to be strongly guarded, and crossed the river and marched to Columbia instead. As the Union army advanced through Georgia and South Carolina, thousands of refugees began to pour into Augusta. By the war's end, the population had swelled to almost fifteen thousand residents and was still growing as migrants continued to arrive from the surrounding countryside seeking employment.

Two of those new arrivals were Lexius and Charles Henson. Though some accounts refer to the men as brothers, they were actually half brothers. Both were the sons of Dr. William James Henson of Columbia County, who appears to have died before the Civil War. Lexius was the son of Pinkey, a mulatto woman, while Charles was the son of Frances, presumably a mulatto woman as well. The identity of William James Henson is a bit uncertain, but multiple records list him as "Dr. Henson," and we can conclude that he was a white man and that the two women with whom he had children were enslaved—a not uncommon scenario in antebellum Georgia.[3]

The Hensons arrived in Augusta at a time of great hope and promise for the local African American community. That community was made up of a small but influential number of residents who had been free persons of color before the Civil War along with a growing number of freedmen, many of whom had left rural farms and plantations and moved to the city after Emancipation to make new lives for themselves. Religion and education were essential institutions for the city's African American residents, and the Springfield Baptist Church, the oldest independent Black church in the state, became the focal point of community life and social activism. In 1866 the Georgia Equal Rights Association—the forerunner of the state's Republican Party—was founded in Augusta. By 1875 sixteen grammar schools for African Americans were in operation in Richmond County, and in 1880, after much advocacy from community leaders, the city's first African American high school accepted its inaugural freshman class.

A sharp divide existed within the city's African American community between the "elite" members, many of whom were of mixed race and had been free before the Civil War, and the poorer, less educated freedmen. The former tended to live in the city's Fourth Ward, while the latter occupied the south end of the city, which became known as the Terri, short for Negro Territory. Lexius and William Henson, thanks perhaps to their mixed-race parentage, were welcomed into elite circles soon after their arrival from Columbia County. In 1866 a notice in the *Loyal Georgian*, the state's first African American–owned newspaper, lists a Mr. L. Henson among the troupe of the Sumner Convivial Association, which was formed to "give tableaux"—that is, to dress in costumes and perform silent, motionless scenes from history in what the French called *tableaux vivants*, or "living pictures." Both Charles and Lexius Henson registered to vote in 1867 and were working as bartenders, though it is unclear at which establishments. Lexius Henson's mother, Pinkey, and his sisters, Olivia and Selina, had joined him in Augusta by the late 1860s.[4]

In 1872 the two brothers set out on their own and opened L & C Henson Saloon and Restaurant. It was located on Ellis Street near the intersection with Macintosh (present-day 7th Street), just one block south of the main commercial district on Broad Street. The Hensons catered to a white clientele, and they promised to serve—in the same vague generalities that had been standard for decades—"none but the best and choicest game, meats, fish, oysters, vegetables, etc to be found at home and abroad." Attached to the restaurant was a "first-class bar" supplied with "the finest of liquors, ales, tobacco, and cigars." The brothers were operating squarely within the standard southern restaurant mode, with an offering that would have been recognizable to travelers from any part of the United States. Known interchangeably as "L & C Henson" and the "Exchange Saloon," the restaurant received fresh oysters daily. The Hensons continued the antebellum marketing practice of offering free turtle soup lunches to draw customers to the bar. In October 1872 they announced that they were introducing "a new feature in the saloon business" and had "fitted up an elegant restaurant above their saloon for the special accommodation of the ladies," who would be waited upon by "polite and attentive female attendants."[5]

Like most medium-sized cities in the early 1870s, Augusta's commercial dining market offered a relatively small number of competing options. When the Hensons opened the Exchange Saloon in 1872, Augusta's population of sixteen thousand residents was served by just five other restaurants. John F. Heuisler operated the Opera House Arcade restaurant in the basement of Girardey's Opera House on Broad Street, where he served meats,

Advertisement for Lexius and Charles Henson's saloon and restaurant, in *Haddock's Augusta, Ga. Directory and General Advertiser, 1872.*

game, oysters, and "everything pertaining to a first-class restaurant." John H. Meinecke operated the Monument Saloon at the corner of Monument and Broad, while Woodson Wood ran the Oglethorpe Saloon and Restaurant at the corner of Ellis and Campbell. Two wholesale liquor dealers, E. R. Schneider and Chas Spaeth, served enough food in the bars of their establishments for them be listed in the Restaurants section of the city directory. Augustans could also dine at the Planters Hotel, which the *Hand Book of Augusta* in 1878 declared to have a "menu unexcelled in the South," or at the city's three other hotels, the Globe, the Central, and the Augusta, all of which were located on Broad Street.[6]

In October, the same month that the Hensons announced their new ladies' dining room, another aspiring restaurateur entered the game. James Hughes opened the Atlantic Saloon just around the corner from Broad Street on Macintosh. Operating out of a space in the back of Christopher Gray & Co.'s dry goods store, Hughes promised "the best of game, oysters, liquors and segars will be dispensed" and declared that he "has had long experience in this business." That experience dated back to the months immediately after the end of the Civil War, but the Atlantic was Hughes's first attempt at running his own establishment. Born in Ireland in 1832, he had arrived in Augusta by 1858. On April 21, 1861, he married a Georgia-born woman named Sarah E. Pritchard and six days later mustered into the Independent Blues, which became Company D of the 10th Regiment of the Georgia Infantry and was part of the Army of Northern Virginia for most of the war. After the fighting ended, he returned to Augusta and signed on to manage the Blennerhassett Restaurant, which opened just across the street from the Georgia Railroad depot. After the Blennerhassett closed in 1868, Hughes moved over to run the restaurant and bar in E. R. Schneider's wholesale liquor establishment, where he stayed for four years before opening the Atlantic Saloon in October of 1872.

Hughes's venture lasted less than a year. In May of 1873 he sold the business to a young German immigrant named Henry P. Heitsch, who ran it for another two years before moving on to Columbia, South Carolina, and opening a restaurant there. Hughes worked for a time as one of Augusta's two city lamplighters, but in 1878 he went back to tending bar, this time at the Globe Hotel. He died in 1885 at the relatively young age of fifty-three, leaving behind a widow and seven children. "He was popular among his associates," his obituary notes, "and had a wide circle of acquaintances in Augusta."[7]

It is difficult to piece together the biographies of operators like Jim Hughes, for they tended to stay in any one location for only a few years. Of all the Hensons' rivals, Woodson Wood of the Oglethorpe Saloon had perhaps the longest tenure. Born two counties to the west in Warrenton, Georgia, he served in the Confederate army and moved to Augusta after the war, where he purchased a half interest in M. T. McGregor's Oglethorpe Saloon in July 1866. Within a year Wood bought the business outright, and he operated the saloon until 1878 when, apparently in failing health, he returned to Warrenton and died the following year. John F. Heuisler of the Opera House Arcade bounced even more. He arrived in Augusta in the closing years of the war and was the proprietor of at least three short-lived Augusta restaurants before he moved into the space below Isadore Girardey's newly remodeled Opera House, which opened in December 1871. Heuisler's restaurant lasted there until Girardey went bankrupt and sold the Opera House in 1876. Heuisler worked as a city bill poster and as a vegetable, ice, and fish dealer in the years that followed.[8]

In comparison to these local competitors, Lexius and Charles Henson were able to establish careers that, though they had plenty of ups and downs, lasted longer and earned them considerably more acclaim. In November 1874, for reasons unknown, the two brothers dissolved their partnership. Lexius continued to operate the restaurant and saloon on Ellis, and Charles opened a restaurant of his own on Broad Street. It was only a few months after the two brothers separated that Lexius Henson was forced to make his critical decision about which kind of clientele to serve as a saloon keeper and restaurateur. As one of the first tests of the Civil Rights Act, the ten men's attempt to get served at Henson's bar was reported in newspapers as far away as Cincinnati and New Orleans. It seems to have been the only such incident that occurred at Henson's establishment, but it was part of a broader effort on the part of Black southerners to test whether the Civil Rights Act would have teeth.

On March ninth in Richmond, Virginia, an African American man took a seat in the orchestra section of a theatre, and the white audience imme-diately responded with cries of "put him out," persisting until the man-ager escorted the Black patron from the building. Similar tests were made in Atlanta, where three African Americans attempted to take seats in the white gallery at the opera house, and in Louisville, where several African American men bought tickets to the dress circle at McCauley's Theatre. In both cases they were confronted by white patrons and ended up leaving the theatre to avoid violence. Two African American men were allowed to sit down and dine at C. C. Rufer's Hotel in Louisville, but upon leaving the building they were attacked and beaten by a white mob.[9]

These and similar efforts to assert public accommodation rights ended unsuccessfully, and the Civil Rights Act was widely ignored throughout the South. In October 1883 the U.S. Supreme Court ruled in an 8–1 decision that the Thirteenth and Fourteenth Amendments did not prevent uncodified racial discrimination, in effect nullifying the act's provisions. The Civil Rights Act of 1875 was the final major piece of Reconstruction legislation, and it would be the last piece of civil rights legislation passed by the federal government for almost a century.

Among the various test efforts, the incident at Lexius Henson's saloon was unusual because it targeted an establishment owned by a person of color. The situation certainly put Henson in a tough spot, for his livelihood and commercial success depended upon white patronage. The path he chose—not to injure his business, at the expense of civil rights—seems to have paid off financially, at least in the short term. Later that year Henson expanded the Exchange Saloon and Restaurant, adding rooms for private dinners and banquets as well as lodging apartments for transient boarders. The facility was now equipped to serve meals any time of the day, and the updates were well received by white diners. "Augusta has long needed a first-class restaurant," declared the authors of the *Hand Book of Augusta*. "Lexius has fully supplied the want."

That 1878 handbook, a guide to the businesses of the growing city, provides one of the few surviving descriptions of Henson's furnishings. "A fine Brussels carpet is on the floor," it notes, "lace curtains adorn the windows, and the tables are dazzling with snowy linens and bright silver." That same year, the *Augusta Chronicle* reported that Henson had outfitted his Ladies Restaurant with "a very handsome set of China, consisting of one thousand and eighty-six pieces," which he had just received from a Savannah importer. "Each piece has a neat monogram upon it, and the whole affair is exquisitely finished and gotten up with much taste."[10]

Accounts from the period, unfortunately, offer fewer details about the food that earned Henson his reputation. The *Hand Book of Augusta* noted only, "Everything that the New York, Savannah, Charleston, and Augusta markets afford, may be called for by the patrons of the restaurant." Though Henson resided in rooms above the restaurant, it seems he had a plot of land where he raised some of the produce used in his restaurant. The *Chronicle* noted in June 1883, "Some fine specimens of large, clear early rose potatoes have been raised upon the place of Lexius Henson, near the city."[11]

By this point Henson's was the venue of choice for banquets and other functions among the city's business community. Such events included a banquet for the members of the National Dental Association, who held their annual meeting in Augusta in 1879, as well as a dinner to honor James B. Randall when he returned home from Washington after serving a stint as the political correspondent for the local newspaper. Like John Dabney and Jim Cook in Richmond, Henson knew full well how to curry favor with the press. At eleven o'clock on a Friday night in September 1877, a white-aproned waiter entered the *Augusta Chronicle* offices bearing a tray with "a tempting array of oysters on the half shell flanked by a bottle of Heidsieck," a prized brand of Champagne. "The bivalves were fresh and delicious," the editors reported the next day, and they sent their compliments to Henson, as they would on many more occasions in the future when they were recipients of his treats.[12]

While Lexius Henson's restaurant was growing in scale and reputation, his half brother Charles wasn't sitting idle. In 1877 Charles Henson announced that he had formed a partnership with John Frazier to open Our House Restaurant on Broad Street. Frazier, an African American man in his midforties, had been born in South Carolina. It is unclear when he arrived in Augusta, but he and Henson advertised boldly that Frazier "possesses abilities as a cook second to none in the South, and his reputation will guarantee that all food will be prepared in first class style." Having arrived in the city during the Civil War, the two Henson brothers had thrived during Reconstruction, establishing themselves as two of the city's leading restaurateurs.[13]

A brief glimpse behind the scenes at Lexius Henson's restaurant is provided in the memoirs of John Hope, who took a job at Henson's in 1881 at the age of thirteen. Like Henson, Hope was the product of an interracial union, the son of a free woman of color and a white Irish immigrant who became a successful local merchant. His family fell on hard times after his father died in 1876, and Hope decided to leave school after the eighth grade to support his mother and siblings. He quickly rose in Henson's trust and became the wine steward at the restaurant and saloon, a position that put him in close contact with Augusta's elite whites. Often he and a fellow employee named Levi White, also a mixed-race teenager, would escort home customers who had sampled a few too many of Henson's "choice wines and liquors," sometimes carrying the patron bodily between them. Hope worked for Henson for five years, eventually keeping Henson's books and helping in the management of the restaurant.

John Hope might have gone on to a long career in the commercial food trade, but African Americans in the postbellum South increasingly had to choose between two incompatible routes for advancement: working in hospitality or pursuing higher education, which often required leaving home and heading north. Though he started down the first path—leaving school after eighth grade to earn money for his family—Hope's life ended up taking a different course when, at the age of seventeen, he fell under the influence of the Reverend John Dart and was baptized in the frigid Savannah River at a revival meeting in February 1886. Dart encouraged Hope to move north to pursue an education, and he enrolled in Worcester Academy in Massachusetts and graduated first in his class in 1890. He then entered divinity school at Brown University, paying for his expenses by working at local restaurants, and after graduation he taught at Roger Williams University in Nashville before becoming professor of classics at Atlanta Baptist College. In 1906 he became the first African American president of the institution, which during his tenure was renamed Morehouse College. In an autobiographical sketch written in 1934, Hope mentions Lexius Henson in only a brief sentence, and he doesn't even call him by name, referring to him only as "that godless man."[14]

New Arrivals and Augusta's Boom

In May of 1882, crowds filled Broad Street to watch as newly installed electric lights were illuminated, making Augusta the first southern city to have full street lighting. The South was transitioning out of Reconstruction, and the city of Augusta was thriving. Its canal had recently been deepened to 11 feet and widened to 150, increasing its power capacity and sparking a wave of industrial expansion. The opening of three new textile mills—Enterprise Factory in 1877, Sibley Manufacturing Company in 1880, and the King Manufacturing Company in 1881—drew an even greater influx of workers from the countryside. The city limits were expanded to incorporate the new mill villages, and residents took to calling their city the Lowell of the South. Each year two hundred thousand bales of cotton passed through the Broad Street exchanges, and with the completion of the Augusta, Greenwood & Knoxville Railroad, the city boasted seven rail connections.[15]

This economic boom drew new entrants into the restaurant and hospitality trade. In October 1882 a man named James Mulhall left his position tending bar at the Planters Hotel to open "an elegant new cafe and restaurant" at 817 Broad Street, which he christened the Windsor Café. To run the kitchen, Mulhall recruited John Frazier, Charles Henson's old partner, "who has made reputation for his skill as chef de cuisine." The Windsor was an immediate success. The dining fare included "daily receipt of the finest New York oysters, fat, luscious bivalves." Its bar was decorated with large paintings, including *Faust's Vision*, which most likely was a nude and possibly a reproduction of Spanish painter Luis Ricardo Falero's 1878 painting. The *Augusta Chronicle*, for its part, gave the Windsor what by then had become the highest form of praise, declaring it "a good representation of especially Stokes' Cafe on Broadway, New York," and an establishment that "would be a credit to any large Northern city."[16]

There were a few southern touches to the fare, though. Just days after the café opened, one of its ads promised "Okra soup and fine lunch to be served tomorrow." Okra soup, an iconic Gullah dish from the South Carolina Lowcountry, was likely a familiar part of the repertoire of the Windsor's South Carolina–born cook, John Frazier. Within weeks Mulhall had secured a number of private events, including a banquet for the members of the Mechanic's Independent Fire Company and another honoring actor Alexander Caufman when his troupe visited the city.[17]

Little is known about Jim Mulhall before he arrived in Augusta, but he is an example of the close interconnections that developed among the bartending and restaurant trades in New York City and in the cities of the South. In addition to sharing common bills of fare, the two regions even shared many of the same cooks and bartenders. The famed Jerry Thomas, for instance, a New York bartender and author of America's first bartender's guide, did a stint in Charleston at the Mills House in 1853. As we've already seen, Charles Ranhofer, before becoming the longtime chef at Delmonico's, spent several years working in New Orleans kitchens. Mulhall himself was a rover, and he didn't stay in Augusta for very long. In June 1883, after less than a year in operation, he sold the Windsor Café and decamped for New York, where he compounded cocktails at various establishments, including the Oriental Bar, the Casino, and Miller's Room on Broadway before opening his own saloon called the Babylon in St. George on the northern tip of Staten Island. That venture ended up going bust, and "when Babylon fell finally," the *New York Herald* reported, "Mulhall sought warmer climes and his mint juleps are now flowing in the Screven House, Savannah." Mulhall appears to have split his time seasonally between Savannah and various northern resorts, keeping bar at the Screven House during the winter and, as the *Augusta Chronicle* noted, dispensing "cobblers and iced punches up north every summer. . . . 'tis said he alone can mix a 'whiskey daisy' for the cultivated taste of E. Berry Wall," a reference to the New York socialite popularly dubbed the King of the Dudes.[18]

When he left Augusta, Mulhall sold the Windsor Café to two young Germans named John and Henry Sancken, who had arrived in the city a decade earlier and established themselves in the grocery and saloon trade. Immigrants like the Sanckens played an outsized role in the evolving southern culinary trade, especially when one considers the relatively small amount of European immigration to southern states. In the late nineteenth century, as millions of central and southern European immigrants crowded into urban neighborhoods in the North or took up homesteads on the midwestern plains, the foreign-born population in the South was actually declining, both in raw numbers and as a percentage of the total population. The generations who had immigrated from the British Isles in the early days of the republic had largely passed away. A trickle of new immigrants continued to arrive from Ireland and from the various German states, but their numbers were small, and they tended to make their way to the South's growing cities, not to the countryside.

The changing demographics of Richmond County, in which Augusta is located, reflect this larger pattern. In 1860, 16 percent of the county's total population of 12,895 were foreign born. A decade later the population had almost doubled, but only 7 percent had been born outside the country. That was a decline from 1,777 to 1,673 in raw numbers, and the number of foreign-born residents in Richmond County continued to shrink. In 1880 only 1,390, or 4 percent of the total population, were foreign born. By 1900 that number had fallen to 1,145—just 2 percent of the county's total population of 53,735.[19]

Augusta's small immigrant community, nevertheless, was very influential in the city's commercial life. Over the decades that followed, its members—especially those born in Germany—played leading roles in the local restaurant, saloon, and grocery trades. In 1880, the earliest year for which the census captured residents' countries of birth, Richmond County's German-born population totaled just 340, but its members were prominent along Broad Street, Augusta's main commercial district. Of the twenty households on the south side of the 500 block of Broad, for instance, twelve were headed by foreign-born men or women and another four by second-generation immigrants. Ten of those families were from Germany or Austria, including John and Henry Sancken, who were living together above a saloon and grocery store. Three families hailed from Ireland, and one each were from Russia, Sweden, and Poland.[20]

There's a recurring pattern to the way that German immigrants came to the South. Young men, typically in their late teens, booked passage to America and settled in a city where they already had a connection with a family member or another native of their German hometown. As was the case in Charleston and Savannah, German immigrants to Augusta tended to enter the grocery trade, starting out as clerks in stores owned by more established immigrants. They earned a small monthly wage and typically lived as boarders in rooms above the store. Once they learned the trade, many would establish their own businesses and then repeat the pattern by hiring a newly arrived young German or two as clerks.

Once established, the first generation of young men usually married within the local German American community—sometimes to a fiancée from back home or to the American-born daughter of an older German immigrant. Judging from census records, it appears that only a few German families immigrated to the United States as nuclear families with small children. For most families in Augusta with German-born heads of household and young children, census records show that those children were born in the United States. This second generation quickly became assimilated into the larger Augusta community, attending local schools, entering the business world, and marrying Georgians of non-German backgrounds.

John and Henry Sancken, natives of Hanover, followed precisely this pattern. Prior to their arrival, there were already two other Sanckens from Hanover—Diedrich and Jacob—living in the city, and we can assume they were related by blood. Diedrich Sancken and his wife, Dora, had arrived by 1870, and Diedrich started working as a clerk at John H. Meinecke's grocery store and saloon at the corner of Broad and Monument Streets. Within five years Diedrich Sancken had taken over the business, and he hired John and Henry Sancken not long after the two teenagers arrived in Augusta in 1878. In 1880 the brothers, then nineteen and eighteen, were living in rooms above Diedrich Sancken's store. Henry was still working there in 1882, but his industrious older brother had caught the eye of John Mohrman, a young German grocer who had recently opened his own store one block east on Broad. Mohrman brought John Sancken on as a clerk for $15 a month—a significant bump over the $6 he was previously earning—and within a year Sancken had worked himself into a partnership stake in the firm, which was renamed Mohrman & Sancken.[21]

John Sancken had his eye out for even bigger opportunities, and when Jim Mulhall put the Windsor Café up for sale in 1883, John and his brother Henry went in together and bought it. They promised "a First Class Restaurant and Bar," with meals furnished at all hours and a free lunch served from eleven to noon in the bar. By June the *Chronicle* reported, "The Sancken boys are making friends at their new stand, and are bound to succeed." Henry Sancken died the following year, but his brother John kept the café going. In September 1885 he moved the Windsor to the south side of Broad Street. The new location featured "bright and artistic" frescoes by local artist T. Sam Tant. In the front was a cigar stand, and behind that a bar, a lunchroom, a pool room, and the main restaurant, and finally the kitchen in the very back.[22]

In these years the temperance movement was just beginning to stir again in the South, and there were few restrictions on the retail sale of alcohol. This allowed the grocery trade to be tightly intertwined with retail liquor sales, saloons, and restaurants. Many businesses managed to serve all four functions within the same building. Some restaurateurs, like Lexius Henson, started out as saloon keepers and then added food and a counter to sell cigars and other items, moving into the restaurant and retail trades. Others evolved in the opposite direction. Retail grocers commonly stocked beer, wine, and spirits alongside their other wares, and many added a bar in the back where patrons could enjoy their purchases on premise, and later began offering food to go along with the libations. Diedrich Sancken's business at the corner of Broad and Monument is described as a "retail grocery" in some city directory entries and a "saloon and restaurant" in others, but its format does not appear to have changed between the 1860s and the 1880s.

In April 1888 John Sancken, after more than a decade in America, made his first trip home to Germany to visit his family. In the process, he served as a recruiter for more aspiring immigrants. In September he returned to the States, bringing with him, as the *Chronicle* noted, "four stalwart young men who will make Augusta their home." Those young men accepted positions with various firms in the city, including Diedrich Sancken's and John Mohrman's, becoming part of the next generation of ambitious young grocers and saloon keepers. In shepherding them to the city, John Sancken was following a long-established practice within the German immigrant community, for Diedrich Sancken had earlier made similar trips back home to Hanover and, as the *Chronicle* noted in a profile, "backed by his glowing accounts of Augusta, has already brought us many young men from his neighborhood."[23]

Despite the influx of new blood, the German community in Augusta remained small. Census records show there were just over three hundred German-born residents in 1880 and a similar number two decades later. But they dominated the wholesale and retail grocery trade, and they operated a large percentage of the saloons and liquor stores, too. In 1888, Edward W. Herman and August J. Schweers, two German American brothers-in-law who previously had been in the brewing business in Louisville and Cincinnati, arrived in Augusta and broke ground on the Augusta Brewery, which within a few years was supplying three states with its Belle of Georgia and Belle of Carolina branded lager. Herman and Schweers were part of a larger trend of German immigrants opening breweries in the South. Atlanta, Birmingham, Charleston, Alexandria, and Jacksonville all gained large-scale German-owned breweries during this period.

As their businesses grew, German and Irish immigrants began to eclipse Augusta's native-born restaurateurs. Sometime around the end of 1888, Charles Henson, who had owned and operated his restaurant on the north side of Broad Street for more than a decade, closed his business and went to work for John Sancken at the Windsor Café. In announcing that he had secured Henson's services as manager of his restaurant department, Sancken declared that "Charles is recognized as one of the leading caterers of the day."[24]

Around the same time, D. W. Connelly arrived in the city. Like Jim Mulhall, he had an Irish name but whether he was native-born or an immigrant isn't captured in public records. Connelly appears to have lived in Savannah before moving to Augusta. By 1888 he and William T. Bugg opened a saloon and retail liquor shop at 730 Ellis Street, just a few doors down from where Lexius Henson's original restaurant had been a decade earlier. Within a year Bugg was out, and Connelly had overhauled the saloon and transformed it into a full-service restaurant. He added a new oyster counter topped with a two-by-eight-foot slab of Georgia pink marble. On October 8 he invited selected guests, including a few members of the press, to a housewarming called the O'Possum Supper. The first course was "the famous Pompinot [*sic*] of the Gulf Stream," followed by roasted opossum and wild turkey along with salads, jellies, and foaming mugs of beer. "Proprietor Connelly has certainly opened up the winter season in a royal manner," the *Chronicle* declared, adding that it was the only all-night restaurant in Augusta and that "the hungry wayfarer can get a first class meal there at 3 a.m. as promptly as at 3 p.m."[25]

Just two weeks later the *Chronicle* reported that "Connelly's all-night restaurant has become one of the most popular points in the city." Like any self-respecting southern restaurateur, Connelly highlighted his oysters, which included Blue Points and Mobile Specialty and could be had stewed, fried, or raw. But his menu also offered woodcock, quail, snipe, doves, squirrels, and rabbits. Connelly boldly dubbed his restaurant Delmonico of the South. A few weeks after opening, he announced that a new shipment of possums was on the way and he was expecting a load of western game to arrive the following week, including bear, venison, elk, prairie chicken, and grouse. Who was cooking this bounty isn't clear, but Connelly's advertisements hint that "his chef has long been recognized as the most thorough and artistic in Augusta," and the *Chronicle* added that the fare was "served by old 'Tom,' the well known chef."[26]

The Fortunes of Lexius Henson

Around the same time that the Sanckens took over the Windsor Café, Lexius Henson, who had long been operating one block away from the main commercial thoroughfare, finally made his move to Broad Street. In August 1883 he secured a new location and moved his saloon and dining rooms to 627 Broad, which the *Chronicle* described as "the handsome iron front store next above Mr. John Bone Moore's hardware stand." This put him two blocks east of the Sanckens' Windsor Café. On the first floor of Henson's new building, his cigar stand and oyster counters were positioned in the front and the barroom in the rear. The second floor held the dining rooms, including private parlors for gentlemen and ladies. When Mayor W. A. Courtenay of Charleston visited Augusta, he was feted at a banquet in one of those upstairs parlors.[27]

But Henson's ambitions were not yet fulfilled. Two years later, when the *Augusta Chronicle* moved into new offices, Henson purchased the old newspaper building at 706 Broad Street and began transforming it, including installing a new ornamental front. The work took more than a year to complete, but by the beginning of 1887 Henson had moved into the newly renovated space and rechristened it the Commercial House Restaurant and Saloon.[28]

Lexius Henson was a southern restaurateur at the peak of his success. In October 1886 the *Cleveland Gazette*, an African American weekly in Ohio, published an article titled "The Colored Race—The Wonderful Progress Which It Has Made in Money Getting." Arguing that African Americans' capacity for business was no longer a matter of doubt, it compiled a list of "rich negroes in various parts of the country." These included a shipbuilder in Bath, Maine, an importer in Boston, and factory owners in New Jersey. The report identified two Augustans as the wealthiest persons of color in Georgia, W. G. Johnson, a general merchant worth $35,000, and Lexius Henson, who "keeps the first-class restaurant of the city" and whose net worth was pegged at $25,000. The tax rolls for 1890 align with that estimate, assessing Henson's property at a total value of $18,500, of which $17,000 was in real estate plus $1,000 of merchandise and $500 of furnishings. Now in his late fifties, Henson not only had secured a prosperous position in the post–Civil War economy but also had earned the patronage of the city's wealthiest citizens.[29]

And that made it all the more surprising when, on January 21, 1892, newspapers across Georgia and South Carolina announced, "Lexius Henson Fails." To build and maintain his first-class restaurant and catering operations, it seems, Henson had highly leveraged himself. "The best known colored restaurateur in the South," as the *Atlanta Constitution* described him, owed the Georgia Railroad Bank $20,000 in loans secured by the property on Broad Street, and he owed another $15,000 outstanding in unsecured debts. That morning, the holders of the unsecured loans met and decided to seize Henson's liquor and cigar stock and other personal property. "He was one of the most prosperous colored citizens in the city," the Charleston *News and Courier* noted, "and had by hard work earned considerable money which he has lost in his old age."[30]

Through public records, we can piece together how Lexius Henson financed his restaurant business. In particular, a man named John S. Davison seems to have played an instrumental role in Henson's fortunes. An Irish immigrant who arrived in Georgia before the Civil War, Davison had quickly established himself as a commission merchant and later as a real estate investor and a director of the Georgia Railroad. At some point in the 1870s he started backing Lexius Henson's ventures. An initial glimpse of Henson's

Detail from a view of Broad Street, Augusta, Georgia, 1903. L. C. Henson's Commercial Restaurant was located at 706 Broad, the second building from the left. By 1903 that location had been taken over by jeweler A. J. Renkl. (Library of Congress, Prints and Photographs Division)

and Davison's business dealings emerged in a lawsuit that Augusta real estate agent Mordecai Hyams brought against a former client named Miller. The actual question was whether Miller owed Hyams a commission, but the transaction involved Lexius Henson's restaurant. Back in 1881, two years before he moved to Broad Street, Henson was already aspiring to secure a spot on Augusta's main commercial avenue. That September, Hyams approached Henson about buying a building on the south side of Broad that was owned by Hyams's client Miller. The asking price was $25,000, with $5,000 in cash down and the balance paid in installments over the next three years.

Henson was interested but didn't have the cash. Hyams assured the restaurateur that John Davison, whom he knew to be one of Henson's regular patrons, would be willing to advance him a loan. Davison was out of town at the time, and when Henson hesitated, Hyams put on the hard sell. He "would not give me time to think," Henson testified later. "Said if I got the property I would have to act that day, as Mr. Harry King was hot after him for it, but he wanted me to have it." Henson's desire for a Broad Street address seems to have gotten the better of his business judgment, for he signed a purchase agreement that day. The deal fell through once Davison returned to town and told Henson that the property wasn't worth the price. Hyams, for his part, maintained that he had completed his end of the bargain by getting the agreement signed and that Miller owed him a commission. The court disagreed, and Hyams lost the suit.

John Davison remained an important patron of Lexius Henson in the years that followed. Just how important emerged after Davison passed away unexpectedly in September 1886, leaving an estate worth almost a million dollars. Lexius Henson filed a claim against the executors, stating that Davison owed him more than five thousand dollars. For the past ten years, it seems, Davison had used private rooms in Henson's establishments for dinners and banquets, and he frequently ordered food, spirits, and other supplies to be sent to his home. Most remarkable, when Davison made trips up north, Henson sometimes accompanied him as his personal valet.

Davison never paid a regular bill for any of these goods or services, though he periodically walked into the restaurant and handed Henson a fifty-dollar or hundred-dollar bill. Henson, for his part, admitted that he didn't keep a regular accounting of Davison's purchases, and he was hardly alone in making this sort of handshake deal with the garrulous Irishman. "It is a well-known fact," the press reported, "that although Davison was worth over $800,000 he would never sign his name to paper, nor would he make bills, even when traveling." Though he asserted that the amount he was owed was actually much larger, Henson sued for $5,143.68—$2,000 for the use of private rooms and another $2,000 for supplies sent to Davison's home, plus $10 a day for 92 days of valet service and another $233.68 for "liquors, etc." Henson ended up losing, most likely because he lacked documentation to substantiate the sums.[31]

Since the colonial era, extending credit to patrons had been the downfall of countless tavern owners and saloon keepers. Having been so liberal in his accommodation of John Davison, Henson probably took a similarly loose approach with other patrons. Henson's failure was an opportunity for his rival D. W. Connelly to make his own move from Ellis Street to Broad. Less than two months after creditors seized Henson's restaurant, Connelly was advertising that he had taken over the building at 706 Broad Street and was opening the New Delmonico, with game and birds as his specialties and Blue Point oysters on the half shell always on hand.[32]

Whether it contributed to his financial collapse or was worsened by it, Lexius Henson's health was failing. Plagued by a lung ailment, he declined over the course of 1892 and died on October tenth. "There were few people in Augusta and in the surrounding counties in this state and Carolina who did not know Lexius," the *Atlanta Constitution* wrote in its obituary. "He was one of Augusta's best and most highly respected colored citizens, and he had many white friends in the city." Henson died intestate, but considering his many debts, it is unlikely there was much left to distribute to his widow and two grown children.[33]

The collapse of Lexius Henson coincided with a general worsening of race relations and African American fortunes not just in Augusta but in the South at large, as the tenuous social bonds that had held together an only partially integrated society were increasingly shaken apart by fear, economic anxiety, and overt racism. In 1897 the county board of education voted to no longer provide secondary education for African American students and closed Ware High School. A group of parents filed a class-action lawsuit to reverse the decision, and the case made it all the way to the United States Supreme Court, which ruled in *Cumming v. Richmond County Board of Education* (1899) that state funds were not under the purview of the Fourteenth Amendment. After four decades at the forefront of the educational movement in Georgia, Augusta's African American community found itself without a school for its teenage children.

For almost three decades the most prestigious restaurant in Augusta had been owned and operated by an African American businessman, as had several other prominent eating establishments in the city. As Augusta entered the twentieth century, those dynamics had shifted. For many of the German immigrants, like John Sancken, the grocery and restaurant trade proved a stepping-stone to larger and more lucrative enterprises. In the late 1880s, John and Diedrich Sancken went in together on a side business manufacturing ice. In 1890, just before his thirtieth birthday, John Sancken married Minnie Ziezenhein, a twenty-four-year-old widow who had been born in Georgia to German parents. Two years later John Sancken sold the Windsor Café to another German immigrant, Diedrich Dryer, and focused his energies on the Augusta Ice Company, for which he was now the general manager. Around 1914, in his early fifties, Sancken retired from the ice business and, after a brief trip to Germany to visit his mother, returned to Augusta and opened a creamery. He soon began buying up small creameries in nearby towns and cities and combining their operations. By the early 1930s the Georgia-Carolina Dairies was the third largest creamery in the United States. When John Sancken died in 1946, the *Augusta Chronicle* hailed him as "one of Augusta's most prominent citizens."[34]

Charles Henson, who had worked briefly for John Sancken at the Windsor Café in the late 1880s, remained in the restaurant business for the rest of his life, but he never owned his own establishment again. He continued to work for D. W. Connelly after the New Delmonico Restaurant moved into his brother's former Broad Street location, but that post was short lived. Connelly died in 1894, and his establishment closed. Henson worked briefly as a butler for a private family, but by 1898 he had returned to the Windsor Café and was working as Diedrich Dryer's headwaiter. In 1903 Jules Heymann, a twenty-five-year-old immigrant from Alsace-Lorraine, opened the Café Metropole, which he billed as the "most elegant liquor house in the South." Heymann hired Charles Henson away from the Windsor to run the café portion of the establishment, which was located in the back of the barroom.[35]

Now nearing seventy years old, "the old reliable caterer," as the *Chronicle* put it, "has bedecked himself and his place at the old stand in keeping with the brilliant palace in the front." Charles Henson remained at the Café Metropole until his death in 1908 at the age of seventy-three. His obituary identified him as "a well known colored restaurant man," and added that "he and his brother always catered to the white trade, and they numbered their clients among the best people of Augusta."[36]

CHAPTER 10

Storifying and Mythmaking

The experiences of Lexius and Charles Henson in Augusta were by no means unique. A great many of the African American entrepreneurs who entered the restaurant business in the wake of the Civil War ended up frustrated in their plans. Those who aligned themselves with the old regime continued to serve their established white clientele and tried not to rock the boat, but they found their status slowly and steadily diminished. Like the Hensons, many others who courted white patrons found themselves reduced to increasingly subservient roles or forced out of the business altogether. On the flip side, those like George T. Downing who aggressively asserted their rights found themselves marginalized, too. It was somewhat easier for European-born restaurateurs to navigate the complex landscape as conservative whites reasserted political control in the South, but amid rising nativist prejudices, these chefs were often pushed toward the margins as well.

In city after city across the South, what had once appeared a promising field of enterprise for entrepreneurs of color—the culinary and hospitality trades—proved increasingly unwelcoming as Reconstruction gave way to Jim Crow. For example, in Nashville, which flourished in the postwar years as a hub of the cotton and dry goods trades, several African American restaurateurs got off to a promising start. Just after the war ended, Henry Harding, an African American blacksmith, opened a boardinghouse and saloon on the corner of Church and Front Streets. William A. Sumner, who had been a hack driver before the Civil War, opened a saloon of his own at 123 North College Street. At first, both establishments appear to have served an integrated clientele, competing for white customers with the grand new Maxwell House hotel, which had been completed in 1869 at the cost of a half million dollars, as well as with Kinney & Wand's Merchant's Exchange Restaurant and Ozanne & Owen's, which offered a confectionery, ice cream saloon, and ladies' restaurant.[1]

Harding and Sumner were both active in local Republican politics, and during the heated election of 1867 the two men were falsely accused of using their saloons to illegally register nonresident African Americans to vote. Harding was also alleged to have lied about selling a city lot to Augustus E. Alden, a recent transplant from Maine, so that the latter could qualify as a resident and be eligible to run for mayor. Alden won the seat, and subsequent lawsuits failed to remove him. In the wake of the divisive election, the *Tennessean* newspaper took to calling Harding's establishment the "Hotel D'Afrique." Though initially serving white patrons, by the 1870s their businesses were routinely identified as "colored hotel" or "colored saloon" anytime they were mentioned in the local papers.[2]

In March 1875, William Sumner was one of several Nashvillians interviewed by the *Tennessean* newspaper after Congress passed the century's last civil rights bill. Asked for his thoughts on how the measure might unfold in practice, Sumner, whom the paper identified as "one of the leading representatives of the colored population of Nashville," said that he considered the law "a simple act of justice to the colored people all over the broad land." Still, he admitted, the African American community wasn't exulting in its passage. On the one hand, they were loath to break social ties with the white community "by taking any advantage offered by the bill." He didn't think the bill would do much to integrate hotels and restaurants, explaining that "very few if any negroes had money enough to dine or lodge in them."[3]

By this point Henry Harding had abandoned the culinary and hospitality trade. He sold his hotel and saloon in 1870 and launched first an employment firm for African American cooks, servants, laborers, and farmhands and then the Freedman's National Life Insurance Company. When Harding died after a sudden illness in 1888, he left an estate estimated at $75,000. He had done well for himself, but not in the hotel or restaurant business. William Sumner looked to get out, too, though via a different route. In February 1877 the Lincoln Colonization Society met at the Sumner House, and it elected the hotelier as its president and Sumner's son George as treasurer. The group's purpose was to explore colonization not to Liberia or anywhere else overseas but instead further west in the United States. A committee traveled to Kansas to scout out suitable farmlands for "colonization" purposes. Before the group undertook an actual move, William Sumner died in 1881, but thousands of other Tennesseans of color did leave the state and settle in Kansas during this period.[4]

Two hundred miles north in Louisville, a pair of African American men established the city's leading postwar restaurant, but they soon experienced the same challenges as Harding and Sumner. George Brown and Daniel Clemmons were both from rural Kentucky and likely were enslaved before the Civil War. They moved to Louisville in the late 1860s and took jobs in the culinary trades, Brown as superintendent of the Louisville Club Rooms on West Jefferson Street and Clemmons as a restaurant cook. In the early 1870s they partnered to open George & Dan's Restaurant on Jefferson Street, which quickly became a hit with the city's gourmands. Like their predecessors in the 1850s, Brown and Clemmons tapped into a national network of game and seafood purveyors. In a single advertisement in December 1873, the two men announced they had just received shipments of sheepshead from Mobile, Spanish mackerel from Long Island Sound, and diamondback terrapin and canvasback ducks from Baltimore, which added to their regular supply of local jack salmon and black bass from the Falls of the Ohio. The restaurant had also engaged "two regular and successful hunters, who make daily returns of their game."[5]

Their early success did not last. In the summer of 1876, despite running "one of the best appointed and finest restaurants in the city," the partners went bankrupt. Their entire stock—wines, whiskies, china, silverware, their kitchen range—was put up for auction. Dan Clemmons went to work as a cook at Charles C. Rufer's hotel, and in 1882 he shifted to cooking for a very different type of clientele when he took the post of cook for the city jail. Suffering from poor health, Clemmons died two years later. His former partner George Brown opened and closed a series of short-lived restaurants, including one he called George and Dan's that lasted only a year and then a plainer establishment called George Brown's New Lunch Rooms and Restaurant on Main Street, which served a clientele of white businessmen.[6]

In July 1884 Brown traveled to Chicago as a delegate to the Republican Convention, where he was interviewed by the *Chicago Tribune* and expressed amazement at seeing whites and African Americans dining at the same table in the Palmer House. "I own a restaurant in Louisville," he said, "but if I were to allow such a thing there I would lose all my customers." Not even the Galt House—Louisville's largest hotel and one of the most respected in the West—could pull it off, Brown added. "If one colored man were received as a guest the day would not pass before every boarder would leave." Not long after, Brown again declared bankruptcy. He worked the remainder of his life as a steward and private caterer. On June 8, 1898, George Brown, "one of the best-known colored men in Louisville," died in the Auxiliary Hospital following a six-month illness.[7]

⇒)(← Who Tells Your Story?

One reason that so many of the South's great chefs and caterers ended up being almost erased from culinary history is that they lost control of their own stories. The business of catering and restaurant keeping became entangled in the larger enterprise of mythmaking that was reshaping the national political and social discourse. In popular novels, poems, and songs, a surge of Old South propaganda advanced a nostalgic, romanticized version of the slaveholding region as a place of kind, noble masters and contented, subservient slaves. Such cultural works went hand in glove with the more overt political maneuverings of Reconstruction-era "redeemers" and acts of political violence by paramilitary organizations like the White Leagues, the Ku Klux Klan, and the Knights of the White Camelia. They were literary weapons deployed in a battle for the hearts and minds not only of southern whites, for whom Old South myths brought reassurance and justification, but also of whites in the North. The effort enlisted emotion and sentiment to persuade American voters that the old white elite in the South should be trusted to manage the region in the interests of future stability and national reconciliation. That appeal to emotion and sentiment ended up recasting the careers and obscuring the achievements of many of the South's great caterers and restaurateurs.

In 1883 the Washington correspondent for the *New York World* filed a report about James Wormley, a "remarkable colored man in Washington," and his success as a hotelier. "The first use he made of his prosperity," the correspondent related, "was to bring his old mistress to his fine hotel and give her the best room in it." Later, upon learning that the granddaughter of his former master had come to Washington to take a government position, he offered to let her stay in the finest room in his hotel for free. The granddaughter declined, explaining, "if it were known that I lived at Wormley's it would be said that my poverty was a pretense and I should lose my office in a week." It's a charming tale that likely struck a chord with the era's white readers, and it contains a trope that we see over and over again in this period: former slaves who still hold warm feelings toward their former owners. In this case, though, there's one small problem with the story: James Wormley was born a free person of color in Washington in 1819. He never had a master or a mistress.[8]

Wormley died the following year, and the portrayal of his career in his obituaries ended up distorting later historical interpretations of his life. Wormley suffered terribly from "calculus," or kidney stones, and in October 1884 he traveled to Boston to undergo what was then a new surgical procedure. He survived the operation but developed peritonitis, an infection that, in an era before antibiotics, proved fatal. He died on October 18 in Boston, surrounded by his family. His body was returned by train to Washington, where it lay in state among the relics in the Charles Sumner parlor at his world-renowned hotel. On the day of his funeral, the city's hotels flew their flags at half-mast. Wormley's pallbearers included the Reverend John F. Cook, the white owners of three of the city's leading hotels—the Arlington Hotel, the Ebbitt House, and the Riggs House—former mayor James G. Barnett, and Blanche K. Bruce, the African American ex-congressman from Mississippi. Wormley reportedly left his family an estate of over $150,000, a stupendous fortune in the 1880s.[9]

Newspapers around the country ran long obituaries for the hotelier and caterer, and many contrasted him with George T. Downing. By highlighting Wormley's supposed avoidance of politics, they offered his life as a lesson for other African Americans. "He was not a public speaker and was not identified with any of the abolition movements before the war," the *Boston Journal* claimed, "or with any of the schemes to ameliorate the condition of the freemen afterward." A correspondent for the *Philadelphia Press* made similar assertions. "Unlike many of his race he never 'talked politics,'" the writer noted. "His policy was a wise one in a business point of view. If any colored man doubts it let him contrast the careers of James Wormley and Geo. T. Downing. The one wouldn't talk politics and 'knew how to run a hotel,' and a first class one at that; the other is deeply absorbed in political problems but is yet to be known as an eminently successful Boniface." This claim manages to mispresent both Wormley's and Downing's careers. The former had indeed been actively involved in efforts to "ameliorate the condition of the freemen" in the years following Emancipation, and to claim that Downing had not achieved a reputation as a hotelier ignores his decades of success in Newport.[10]

George T. Downing's story ended up being subjected to even more myth-making and fictionalization than Wormley's. The most egregious example is a bizarre dramatic work created by Colonel William Foote, a white man-ager of minstrel shows. In 1894 the promoter announced a "golden oppor-tunity" for investors to buy shares in his upcoming production *Afric-America*, which promised to depict "every character of darky life, from the cradle to old age" in a "most realistic and sensational manner." Its central char-acter is a man named Joe Downing, and the parallels of his story with the career of George T. Downing would be obvious to Foote's audience. The fictional Downing establishes a catering operation in New York City and, after that business flourishes, extends it to Newport, Rhode Island. "Visitors to Newport today," Foote's prospectus noted, "can be pointed out Downing Street, and will be told that it was named after Downing, the popular col-ored caterer of New York City."

That's where the similarities between the two Downings end. Foote's hero is born not in Manhattan but on the Gold Coast of Africa, the son of a tribal chief. At the age of thirteen "Nasa," as he was named at birth, is captured in battle, sold into slavery, and shipped to Charleston, where he is bought by a planter named Joe Downing and taken to work on his plantation in Georgia. The white Downing is famous among his neighbors as "a humane master," and he immediately wins the young Nasa's loyalty. The faithful slave for unexplained reasons decides to change his own name to Joe Downing, then promptly falls in love with a young enslaved woman named Lucy. When they learn they have been emancipated, all the slaves refuse to leave "Old Marse," and they stage a lot of impromptu entertain-ments on the plantation lawn featuring "comical negro songs" accompa-nied by banjos, fiddles, and jawbones. Young Joe Downing next enlists in the U.S. Army, fights Indians on the frontier, then finally moves east to New York City and establishes a successful oyster business. After earning a for-tune, he journeys back to Georgia to find his old sweetheart, Lucy, and pay for her to study music at Shaw University in Raleigh. He then waits a year while she tours Europe as an acclaimed vocalist before finally returning to New York to marry "the wealthy caterer."

Foote could have ended things there and had a singularly ludicrous story. But that would have left unresolved the fate of "Ole Marse" Downing. One evening in New York the formerly enslaved Joe Downing has staged a grand party at his home for "the leaders of colored society in America." Just after the orchestra and celebrated vocalists finish their big number, a servant in-forms Downing that "an old white man" is at the door. It's the old master, of course, who has fallen upon hard times and is now homeless and penniless, though he somehow managed to pay for passage to New York. The younger Joe Downing announces to the assembled crowd that he will contribute $1,000 to his old master "in order that the world might know that there was one slave, who having had a kind master, now that he had found him destitute, rejoiced in being able to show his good will and appreciation." By sheer coincidence, several of the other guests had also been enslaved on Ole Marse Downing's Georgia plantation back in the good old days, and they too pony up contributions. Then they all sing songs of celebration, break out banjos and mandolins, and bring the production to a rousing conclusion.[11]

Foote's *Afric-American* was perhaps the most absurd example of a white writer co-opting the lives of real African American restaurateurs and twisting them for ideological ends, but it was hardly the most pernicious. Over time, these distortions appeared as entertainment in poems, stories, and plays and as popular histories in magazines and newspapers, and they had the cumulative effect of erasing the achievements of the very entrepreneurs who helped create the South's commercial cuisine. They replaced their subjects with caricatures and, inevitably, transposed their stories to an idealized version of rural plantation life, even though most of their subjects had achieved success in cities. In the process, they wiped out the history not just of African American chefs but of their European counterparts, too.

In 1932, when the syndicated writer "Colonel Goodbody" dedicated his weekly food column to "A Meal in the Nation's Capital," he made no mention of Absalom Shadd or James Wormley. Nor did he mention the many European immigrants who shaped the city's cuisine, like Charles Gautier or Joseph Letourno. Instead, Goodbody invoked the image of "the Virginia mammy" whose "kitchen was her castle. If a plantation owner poked his nose under the kitchen lintel, she would grab a hickory stick and run him until his hip pockets dipped sand." In Goodbody's take, it wasn't free persons of color or recent immigrants who fed the great politicians of the day. "When a Southern gentleman went to Washington to represent his state in the House or the Senate," Goodbody explained, "he took his cook along. . . . It was here that Mammy turned professional and went to cook for the famous restaurants, and Washington's culinary reputation was born."[12]

Of all the great southern caterers, none had his story more twisted than John Dabney of Richmond. In the years just after the war, Dabney's restaurant and saloon flourished, and he remained the most sought-after caterer in the city. He maintained his practice of treating the editors of the Richmond papers to the occasional tray of turtle soup and mint juleps, for he understood well the importance of getting others to spread his story. "He knows how to make a julep," the editors of the *Whig* commented after receiving one such delivery in July 1868. "And where to send it when made—two rare talents."[13]

In 1869 Dabney moved his restaurant from 14th Street to 806 Main Street, just around the corner from where he had operated the Senate-House Restaurant in the early 1860s. In 1872 he moved again, to 803 Byrd Street. Dabney's son Wendell recalled being filled with pride and admiration whenever he went anywhere with "Pop," for "his reputation and business standing rendered him almost immune to segregation, ostracism or racial prejudice." Wendell Dabney's autobiography offers us a rare personal view of the personality and motivations of a successful nineteenth-century African American caterer, including the many lessons the father tried to teach his son. John Dabney had little truck with ignorant people. "You can make money easier out of white folks if you can do anything," he told his son, "as they are not so suspicious as cullud folks." Wendell described his father as "reddish brown complexion, fat, rotund as a high liver should be, long black hair, curling under his dark silk beaded round cap." That long black hair was a wig, for Dabney had been bald since reaching adulthood.[14]

Behind the bar, John Dabney was the consummate showman. "When a big crowd was present," his son recalled, "Pop was in his glory, and nobody could move faster." He mixed cocktails and cobblers with speed and grace, juggling the liquid between mixing cup and glass before sliding the finished concoction "with a single movement of the hand" down the counter to the waiting customer. Sometimes Dabney would throw the entire contents of the mixing cup up in the air and catch them in a waiting glass. The few times Wendell tried to duplicate his father's trick, his "misguided drinks" ended up on the floor, earning jeers from the customers. His father had another invaluable asset for a caterer and bartender: a splendid memory. Almost none of his patrons paid cash for their drinks or meals, and Dabney tallied their accounts in his head and never missed a penny.[15]

The pinnacle of John Dabney's art remained his mint juleps. "A julep a la Dabney," one reporter enthused, "is a world-wide art upon personages whom he holds in high esteem." He started with a fourteen-inch-tall silver goblet, and within it he mixed sugar, brandy, mint, and what his son described as "a very delicate essence lost to the world when Pop passed away." Next he took shards of crystal-clear ice, shaved with a carpenter's plane

Stereoscopic view of Main Street above 8th Street, Richmond, Virginia, ca. 1870. The sign for John Dabney's restaurant at 806 Main Street is visible in the foreground. (Library of Congress, Prints and Photographs Division)

inverted over a wooden box, and pressed them into an obelisk-shaped mold. The resulting pyramid was fitted into the top of the tumbler and decorated with a bouquet of fruits and flowers—grapes, sliced peaches, bananas, strawberries, raspberries, blackberries, and raisins; roses, carnations, and violets. Then Dabney took more ice, formed it into ornamental shapes, and pressed them onto the sides of the goblet. Finally, he took several silver straws—a Dabney julep was a multiperson drink—and inserted them through the ice into the amber fluid beneath.[16]

Wendell was the Dabneys' fifth child, named for the prominent abolitionist Wendell Phillips, which suggests something about his parents' political leanings. John Dabney himself was not particularly active in politics, focused as he was on making money. He was a soft touch, though, for local African American politicians, and he gave freely to the Republican Party to the point where he nearly went broke. After that, his son recalled, "He finally ceased taking an interest in politics but was strong for 'race rights.'"[17]

In the summer of 1879, John Dabney headed west as usual to work the season at one of the resort springs, this time at Sweet Chalybeate, which was also known as Red Sweet Springs. That year Wendell Dabney, having turned thirteen, accompanied his father to become "initiated into the art of making a living," and he wound up being initiated into much more than that. In addition to presiding over the bar, John Dabney served as the resort's *chef de cuisine*, responsible for hiring the cooks and the waiters as well as procuring the provisions for the kitchen. One day while out buying supplies, Dabney and his son met Thomas Nelson Page, whom the elder Dabney had frequently served as a guest at the various resorts.

A lawyer and diplomat, Page was the son of a wealthy Virginia plantation owner. Impoverished after the war, he put himself through law school at the University of Virginia and started practicing in Richmond, where he also began publishing poems and stories. Page's literary works proved so successful that he eventually gave up the law to write full-time. His 1887 collection *In Ole Virginia*, which included the immensely popular dialect-heavy tale "Marse Chan," helped establish the "plantation" or "Lost Cause" genre of southern fiction. Page's poems and tales paint an idealized version of life before the Civil War, complete with happy slaves devoted to their noble masters, and they often contrasted that nostalgic image against a sensationalized depiction of the "modern negro"—a dangerous, brutish threat to white society.

When John Dabney and Thomas Nelson Page met on the street, Wendell Dabney recalled, they shook hands and said to each other, "Hello, John," and "Howdo, Mr. Page." Dabney then introduced his son to the great southern author, who replied, "I am glad to meet you. If you turn out to be half as good a man as your father, you will be alright." After some small talk they parted ways, but something in Page's manner didn't sit well with Wendell. When his father asked him later what he had thought of Mr. Page, Wendell replied that he figured Page liked his father well enough but didn't like young Wendell at all.

The next time John Dabney met Page, he told him what his son had said. "The boy is right in a way," Page told him. "I don't like him as I like you. That boy looked me right in the eye, cold and calm, and showed that he felt that he was just as good as I was." Page explained that he knew the elder Dabney had a terrible temper and wasn't scared to fight any man, but, being old and uneducated, was "not in our way. . . . Young Negroes coming on like that boy of yours, going to school, and with the proud feeling of independence, that only knowledge brings, are going to make a great deal of trouble for our sons and daughters that are now coming into our world."[18]

Four years later, in March 1887, Thomas Nelson Page published a poem titled "Little Jack" in the *Century* magazine. Directly beneath the title was the inscription "Dedicated to John Dabney, Richmond, VA." The poem's fifteen six-line stanzas have a turgid ABABAA rhyme scheme, but even more tortured is the dialect, which includes bits like this: "Dat's what de Marster said, / An' Marster warn' gwine tell me lie, / He'll come bym'bye." Little Jack is an elderly former slave still living on his "old Marster's" land. Back during slavery days, that master had sold Little Jack but then missed him so much that he bought him back. Little Jack remained loyal to his master's family ever after, even once Emancipation came and old Marster died.

Now on his own deathbed, Little Jack asks his son to retrieve a hidden stocking filled with money, "de sweat of many days." Back during slavery, he had toiled and saved that money, intending to use it to buy his son's freedom. But "de Lord he sot free all de n———s" before he could do so. Take that money, he tells his son, and take it to "young Marster"—his old owner's son. "You kin work, an don't need none," he explains to his son. "He ain't been used to diggin' / His livin' out de dirt." Having taken his own son's inheritance and given it to the shiftless offspring of the white man who once enslaved him, Little Jack dies.[19]

A footnote to Page's poem identified John Dabney as "a former slave of Miss DeJarnett of Caroline Co.," and it repeated the story of Dabney's paying off the money he had promised her for his freedom. It makes no mention of Dabney's career as a caterer and businessman in the city of Richmond, nor of the fact that the sum he paid DeJarnette was but a small fraction of the considerable wealth he had amassed. Wendell Dabney recorded in his autobiography that his father "scarcely appreciated" Page's dedicating "Little Jack" to him. Curiously, what really irked the caterer was not that his name was linked to a story that bore no resemblance to his own life. John Dabney's biggest objection, according to his son, was that "he never used the typical distorted Negro dialect. . . . though unable to read and write, his contact had always been with cultured white people."[20]

John Dabney took pride in his wits and eloquence, and he was self-conscious about his lack of formal education. When he was a boy, a relative of his owner started to teach him to read and was caught doing so. The girl was sent away, and Dabney was whipped. For the remainder of his life he was determined that his children would be well educated. As an older man, his son recalled, Dabney once got into a confrontation in a bank with "a very officious young clerk," who expressed surprise that a man as successful in business as Dabney was could not write his own name. "Naw, God durn it," Dabney bellowed at the clerk, "I can't write 'cause I was kept a slave all my life and after the war I took all of my time working to send my children to school. They could learn a lot while I would learn only enough to make a fool of myself."[21]

Dabney was proud as well of his commercial success, starting with his attaining the position of headwaiter at the Gordonsville hotel by the young age of eighteen. It was an achievement, Wendell recalled, that "he used to tell me during the frequent occasions necessary to impress upon my egotistical mind the worthlessness of modern young Negroes." But Dabney's single-minded pursuit of money had less to do with greed or the need for social status than with providing his children with the opportunities than he had been denied. "All your books haven't taught you never to let a white man know how much you really do know about anything but hard work," Dabney lectured his son. "If you ever expect to get money or anything worthwhile out of a white man, always make him feel that he knows more than you and always act as if you think he is the greatest man in the world."[22]

John Dabney's eldest son, Clarence, was a star baseball player, but he also was a hot-tempered brawler. As a teenager he got into repeated fistfights, many of them with white teens, and also with the white police officers who came to break up the disturbances. His father's wealth and connections kept Clarence out of jail, but each fight, Wendell Dabney recalled, "meant one or two hundred dollars in 'hush money' from 'Pop.'" Finally John Dabney sent Clarence north to Boston to attend school. Clarence returned to Richmond after graduation, claiming to have been fully reformed. Just four nights later he and a cousin went out drinking and got into a fight with a group of men outside a saloon. The police were summoned, and all the combatants fled except Clarence who, now even bigger and stronger after his years in Boston, battled six policemen until they clubbed him to the ground. This time around, the expense John Dabney had to pay for his son "was something awful," and the judge warned the caterer that he had better send his son away from the city, for the next fight would land him in the penitentiary.

After this incident, the Dabney family sat down and had a serious discussion about whether they should move north. "The younger members of the family did not expect to stay in the South anyhow," Wendell Dabney recalled. "The chains of race prejudice were getting tighter and far more irksome. We were now old enough to notice outside conditions." The question wasn't so simple for John Dabney. "Pop said if he wasn't so durned old, and his business was not so durn good, he would go at once."[23]

That summer Clarence headed to New York, where he found work in the resort hotels on Long Island, and his brother John Milton made his way to Washington, D.C. Wendell headed west with his father to Allegheny Springs in Montgomery, Virginia, to spend another summer working the resorts. During previous seasons Wendell had reveled in his father's prominence behind the bar, but now he chafed at their subservient status. "I hated to 'wait' on anyone, particularly white people," he recalled. "I had grown sensitive and had begun to look upon whites as enemies." What bothered him more than anything was the fact that, despite his father's proven business acumen, integrity, and reliability, "no white man, woman, boy, or girl would call him Mr. Dabney. 'Twas always, 'John' or 'Uncle John.'"

That summer Wendell used some of his wages to buy a guitar, and he spent all his free time learning to play it. His father initially looked upon that enthusiasm with contempt, telling his son that back in slavery days African American musicians were petted and pampered and ended up drunk and dissolute. But he warmed to Wendell's musical ambitions over time. The following year, after Wendell graduated from high school, his father paid to send him to Oberlin College. Wendell went on to teach elementary school and then opened a music school in Boston. In 1894 he moved to Cincinnati and ran a hotel for a few years before going to work

Engraving of the Old Sweet Springs resort, where John Dabney worked summers during the 1890s. (Library of Congress, Prints and Photographs Division)

in city government, first as a license clerk and then as paymaster. In 1907 he established the *Union*, an influential African American newspaper, and he used it to campaign against injustice and segregation. In 1914 Wendell Dabney became the first president of the Cincinnati branch of the NAACP, and he remained a fearless advocate for civil rights for the rest of his career.

Though their children headed north, John and Elizabeth Dabney remained in Richmond. After closing his Byrd Street establishment in the late 1870s, Dabney never again operated his own restaurant or saloon. He focused his efforts instead on catering during the fall and winter and working the summers at the resort springs. In 1894 a correspondent for Kentucky's *Lexington Leader* reported that "Northern visitors returning from Old Sweet Springs are talking still of the old uncle down there, who is so entirely a picturesque figure of the past, a type of the negro in ante-bellum days." The article repeated the requisite story of Dabney's paying off his debt (the outstanding sum now inflated to $1,000) and declared Dabney to be "the last connecting link to a class of colored men and women to whom the South owes an eternal debt of gratitude." Though Dabney had actually spent the Civil War years selling whiskey and juleps in Richmond, the reporter insisted that "it was his kind who during the war stayed at home and faithfully cared for and protected women and children when the men were fighting at the front."[24]

On June 7, 1900, John Dabney died at his home at 1414 Broad Street. He was seventy-five years old. His passing received only brief notices in the local papers. The *Dispatch* identified Dabney simply as "the caterer," while the *Times* summarized the career of "the celebrated julep maker" in a single paragraph, noting that he was "for many years one of the best-known caterers in the South." The *Baltimore Sun* offered a few additional details, noting that Dabney had officiated at great political barbecues and dinners in Richmond and "was known to all of the leading Virginia politicians of a quarter of a century ago." It closed by noting that it was Dabney's julep that "made such an impression on the youthful Prince of Wales."[25]

A few weeks later the *Richmond Dispatch* ran a much longer article that belatedly commemorated the life of the city's greatest caterer. It was headlined "'Little Jack': Thomas Nelson Page's Tribute to the Memory of the Well-Known Old Richmond Negro, John Dabney." The text explained how Page's poem had captured an incident from Dabney's life that was "one of the most remarkable ever recorded of a negro." It related how Dabney paid off the balance of his debt to "Miss De Jarnette," and followed that with a story of how, in the early days of Reconstruction, Dabney had ejected an African American man who had taken a seat in his restaurant and tried to "put the negro upon a footing of equality with the whites." The tribute closed by quoting a letter that Page had written to the *Dispatch* in the days following Dabney's passing. "John," Page asserted, "was a type of a class which is rapidly passing away, and when it shall have passed entirely away few will believe it ever existed." For good measure, the editors then reprinted the entire text of "Little Jack."

Thomas Nelson Page got the last word.

CHAPTER 11

The Decline and Fall of Southern Restaurant Cuisine

We've wrapped up the stories of most of the great culinary figures profiled in this book, but we've left a few hanging. Fields Cook never returned to the culinary business, serving as the pastor of Ebenezer Baptist Church in Alexandria until his death in 1897 at the age of eighty. He remained justly proud of the success and independence he had achieved as a Black restaurateur in the slaveholding South, and he wasn't one to let careless newspaper reporters tarnish that reputation. When the *Alexandria Gazette* and the *Richmond News* published brief stories recalling his brother Jim's making juleps for the Prince of Wales at the Ballard House, they mentioned that Fields Cook "in old times . . . was head waiter there." Cook promptly dashed off a correction to both papers. "I never served a day in my life under John P. Ballard," he wrote. "I at one time leased a portion of the Ballard House, for which he paid me $2,000 to relinquish my claim."[1]

In Charleston, Tom Tully, who had succeeded Nat Fuller and Eliza Lee as the city's leading caterer, struggled to adapt to the post–Civil War market. He maintained his lunchrooms and catering operation on King Street and sold game from the City Market, and he was still regarded as the best cook in the city. He had no peer, one newspaper declared, "in the preparation of oysters and shell fish. His 'stews' were unapproachable. . . . no one to this day has ever attained the art of frying an oyster like Tully." The caterer endorsed the politics of the elite whites who were his regular customers—in public, at least. "He was a staunch Democrat in politics," his obituary recalled upon his death in 1883. "But always conservative in views." For almost half a century Tully had made his living catering to the likes of the Hibernian Society and the Society of the Cincinnati, but as one commentator noted, "He seemed unable to realize the results of the war, and his prices were found to be too high." Many of Tully's former apprentices went on to open their own businesses and began undercutting him on rates. Still, the *News and Courier* noted, "no one could equal Tully in preparing a feast, and those who desired epicurean repasts, independent of expense, always went to Tully."[2]

After Tully died in 1883, no other Charleston caterer achieved the same prominence, and the stature of African Americans in the culinary industry was steadily diminished. George E. Johnston, after making his name in the kitchens of the Charleston Hotel and the Mills House before the war, had in 1866 ambitiously launched his own restaurant, which he declared would be "second to none in the country." In the years that followed, his business evolved into more of a saloon, and by 1872 he had closed its doors. Johnston briefly worked as a grocer before taking a position at the Carolina Club that was described in various city directories as janitor, superintendent, and waiter. His fellow freedman-turned-restaurateur Archibald Wigg continued operating his establishment at 41 Market Street, advertising it variously as an eating house, eating saloon, and lunchroom. He closed the business around 1880 and for the next several years was listed as a caterer and a steward in the city directories. By 1888 he had moved to Savannah, where he signed on as the watchman on the steamer *David Clark*, which made regular runs carrying passengers, rice, and cabbage between Savannah and Brunswick, Georgia. George Johnston passed away in 1888, and Archibald Wigg died of fever the following year at the age of sixty.[3]

It's instructive to contrast the careers of Johnston and Wigg with that of Francis J. Moultrie, another formerly enslaved South Carolinian who pursued the culinary trade. Moultrie was born in Charleston in 1842 and apparently escaped at least briefly from enslavement in 1862. Shortly after the war, Moultrie decided to make his living as a professional cook, but he headed north to do it. He worked at various catering houses in Manhattan, then moved out to Yonkers. In 1870 he married Fannie J. Alston, herself a Charleston native, and took work in private homes while his wife ran a catering business out of their rented house. Her income allowed Moultrie to save his entire earnings, and the couple soon put away enough to buy a house and establish a permanent place of business. In 1878 they leased a storefront in the heart of downtown Yonkers and gradually grew the Moultrie Company into the largest catering establishment in Westchester County, doing $25,000 a year in business and owning ten wagons for deliveries. By the time he retired, Francis Moultrie owned the largest apartment house in Yonkers, held stock in the city's two Black-owned banks—serving as president of one and treasurer of the other—and was the only African American member of the Westchester Citizens Association. In 1903 the Washington *Colored American* newspaper declared him "The Delmonico of Westchester." By 1904, Francis and Fannie Moultrie had moved to a newly built five-thousand-square-foot house at 140 Warburton Avenue, then the most prestigious residential street in the city. The house still stands today.[4]

The stories of those who stayed in the South tended to end more like Johnston's and Wigg's. African Americans in the culinary industry were increasingly limited to less prominent roles as waiters and cooks in white-owned restaurants and hotels. Those who did own their own businesses—and most southern cities had several African American–owned restaurants—served primarily an African American clientele. After the 1880s, in sharp contrast to the previous half century of southern culinary life, the names of African American cooks and restaurateurs appear much less frequently in the local newspapers.[5]

As was the case in Augusta and elsewhere, Charleston's rising class of restaurateurs during this period was dominated by recent German immigrants, many of whom entered the field by way of the grocery trade. Patjen's on East Bay, George Rouse's Grand at 278 King, and C. W. Meyer's at 108 Meeting were among the city's more prominent restaurants at the close of the century. The quality of the city's public dining seems to have suffered, though. In 1899 the editors of the *Evening Post* complained of "the woeful lack of a modern and thoroughly first-class restaurant in Charleston" and lamented that it threatened to prevent the city from being "an enviable place in the estimation of travelers and visitors."[6]

The experience of European immigrants in the closing decades of the century was a mixed one as well. For those who, like John Sancken, arrived at an early age and were driven by larger commercial ambitions, owning a restaurant could be a springboard to bigger and better things. For others, like Joseph Boulanger in Washington, D.C., it turned into a long, slow grind. The life of a restaurateur was one of boom and bust, and in the last half of the century it became increasingly peripatetic, as chefs, bartenders, and restaurateurs bounced from one city to the next seeking a new start. It was common for caterers and chefs to go bankrupt at some point in their careers. Many went broke multiple times, and they had no pension plans. Rare was the caterer like Fritz Huppenbauer, who in New Orleans had operated the United States Restaurant and then the Confederate States Restaurant and then the United States Restaurant again. According to his obituary, Huppenbauer spent "his declining days with his venerable consort in happiness and prosperity, in the midst of a large and loving family." Huppenbauer, admittedly, had gone bankrupt several times, and he spent the last decade of his career overseeing the kitchen at the West End Hotel out by the lake, an establishment owned by his son-in-law Ferrole Michelet.[7]

As the twentieth century approached, a new pattern began to appear in the way the press treated immigrant restaurateurs. In the 1840s and 1850s, few newspaper and magazine accounts of immigrant chefs and caterers noted their "foreign" characteristics—speaking with an accent, for instance, or having unusual mannerisms or turns of phrase. A half century later, it was almost obligatory for a treatment of a foreign-born restaurateur to throw in a quote or two that highlighted the subject's heavily accented English.[8]

Adolph and Théonie Rutjes, who had given up their old confectionery and catering establishment in Charleston after the war, remained in Raleigh for a time, operating the National Hotel. Adolph declared bankruptcy again in 1872, and the hotel was sold. He and Théonie ended up moving north to Greenwich, Connecticut, where they operated a hotel called the Lennox House. Théonie Rutjes died there of a stroke in 1875. Her husband bounced around various New York establishments until he went bankrupt (again) in 1878. Rutjes ended up back in North Carolina, where he managed the hotels at several resorts in the Blue Ridge Mountains for a decade. He remarried and moved back to Raleigh around 1890, and two years later, on the verge of yet another bankruptcy, he abandoned his new wife and his latest hotel and skipped town. The last anyone heard, Rutjes was "somewhere in Germany." The last mention of Adolph Rutjes's name in a southern newspaper captured only his accent. "The city is too big," the *Morning Post* commented in 1898, "and, in the language of the late Col. Rutjes, 'does not know how big its britches vas.'"[9]

In Richmond, Spiro Zetelle did not face the same racial prejudice and legal barriers that restaurateurs of color like John Dabney and the Cook brothers had to overcome, but he was never fully accepted as part of Richmond's white community, either. "Mr. Zetelle never acquired a correct pronunciation of English," the *Richmond Dispatch* recalled in its obituary of the caterer. "His pronunciation was essentially his own, and this, with his excitable, generous, impulsive nature made him a character." It also made him the frequent butt of practical jokes. Once, after Zetelle expressed his desire to cook some frog legs, a group of customers contrived to take him frog hunting along the canal, where they claimed frogs grew larger than anywhere else in the region. Zetelle soon came across "the father of all frogs, a giant in size." He took aim with his pistol and fired, only to be greeted by a loud "kerchunk," so he aimed and fired again and again with the same result. As he heard the growing laughter from the party behind him, he finally realized he had been shooting at a large iron doorstop in the shape of a frog.[10]

Zetelle had struggled financially ever since he returned to Richmond after the war and found his fortune converted to worthless Confederate bonds. He managed to resume a regular business in his restaurant and saloon at the corner of 11th and Bank Streets, and he catered many events for the city's civic organizations and business clubs during the 1870s. An 1875 tabulation of "the famous restaurants of our country" in Washington's *Daily National Republican* included "Zitelle's, of Richmond" alongside the Parker House of Boston, Moreau's of New Orleans, and Delmonico's of New York. Zetelle's life soon became the subject of mythmaking, too, albeit with less pernicious overtones than the stories fabricated about restaurateurs of color. In 1900 a nostalgic piece in the *Richmond Dispatch* noted that the famous caterer "found himself almost penniless a few years ago, after once having been well-to-do." A wealthy man visiting from Chicago heard of Zetelle's misfortunes and offered to set him up "in a handsome way" in a restaurant in Chicago. Zetelle conferred with his Richmond friends, who advised him it was the chance of a lifetime. Two days later the millionaire came to hear the restaurateur's decision, finding him in his kitchen wearing his usual paper cap and long white apron. Without saying a word, but with "a tear resting on each cheek," Zetelle took the man by the arm and led him to the front door, where he pointed out a star shining dimly above the green trees in Capital Square. "You are very, very kind," Zetelle said, "but do you see that little star above the trees there? Well, I would rather see that little star twinkle night by night in Richmond than to see the whole damned Aurora Borealis in Shee Cargo."[11]

This story was included in a newspaper article titled "A Patriotic Letter" that praised Richmond's civic virtues, but the facts of Zetelle's life don't quite match the sentiment. In 1880 the "Napoleon of cooks" did indeed leave Richmond, heading to North Carolina, where he briefly operated the Bellevue Hotel in High Point. The following year he made his way to Atlanta, where he took charge of the culinary department of the Grand Hotel at the Atlanta Cotton Exposition. He stayed on in Atlanta after the exposition ended, running a lunchroom for a while, before trying his luck one last time in Virginia's capital. He operated a restaurant on Bank Street for three years, then finally left Richmond for good. This time Zetelle headed west to sunny California, where he opened not a restaurant but the Zetelle Cigar Store in San Pedro. He no longer hosted grand banquets for hundreds of guests, but the warm climate apparently suited the restaurateur in his final years. In the winter of 1891 he wrote to a friend back in Richmond, "I am in paradise once more. . . . I am now amongst orange orchards and valleys of flowers and have strawberries for dinner every day. The climate is supreme here to-day. It looks as a day in May." Spiro Zetelle died in San Diego in 1894.[12]

⇒✺⟵ Shifting Fashions

In the decades just after the Civil War, the ingredients and styles of the southern table—especially those of the Mid-Atlantic—had been at the forefront of American dining fashions, but that prominence faded as the twentieth century approached. The larger trajectory of southern fine dining is reflected in Baltimore's cuisine. The city's culinary reputation surged just after the Civil War, thanks in large part to New Yorkers looking south for inspiration. By 1880 an almost fixed menu for a "Maryland dinner" had crystalized. An article in the *Cincinnati Daily Star* that year defined it like this: four cherrystone oysters, terrapin and sherry, then roasted canvasback served with "large hominy fried in cakes, potatoes a la Saratoga, celery salad or in the stick"—all washed down with plenty of Champagne and Burgundy. The *San Francisco Bulletin* sang the praises of canvasback that same year, calling it "the most splendid wild fowl of its kind in the world." A three-pound duck roasted from 14 to 18 minutes, the correspondent asserted, "served on 'red hot' plates with a quart bottle of chablis and baked hominy as accompaniments, at Guy's famous hotel on Monument Square, has, upon many occasions, convinced me that this world was not made in vain." Hominy had often appeared on restaurant and banquet menus in earlier years, but it was usually just listed among the many other offerings in the vegetable course. By the 1880s it had become the inseparable companion to roast canvasback.[13]

Soon Maryland-style cooking was in vogue throughout the country, and especially in New York. In 1887 the *New York Times* declared, "In Maryland, one of the roads to Paradise begins in the kitchen and ends in the dining room. Nowhere in the world do people as a class live better." It sang the praises of Baltimore's cantaloupe, oysters, soft crabs, trout, rail birds, luscious peaches, and watermelon. Just a few years before, the reporter noted, diamondback terrapins "were cheaper than beefsteak and canvas-back ducks as accessible as chicken." Now, though, "the boom in all parts of the world for Maryland delicacies" had forced prices sky high. Gentlemen's clubs in the Northeast became enthralled with Chesapeake cuisine and began featuring Mid-Atlantic dishes on their menus. At first their local contingents of French-trained chefs adopted these dishes and added them to their menus, but later it became popular for clubs to hire experienced African American cooks from Maryland or Virginia, who amid the worsening social conditions in the Jim Crow South were increasingly willing to seek new opportunities in the North.

A menu for a dinner given at Delmonico's in honor of the Maine statesman and politician James G. Blaine in October 1884 is overwhelmingly French, at least in language. Southerners from the Mid-Atlantic states, though, would be quite familiar with many of the dishes, like the "Terrapène à la Maryland" in the Entrées course and the "Canvas-back ducks" in the Rôti. They might not recognize the *éperlans frits* in the Poisson course until the dish arrived at the table and proved to be fried smelt.[14]

The vogue of the Maryland dinner was short lived. Even as bon vivants in New York luxuriated over canvasback with hominy and terrapin à la Maryland, culinary fashions were shifting, and the hotels and restaurants that helped establish the southern culinary style started to be eclipsed by more modern competitors. Before the Civil War, the Charleston Hotel in Charleston, the Ballard House in Richmond, and the St. Charles and St. Louis Hotels in New Orleans had been physical manifestations of their respective cities' ambition, signaling their arrival among the ranks of great commercial centers. A half century later those same structures had become obsolete. One by one they slipped into the ranks of second-tier hotels and often slid even further to become seedy apartments or boardinghouses. The Ballard House closed in 1896, and the building was demolished in 1920. The St. Charles burned to the ground in 1894; rebuilt in a thoroughly modern form, it stayed in operation until the 1970s. The St. Louis languished for decades before finally closing its doors around the turn of the century, then sat decaying until a hurricane reduced it to rubble in 1915. The Charleston Hotel lasted the longest of the antebellum structures. After repeated remodeling, it closed in 1958, and the building was demolished in 1960.[15]

These venerable establishments were replaced by modern commercial hotels like the Francis Marion in Charleston, the Grunewald in New Orleans (later renamed the Roosevelt), and the Jefferson in Richmond—all of which are in operation today. Thanks to steel-beam construction, these newer buildings were larger and taller, and they boasted more rooms, electric lights, improved elevators, and amenities like bathrooms en suite with hot and cold water. A fancy bar and a high-quality restaurant remained essential to any hotel, and their new dining rooms quickly became the top dining spots in their respective cities and remained so until Prohibition.

The fare served in those dining rooms was modernized, too. In the 1870s and 1880s, French dishes became more and more fashionable, and French cooks—or, at least, cooks with accents that could be mistaken for French—were in high demand. French words became ubiquitous on menus, even if the dish being described was not remotely French in origin. As newly moneyed northern industrialists eclipsed southern planters as the nation's wealthiest class, they borrowed many of the social trappings of the old elite South. They bought stores of old Madeira wine from insolvent southern families, purchased old plantations to use as hunting estates, and styled themselves as the new aristocrats of the Gilded Age. Those aspiring aristocrats adopted many of the classic dishes of the southern commercial tables, too, like canvasback duck and Lynnhaven oysters, though they insisted upon gilding them with a veneer of French.

It's not surprising that visitors like Grand Duke Alexis of Russia, who during his tour of the United States dined at Delmonico's and other high-end restaurants, would conclude that in the United States all the cooks were French and "there were no American dishes," for all the names on the menu were in French. Yet a closer look at menus from the period, including those at Delmonico's, reveals that beneath the French verbiage, much of the fare was thoroughly American and even decidedly southern in character. We have already noted that Charles Ranhofer, the famed Delmonico's chef during the period of the New York restaurant's greatest vogue, early in his career made a tour southward through Washington to New Orleans, where he worked for several years before returning to New York and assuming his post at Delmonico's. He likely made later trips south to sample the cuisine, too. In his autobiographical sketch, John Dabney's son Wendell recalled that "a Chef of Delmonico's" once came to Richmond "to show the natives what real cooking meant" and left saying, "No man ever made a better terrapin stew than John Dabney." Wendell Dabney doesn't name the chef, but it almost certainly would have been Ranhofer. Indeed, Ranhofer's influential 1893 cookbook *The Epicurean* includes many of the great delicacies of the mid-nineteenth-century South, including planked shad, chicken à la Maryland (fried chicken with white cream gravy and "small corn fritters"), and one of the most detailed discussions in print of the technique for preparing turtle soup.[16]

Though they had once owned their own restaurants, hotels, and catering operations, by the end of the century African Americans had been largely relegated to cooking in the kitchen or serving guests as waiters. The most prestigious position remaining was that of headwaiter. E. A. McCannon's *Commanders of the Dining Room*, a 1904 collection of sketches of noted headwaiters, shows that a great many of these men were born and raised in the South, especially in Virginia, but most had gone north to find employment. "The South can point with reasonable pride to the long list of men whose names have gone down in history as head waiters," McCannon wrote. "With few exceptions, all the men who have risen to the position of head waiters throughout the country came from the South." By 1904, that "old regime" of headwaiters—"born in time of travail and trouble" with "little chance and less opportunity for books," who had made their fortunes in one of the few industries that accepted them—was already fading away.[17]

⇒҉⇐ Lost Ingredients

As the end of the century neared, the same demand that had created the national game and seafood trade was threating to destroy it. The American mania for oysters continued unabated, and the packing operations in Norfolk and Baltimore, joined by newly founded oyster centers like Crisfield and Solomons in Maryland, produced millions of cans each year, which were shipped north and south by boat and west by rail. By the late 1800s, oyster poaching was rampant on the Chesapeake, and violent battles over territory began breaking out among watermen. Hand tongs were replaced by dredges dragged over the beds by steam-powered boats, harvesting oysters in massive quantities but destroying centuries-old beds in the process. The damage was compounded by urban growth and agricultural expansion, which increased the nutrients and sediment running off into the rivers and streams of the Chesapeake. These fueled the growth of algae blooms and created low-oxygen "dead zones" that hindered the development of oyster larvae and made the shellfish more susceptible to disease. As a result of overfishing and environmental degradation, the oyster harvest in Maryland declined from a peak of 615,000 metric tons in 1884 to around 200,000 in 1900. It continued to fall during the twentieth century, reaching just 12,000 metric tons in 1992.[18]

Lynnhaven River oysters, long the most prized on the Eastern Seaboard, remained vibrant into the twentieth century, thanks to careful cultivation by local oystermen. Lynnhavens were always shipped in the shell, never canned. In 1888 an admirer of the actress Sarah Bernhardt sent a bushel of them to her in Paris, having them fed en route on oatmeal and saltwater. The famous gambler Diamond Jim Brady ate three dozen Lynnhavens during one of his legendary feasts. But even the most fastidious cultivation could not protect the oysters from environmental changes in the Lynnhaven Basin. In 1915 the oysters began developing green gill from the increased algae blooms in the water, and that green tint gave them a bad name in the market and sent demand plummeting. Within a few years Lynnhaven oysters were but a distant memory.[19]

Shad stocks spiraled downward in the late 1800s, too, due to many of the same factors, including excessive harvesting and loss of spawning grounds. The widespread damming of eastern rivers limited their famed spawning runs, which once took them up the Santee and Congaree Rivers as far as Columbia in South Carolina and a hundred miles beyond Richmond on the James. Things worsened in the twentieth century. The shad catch in the Chesapeake fell from 17.5 million pounds at the turn of the century to fewer than 2 million by the 1970s. Pollution likewise took its toll on the canvasback duck. Starting in the twentieth century, the beds of *Vallisneria americana*—the wild celery, also known as eelgrass or tape grass, on which the famed ducks fattened themselves each fall—began to disappear, with a disastrous effect on the game bird's most prized quality. When "obliged to content itself with a diet chiefly of animal food," wrote Alessandro Filippini, the chef at Delmonico's Pine Street outpost, in his 1889 *Delmonico Cook Book*, "it becomes merely a very ordinary table bird."[20]

The game trade of the 1850s, a miracle of modern rail and steamship transport, faltered in the last half of the century. Even before the Civil War there had been growing efforts to rein in the so-called market hunters—those who hunted commercially and shipped their kill back east—"lest the war be carried on," as one report put it in 1856, "to an extermination of those animals and feathered tribes." These "unseasonable meats," the report noted, were typically killed during the coldest months of winter, when local hunters avoided the fields because downed carcasses would quickly freeze. But the cold temperatures were just fine with market hunters, who would "lumber up the eastward express companies at such seasons, to supply the sea-board epicure's demand."[21]

As the insatiable hunger for game depleted the western prairies, states began instituting bag limits and greatly restricted commercial hunting. By 1900 most states had outlawed the export of deer, quail, prairie chickens, and most other wild game, and the federal government passed additional measures making it illegal for common carriers to ship game that had been killed in violation of local laws. Today it is illegal in most places for restaurants to serve wild game, so chefs are limited to farmed meat. Little wonder we don't see canvasback duck or woodcock on fine-dining menus today, even in restaurants whose chefs are passionate about traditional southern cuisine.[22]

AFTERWORD

The Legacy of the Lost Southern Chefs

This book is called *The Lost Southern Chefs* because it profiles culinary figures who were all but lost to history. Their restaurants were shuttered, their stoves and ovens removed, their buildings eventually taken apart brick by brick or brought down by the wrecking ball. Their signature dishes were forgotten, supplanted by new waves of French and Continental fashion. Few of these chefs' recipes were written down or made their way into cookbooks, so their methods and techniques were lost, too. After decades of overharvesting and environmental degradation, the ingredients that formed the foundation of their cuisine vanished from the market. Thanks to those who rewrote the narratives of the antebellum South to suit their own ends, the very names of the great chefs and caterers were erased from history.

Or at least they almost were. It is important for us to rediscover those names, piece together their repertoires, and begin telling their stories again, for they left a rich and vital legacy—one that we might profit from today.

Stories matter. By the early twentieth century, the romanticized view of the old South—and, in particular, the fetishizing of cotton plantations—left no place for memories of the South's once-famed chefs. The WPA *Guide to the Palmetto State*, a guidebook created by the Depression-era Federal Writers Project and published in 1941, summarized South Carolina's cookery this way: "Unfortunately, it is hard to find many dishes of local renown on the menus of public eating places. Only in private homes and at barbecues . . . can one, as a rule, sample the distinctive cookery of the affluent past."[1]

The irony isn't lost on me that this book came into being because of an act of storytelling and mythmaking. The Nat Fuller Feast in Charleston in 2015 had its genesis in a seemingly trivial scholarly error—misinterpreting a single line from a 150-year-old letter and assuming that Nat Fuller had staged an integrated dinner at the Bachelor's Retreat with reconciliation as its theme. In their companion pamphlet, the organizers of the reenactment erred in stating that the letter writer, Mrs. Porcher, had "returned from her evacuation of the city," not realizing that she was actually writing from two hundred miles away in Greenville. Thinking her letter a firsthand account, they took at face value her assertion that "blacks and whites sat on an equality" and from there extrapolated that the supposed feast must have "heralded a new kind of civil society and promised a new grounds of civility." That led to a chain reaction of suppositions, including that the "African Americans at the table belonged to that society of freedman who dominated the black community since the 1840s" and that "Charleston's old white elite" in all likelihood came to Fuller's "miscegenat feast," too.[2]

It is an understandable error, and the tales it spawned were conceived with the best intentions. "Of all the actions in the defeated South in that Spring of 1865," David Shields wrote in the invitation to the event, "Fuller's Feast was the most hopeful and forward looking, anticipating a civil society in which tolerance, shared pleasures, and a willingness to converse might exist. To honor these ideals we are staging a commemorative dinner." It's a noble sentiment, and those ideals are ones we very much should pursue today. But, as we've seen in this study, things didn't play out that way at all in the years that followed Nat Fuller's return to the Bachelor's Retreat. Charleston's old white elite had no intention of dining side by side with newly freed African Americans, and they violently resisted that prospect for more than a century. It would be nice to believe that a feast of reconciliation brought the Civil War to completion in Charleston, but that isn't what actually happened.

The scholarship that underlay the commemorative event has considerable value nonetheless. In his contribution to the companion pamphlet, chef Corey Green, who helped research and reconstruct Fuller's recipes, thanks David Shields for his efforts. "Shields' work," he writes, "has brought Fuller's remarkable achievements out of forgotten archives back to the forefront of southern cuisine where it belongs." Chef Kevin Mitchell, who at the time was an instructor at the Culinary Institute of Charleston and played the role of Nat Fuller in the reenactment, subsequently decided to pursue a master's degree in Southern Studies at the University of Mississippi and to delve further into the history of the South's forgotten chefs. His voice has now been added to other researchers who are telling these important stories, and hopefully their efforts will correct more mistaken assumptions, fill in more factual gaps, and tell the story from new and different vantage points.

The effort could pay off at the table, too. In recent years, as southern chefs have looked to the past and rediscovered traditional ingredients and cuisines, they've focused on the plantation fields and farmhouse kitchens of the rural South. In the process, they have resurrected an incredible bounty of recipes and ingredients—stoneground grits from heirloom corn, Sea Island red peas, Carolina gold rice, traditionally cured bacon and hams, pickles and preserves of all kinds. We now recognize that gumbo descends directly from African okra preparations, not French bouillabaisse, and that there's much to admire in a platter of fried whiting or a pot of slow-simmered greens.

But if we add other stories into the mix, our culinary boundaries expand even wider. The Chesapeake has rebounded remarkably in just the past few decades, the result of concerted efforts by activists, nonprofits, and local governments. In 2004 Cameron Chalmers founded the Lynnhaven Oyster Company in an attempt to resurrect the once-famed Lynnhaven oyster, and in recent years other producers have revived oyster cultivation in waters up and down the South Atlantic coast. Canvasback may no longer be viable for commercial tables, but fire-roasted duck with fried hominy would be a fine addition to the Mid-Atlantic table alongside all that blue crab. Craft distillers are starting to make brandies from apples and peaches again, which our bartenders could use instead of bourbon in juleps—and they might start serving them in large goblets crowned with a pyramid of ice and adorned with fruit and flowers.

These are all important facets of the South's culinary legacy. If we dig a little deeper and brush aside the cobwebs of myth and received wisdom, there are surely even more stories out there to inspire us.

NOTES

Introduction

1. Qtd. in David S. Shields and Kevin Mitchell, *Nat Fuller, 1812–1866: From Slavery to Artistry* (Columbia: Institute for Southern Studies and McKissick Museum, University of South Carolina, 2015). The original source of this quotation proved remarkably hard to track down. Shields's and Mitchell's pamphlet, which was produced as a companion to the commemorative banquet, cites Wilbert L. Jenkins, *Climbing Up to Glory: A Short History of African Americans During the Civil War and Reconstruction* (Wilmington, Del.: Scholarly Resources, 2002), 94. Jenkins, in turn, cites Benjamin Quarles's *The Negro in the Civil War* (Boston: Little, Brown, 1953), which does not have footnotes, and Quarles does not cite a source in his bibliographic essay. Quarles—and Jenkins, Shields, and Mitchell after him—misspell the Charlestonian's name as "Frances." It actually was not her first name but her husband's, for Louisa Porcher was married to Francis J. Porcher. In 2018 Ethan J. Kytle, an associate professor of history at California State University, Fresno, uncovered the original letter, which I discuss in chapter 6.

2. Jessica B. Harris, *High on the Hog: A Culinary Journey from Africa to America* (New York: Bloomsbury, 2011); Toni Tipton-Martin, *The Jemima Code: Two Centuries of African American Cookbooks* (Austin: University of Texas Press, 2015); Michael W. Twitty, *The Cooking Gene: A Journey Through African-American Culinary History in the Old South* (New York: Amistad, 2017).

3. Ginnie Mulkey, "Southern Cooking Full of Down-Home Goodness," *Evansville Courier*, February 18, 1977, 13.

4. Joe Gray Taylor, *Eating, Drinking, and Visiting in the South* (Baton Rouge: Louisiana State University Press, 1982), 67–68.

5. Taylor, *Eating, Drinking, and Visiting*, 67. Paul Freedman's survey of American restaurant cuisine in the mid-nineteenth century gives a similar short shrift to

southern restaurants. He assesses the menus of multiple New York and Boston restaurants between 1836 and 1860 but inexplicably picks up his discussion of restaurants in the South in 1863, and then just to note the high prices in wartime Richmond. He gives no indication that there were any restaurants worthy of notice outside of New Orleans. Freedman, "American Restaurants and Cuisine in the Mid-Nineteenth Century," *New England Quarterly* 84 (March 2011): 5–59.

CHAPTER 1. Commercial Dining in Early Nineteenth-Century Charleston

1. For more information about the character of colonial taverns and early drinking habits, see Sharon V. Salinger, *Taverns and Drinking in Early America* (Baltimore: Johns Hopkins University Press, 2002); Daniel B. Thorp, "Taverns and Tavern Culture on the Southern Colonial Frontier: Rowan County, North Carolina, 1753–1776." *Journal of Southern History* 62, no. 4 (1996): 661–688.

2. For a general history of the evolution of American hotels, see A. K. Sandoval-Strausz, *Hotel: An American History* (New Haven: Yale University Press, 2007).

3. "Jessop's Hotel, No. 63, East Bay," *Charleston City Gazette*, July 19, 1799, 3.

4. "St. Mary's Hotel," *South-Carolina Gazette*, December 24, 1801; "St Mary's Hotel," *Charleston City Gazette*, January 14, 1801, 1; *Charleston City Gazette*, May 6, 1801, 6. In 1786 a Miss Fletcher advertised in the local paper that she had just taken occupancy of "a large, pleasant, and commodious new house" on Meeting Street which she called the City-Hotel. She promised gentlemen would have "the best Liquors and attendance the City can afford, with Tea, Coffee, Beef Steaks &c. by a professed cook" and that non-boarders could have "dinners provided at the shortest notice." Her short-lived City-Hotel seems to have been more a boardinghouse than something we would recognize today as a hotel or restaurant. When the building was put up for sale the following year, it was described as "A comfortable dwelling-house . . . intended originally for a store." "City-Hotel," *Charleston Morning Post*, August 16, 1786, 3.

5. "To the Public," *Charleston City Gazette*, September 17, 1803, 4.

6. "A Large Fine Green Turtle," *Charleston City Gazette*, September 2, 1806, 3. Thompson ran a half dozen similar ads for green turtle in November and December of the same year.

7. These descriptions of turtle preparations are digested from various cookbooks of the period, including Hannah Glasse's *Art of Cookery, Made Plain and Easy* (1774), Mary Randolph's *Virginia Housewife* (1836), and Sarah Rutledge's *Carolina Housewife* (1839).

8. "The Merchant's and Planter's Hotel," *Charleston City Gazette*, October 15, 1806, 2. The building at 60 East Bay still stands today. Until just recently it housed the renowned McCrady's Restaurant, and its Long Room was the site of the anniversary Nat Fuller Feast in 2015. As of this writing the building stands empty,

since the latest incarnation of McCrady's Tavern closed its doors in the summer of 2019 and the owners put the historic building up for sale.

9. "To the Publick," *Charleston Courier*, December 29, 1809, 1; Martha A. Zierden et al., *The Dock Street Theatre: Archaeological Discovery and Exploration*, Archaeological Contributions 42 (Charleston, S.C.: Charleston Museum, 2009).

10. Larry Koger, *Black Slaveowners: Free Black Slave Masters in South Carolina, 1790–1860* (1985; rpt., Jefferson, N.C.: McFarland, 2011), 147, 153–154.

11. "Harriet P. Simons and Albert Simons, "The William Burrows House of Charleston," *Winterthur Portfolio* 3 (1967): 186; Sheriff's Sales," *Charleston Courier*, March 15, 1827, 3; "By William Lloyd," *Charleston Courier*, September 23, 1831, 3.

12. Thomas Hamilton, *Men and Manners in America* (Philadelphia: Carey, Lea and Blanchard, 1833), 347–348.

13. 1820 United States Federal Census, Charleston, Charleston County, South Carolina, page 48, NARA roll M33_119, image 111, digital image s.v. "Jehu Jones," accessed via Ancestry.com; "For Private Sale," *Southern Patriot* (Charleston), April 29, 1826, 3. How other African Americans in Charleston felt about free persons of color like the Joneses owning slaves is a difficult question to answer. In fact, there has been considerable debate among historians about why African Americans elected to own slaves in the first place. For many decades, scholars of Black slaveholding followed the lead of Carter G. Woodson, author of the pioneering study *Free Negro Owners of Slaves in the United States in 1830* (Washington, D.C.: Association for the Study of Negro Life and History, 1924), and asserted that the vast majority of such slaveowners had actually purchased a spouse or child to preserve their families or for other philanthropic motives. Beginning in the 1970s, other scholars advanced the argument that many free persons of color were in fact economically exploiting the people they purchased. These include Larry Koger, who in *Black Slaveowners* concludes that "the Woodson thesis that most free black slaveowners were benevolent masters may be a myth" (80). Koger points specifically to Charleston's urban trades, including innkeeping and catering, as examples of slave labor being enlisted in profit-seeking enterprise. For a summary of the evidence on both sides of the debate, see David L. Lightner and Alexander M. Ragan, "Were African American Slaveholders Benevolent or Exploitative? A Quantitative Approach," *Journal of Southern History* 71, no. 3 (August 2005): 535–558.

14. For information on the commercial and social seasons in early nineteenth-century Charleston, see Walter J. Fraser Jr., *Charleston! Charleston!: The History of a Southern City* (Columbia: University of South Carolina Press, 1989), 195–198.

15. *Charleston Courier*, July 31, 1807, 1; "For Sale," *Southern Patriot*, March 28, 1820, 1; "Jones' Establishment," *Southern Patriot*, April 28, 1820, 1.

16. "Gaston," *Charleston City Gazette*, March 19, 1804, 4; David S. Shields, *Southern Provisions: The Creation and Revival of a Cuisine* (Chicago: University of Chicago Press, 2015), 112.

17. *Charleston City Gazette*, May 11, 1798, 1; *Charleston City Gazette*, October 4, 1800, 1. For the full story of Frederic Tudor and the development of the intracoastal ice trade, see Gavin Weightman, *The Frozen-Water Trade: A True Story* (New York: Hyperion, 2003).

18. *Charleston City Gazette*, May 18, 1821, 1; *Charleston Courier*, May 3, 1828, 3; *Charleston City Gazette*, June 25, 1829, 1.

19. Koger, *Black Slaveowners*, 38–39.

20. Robert L. Harris Jr., "Charleston's Free Afro-American Elite: The Brown Fellowship Society and the Humane Brotherhood," *South Carolina Historical Magazine* 82 (1981): 289–310.

21. Koger, *Black Slaveowners*, 39; Shields, *Southern Provisions*, 115. Those seven were Camilla Johnson, Eliza Dwight, Martha Gilchrist, Hannah Hetty, Elizabeth Holton, Mary Holton, and Cato McCloud.

22. Koger, *Black Slaveowners*, 38–39; *Charleston City Gazette*, December 3, 1824, 3.

23. "Ranaway," *Charleston City Gazette*, December 18, 1821, 1; "At Private Sale," *Charleston Times*, August 18, 1817, 3.

24. "Notes on America," *Museum of Foreign Literature and Science* 21 (1832): 221; James Stuart, *Three Years in North America* (New York: Harper, 1833), 2:131–132.

25. Stuart, *Three Years in North America*, 2:142–143.

26. Koger, *Black Slaveowners*, 154.

27. Fraser, *Charleston! Charleston!*, 200–206. A considerable debate over the details and nature of the supposed Vesey plot was sparked by the work of Michael P. Johnson, who concludes that the charges against Vesey and his alleged coconspirators were trumped up by a corrupt Charleston court. See Johnson, "Denmark Vesey and his Co-Conspirators," *William and Mary Quarterly* 58 (2001): 915–917. For a summary of the historical reevaluation of Vesey, see Philip D. Morgan, "Conspiracy Scares," *William and Mary Quarterly* 59 (2002): 159–166.

28. *Jehu Jones: Free Black Entrepreneur* (Columbia: South Carolina Department of Archives and History, 1989).

29. "Sullivan's Island," *Southern Patriot*, April 11, 1826, 1; "Sullivan's Island," *Charleston Courier*, June 3, 1826, 1; "Jones' Hotel," *Southern Patriot*, October 21, 1829, 3.

30. "Sheriff's Sales," *Charleston Courier*, March 15, 1827, 3.

31. For an example of a work citing the Huguenot influence on Charleston's cuisine, see John Egerton, *Southern Food: At Home, on the Road, in History* (Chapel Hill: University of North Carolina Press, 1993), 14. James Beard incorrectly asserted that "the Huguenot influence in Charleston produced the famous she-crab soup," a dish that was actually created by the African American cook William Deas in the early twentieth century. *James Beard's American Cookery* (1972; rpt., New York: Little, Brown, 2010), 82. Charleston had had coffeehouses since the late eighteenth century, but the nature of those establishments evolved considerably in the early

decades of the nineteenth century, becoming more like a modern restaurant. The Carolina Coffee-House on Tradd Street had been operated by various proprietors since at least 1802, and in its early incarnations it seems to have served more booze than coffee. When J. R. Mauran, one of the establishment's numerous owners, put the business up for sale in 1809, his advertisements emphasized the generous stock of liquors that came along with the deal, including London porter, Madeira wine, claret, "Old Cognack Brandy," and Jamaica rum, plus one thousand "Spanish segars" and two billiard tables. He soon found a buyer, and it was none other than James Thompson, who had briefly operated the Planter's Hotel before selling it to the Calders. Thompson played up the culinary side of his new business, saying he was opening "for the purpose of Entertaining Societies, furnishing Public Dinners, &c." During the 1820s the Carolina Coffee-House hosted the meetings of the city's leading societies and clubs—the Republican Artillery, the Charleston Library Society, the Society of the Cincinnati, the Hibernian Society, the Charleston Marine Society. "Carolina Coffee House," *Charleston Courier*, September 8, 1808, 3; "Carolina Coffee House," *Charleston City Gazette*, February 13, 1809, 4.

32. John W. Coffey, "Biographical Sketch of Rémy Mignot," Find a Grave, https://www.findagrave.com/memorial/34185167/rémy-mignot; "Council Chamber," *Charleston City Gazette*, October 11, 1823, 3.

33. "United States Coffee House," *Charleston Courier*, January 14, 1837, 3; David S. Shields, *The Culinarians: Lives and Careers from the First Age of American Fine Dining* (Chicago: University of Chicago Press, 2017), 25–28.

34. Shields, *Southern Provisions*, 115–117.

35. "25 Dollars Reward," *Charleston Courier*, February 16, 1832, 3.

36. "Charleston," *Charleston Courier*, September 9, 1842, 2.

37. "Oysters," *Charleston Courier*, November 12, 1829, 3; "Oysters," *Charleston City Gazette*, March 18, 1830, 3; "D. Truesdell," *Charleston City Gazette*, January 16, 1826, 3; "Terrapin Soup," *Charleston Courier*, May 26, 1825, 3.

38. "Oysters," *Charleston Courier*, May 8, 1834, 3; Cindy Lee, *A Tour of Historic Sullivan's Island* (Charleston: History Press, 2010), 42–46.

39. William Gilmore Simms, *Father Abbot; or, The Home Tourist* (Charleston: Miller and Browne, 1849), 61–62.

CHAPTER 2. Early Commercial Dining in the Mid-Atlantic

1. Jefferson Morley, "The 'Snow Riot,'" *Washington Post Magazine*, February 6, 2005.

2. John DeFerrari, *Historic Restaurants of Washington, D.C.: Capital Eats* (Charleston: History Press, 2013), 19–20.

3. DeFerrari, *Historic Restaurants of Washington*, 51–52; "Life at Gadsby's," *Alexandria Gazette*, December 24, 1835, 2.

4. Benjamin Perley Poore, *Perley's Reminiscences of Sixty Years in the National Metropolis* (Philadelphia: Hubbard Brothers, 1886), 1:43; DeFerrari, *Historic Restaurants of Washington*, 53–54.

5. "Social Retreat—Monsieur Boulanger—The First Ward," *Daily National Intelligencer*, March 31, 1851, 1;

6. Andrew Jackson Papers, Series 1, General Correspondence and Related Items, 1775 to 1885, Library of Congress, s.v. "Joseph Boulanger," https://www .loc.gov/collections/andrew-jackson-papers.

7. "Furniture Sale," *Poulson's American Daily Advertiser*, December 23, 1824, 2; "Washington Coffee House," *United States' Telegraph*, September 7, 1826, 3.

8. "Fountain Inn for Rent," *United States' Telegraph*, September 6, 1827, 2.

9. "Congress Hall Hotel & Refectory," *Baltimore Republican*, October 4, 1832, 4.

10. "Two Refectories," *Daily Pennsylvanian*, August 21, 1837, 2; "Removal," *Daily Union*, January 28, 1848, 2.

11. Poore, *Perley's Reminiscences*, 1:156; "A Lunchroom Called Capitol Hill," *New York Times*, March 6, 2013, D1.

12. John Sharp and Gene Sharp, "Beverly Randolph Snow," Find a Grave, https://www.findagrave.com/memorial/180437190/beverly-randolph-snow.

13. "Beverly Snow," *United States' Telegraph*, January 27, 1831, 3; "Snow's Epicurean Eating House," *United States' Telegraph*, March 4, 1833, 4; "Tumultuary Movements in Washington," *Washington Globe*, rpt. *New York Evening Post*, August 15, 1835, 2.

14. Donet D. Graves, "Wormley Hotel," White House Historical Association, https://www.whitehousehistory.org/wormley-hotel-1.

15. *Liberator*, August 6, 1831, 125; George W. Williams, *History of the Negro Race in America from 1619 to 1880* (New York: G. P. Putnam's Sons, 1883), 2:205–206.

16. Qtd. in Morley, "The 'Snow Riot.'"

17. Qtd. in Morley, "The 'Snow Riot.'"

18. "Tumultuary Movements in Washington," *Washington Globe*, rpt. *New York Evening Post*, August 15, 1835, 2; Morley, "The 'Snow Riot'"; Williams, *Negro Race in America*, 2:253–254.

19. "Beverly Snow," *National Intelligencer*, rpt. *Philadelphia Inquirer*, April 28, 1835, 2.

20. "Beverly Snow," *Liberator*, September 24, 1836, 155; Sharp and Sharp, "Beverly Randolph Snow."

21. Williams, *Negro Race in America*, 2:253–254; Morley, "The 'Snow Riot.'"

22. Paul Freedman, *Ten Restaurants That Changed America* (New York: Liveright, 2016), xliv.

23. Charles Dickens, *The Life and Adventures of Martin Chuzzlewit* (London: Chapman and Hall, 1843), 204–205. The "barbarous" characterization was made by Andrew P. Haley, who claims that Dickens, "whose aspirations to respectability

included a love of French cuisine, found the culinary life of America barbarous." *Turning the Tables: Restaurants and the Rise of the American Middle Class, 1880–1920* (Chapel Hill: University of North Carolina Press, 2011), 19.

24. Haley, *Turning the Tables*, 18–21.

25. "National Eating House," *Daily National Intelligencer*, December 5, 1835, 3.

26. "Fresh Shad and Oysters!" *Daily National Intelligencer*, February 24, 1839, 3; "The Shad," *Alexandria Gazette*, August 9, 1843, 2.

27. "Shad," *Boston Daily Times*, rpt. *Charleston Courier*, May 4, 1839, 2.

28. David S. Shields, *Southern Provisions: The Creation and Revival of a Cuisine* (Chicago: University of Chicago Press, 2015), 101.

29. DeFerrari, *Historic Restaurants of Washington*, 42–45.

30. David Wondrich, "The Cunningest Compounders of Beverages: The Hidden History of African-Americans Behind the Bar," *Bitter Southerner*, August 2016, https://bittersoutherner.com/a-history-of-black-bartenders; DeFerrari, *Historic Restaurants of Washington*, 42–45.

31. "American and French Restaurant," *Daily National Intelligencer*, January 10, 1837, 3; "American and French Restaurant," *Daily National Intelligencer*, February 13, 1837, 2.

32. Poore, *Perley's Reminiscences*, 1:179; "American and French Restaurant," *Daily National Intelligencer*, January 10, 1837, 3; "American and French Restaurant," *Daily National Intelligencer*, February 13, 1837, 2; "American and French Restaurant," *Daily National Intelligencer*, January 5, 1838, 4.

33. "Picayune Express," *New Orleans Daily Picayune*, December 16, 1841, 2; Poore, *Perley's Reminiscences*, 1:179.

34. "Boz at Washington," *Boston Post*, March 19, 1842, 2.

35. Charles Dickens, *American Notes for General Circulation*, 2nd ed. (London: Chapman and Hall, 1842), 1:272, 281.

36. Dickens, *American Notes*, 1:275. In his 1842 travelogue Dickens touches on American food only in passing, and when he does, it is usually to note its deliciousness, as in the case of canvasback ducks. In another passage, discussing the streets of New York, he seems to have found the city's famed oysters quite delicious, too. Oyster-cellars are "pleasant retreats, say I: not only by reason of their wonderful cookery of oysters, pretty nigh as large as cheese-plates (or for thy dear sake, heartiest of Greek Professors!), but because of all kinds of eaters of fish, or flesh, or fowl, in these latitudes, the swallowers of oysters alone are not gregarious; but subduing themselves, as it were, to the nature of what they work in, and copying the coyness of the thing they eat, do sit apart in curtained boxes, and consort by twos, not by two hundreds" (1:208–209).

In the apology that Dickens penned in 1868 after the banquet at Delmonico's, he does admit to being astounded by the changes he saw all around him in America a quarter century later, but here again he makes no mention of food.

He harps mostly on the press and its treatment of him, and—after being mobbed by fans and overwhelmed by the sheer volume of invitations to attend public gatherings in 1842—he expresses gratitude for his having been "received with unsurpassable politeness, delicacy, sweet temper, hospitality, consideration, and with unsurpassable respect for the privacy daily enforced upon me by the nature of my avocation here and the state of my health." See "Postscript" in *American Notes; Pictures from Italy; and, A Child's History of England* (London: Chapman and Hall, 1891), 201–202. It was American crowds and manners, not American cuisine, that had so plagued Dickens on his first tour.

37. "Congress Hall and Eating Saloon," *Washington Globe*, December 4, 1844, 3; "At Private Sale," *Daily National Intelligencer*, January 23, 1846, 4; "Villainous Vandalism," *Baltimore Sun*, April 17, 1846, 4.

38. "American and French Restaurant," *Washington Union*, December 27, 1847, 3.

CHAPTER 3. Commercial Dining in Old New Orleans and the West

1. "Lavishly festooned with magnolia and bougainvillea," John DeMers writes in *The Food of New Orleans: Authentic Recipes from the Big Easy* (Clarendon, Vt.: Tuttle, 1998), "New Orleans is an American city unlike any other. . . . Its French roots may be why New Orleanians are known for their love of good food" (5). More egregious is Dorothy Dix's introduction to Elaine Douglass Jones's *Gourmet's Guide to New Orleans: Creole Cookbook* (1933; rpt., Gretna, La.: Pelican, 1975), which asserts that the city's cooking, "Founded originally on the French cuisine," was then "pepped up, so to speak, by the Spanish, given body and strength by the New England influence, a bit of warmth by the hot breads of Virginia, and finally glorified by the touch of the old Negro mammies who boasted that they had only to pass their hands over a pot to give it a flavor that would make your mouth water" (i). More recent works, like the fourteen essays in Susan Tucker, ed., *New Orleans Cuisine: Fourteen Signature Dishes and Their Histories* (Jackson: University Press of Mississippi, 2009), are careful not to overemphasize the French roots of New Orleans's cuisine, portraying it instead as "a blending of culinary habits" of dozens of European and African cultures along with Native American traditions. That "gumbo pot" approach still advances the notion of a New Orleans culinary exceptionalism that isn't particularly apparent in the restaurant cuisine before the Civil War. That came considerably later in the century.

2. Joseph Holt Ingraham, *The South-West, by a Yankee* (New York: Harper Brothers, 1835), 1:113.

3. Much of the early story of the Exchange can be found in Samuel Wilson Jr., "Maspero's Exchange: Its Predecessors and Successors," *Louisiana History* 30 (1989): 191–220.

4. Robert F. Moss, *Southern Spirits: Four Hundred Years of Drinking in the American South* (Berkeley: Ten Speed, 2016), 82–83; Ingraham, *The South-West, by a Yankee,* 1:115.

5. H. Didimus [Edward Henry Durell], *New Orleans As I Found It* (New York: Harper and Brothers, 1845), 21–22.

6. For sketches of early New Orleans, see Didimus, *New Orleans As I Found It.* For an overview of New Orleans's rapid growth in the 1830s and 1840s, see Scott P. Marler, *The Merchants' Capital: New Orleans and the Political Economy of the Nineteenth-Century South* (New York: Cambridge University Press, 2013), 15–52.

7. Moss, *Southern Spirits,* 84–87.

8. A. Oakey Hall, *The Manhattaner in New Orleans* (New York: J. S. Redfield, 1851), 9–18.

9. *Historical Sketch Book and Guide to New Orleans and Environs* (New York: W. H. Coleman, 1885), 76–78.

10. Qtd. in David S. Shields, *Southern Provisions: The Creation and Revival of a Cuisine* (Chicago: University of Chicago Press, 2015), 63; "Walter's Grand Oyster Saloon and Restaurant," *New Orleans Daily Picayune,* November 4, 1846, 4.

11. "Victor's Restaurant Burned," *New Orleans Daily Picayune,* April 11, 1874, 1.

12. "Victor's Restaurant," *New Orleans Daily Picayune,* September 5, 1849, 2, 3; "Victor's Restaurant Burned," *New Orleans Daily Picayune,* April 11, 1874, 1.

13. "Hewlett's Exchange," *New Orleans Daily Picayune,* November 15, 1843, 2; Shields, *Southern Provisions,* 69.

14. "Refreshments," *New Orleans Crescent,* May 19, 1848, 3; "Wholesale and Retail," *New Orleans Daily Picayune,* December 26, 1850, 1; "M. V. Lefort's," *New Orleans Daily Picayune,* December 31, 1850, 2; Shields, *Southern Provisions,* 76.

15. Louis C. Hennick and E. Harper Charlton, *The Streetcars of New Orleans* (1965; rpt., Gretna, La.: Pelican, 2005), 5–8.

16. "Death of Miguel," *New Orleans Daily Picayune,* October 6, 1889, 4; William Makepeace Thackeray, "A Mississippi Bubble," in *The Works of William Makepeace Thackeray,* vol. 25, *Roundabout Papers* (Cambridge, Mass.: Jenson Society, 1907), 187.

17. David S. Shields, *The Culinarians: Lives and Careers from the First Age of American Fine Dining* (Chicago: University of Chicago Press, 2017), 109–113; "Washington Hotel," *New Orleans Daily Picayune,* October 20, 1846, 5.

18. "Our First Frost Dinner," *New Orleans Daily Picayune,* November 2, 1843, 2.

19. "Holbrook's Oyster Saloon," *New Orleans Daily Picayune,* September 6, 1843, 2; "Crescent Oyster Saloon," *New Orleans Daily Picayune,* September 3, 1844, 2.

20. "Walter's Grand Oyster Saloon," *New Orleans Daily Picayune,* November 4, 1846, 4.

21. "Holbrook's Oyster Saloon" and "Walter's Grand Oyster Saloon and Restaurant," *Concordia Intelligencer*, February 27, 1847, 4; *New Orleans Daily Picayune*, October 8, 1845, 2; "Crescent Oyster Saloon," *New Orleans Daily Picayune*, September 6, 1844, 3.

22. For details on the evolution of gumbo, see Robert Moss, "The Real Story of Gumbo, Okra, and Filé," *Serious Eats*, September 2014, http://www.seriouseats .com/2014/09/history-new-orleans-gumbo-okra-file-powder.html. A version of gumbo (also known as okra soup) was a staple in the Lowcountry of South Carolina, too, but it does not appear to have made its way into Charleston's early restaurants.

23. Henry Bradshaw Fearon, *Sketches of America: A Narrative of a Journey of Five Thousand Miles through the Eastern and Western States of America* (London: Longman, Hurst, Reese, Orme, and Brown, 1819), 246–250. Washington Hall was operated by a man named Archibald Allan, not Allen. In January 1819, Allan purchased the Indian Queen (also known as Union Hall) from John Gwathmey, who moved to New Orleans and opened a coffeehouse. Allan consolidated his operations into the larger Union Hall building, where the Marquis de Lafayette lodged during his visit to Louisville in 1825. See Margaret M. Bridwell, "At the Sign of the Indian Queen," *Louisville Daily Journal*, November 11, 1856, 255–258.

24. Fearon, *Sketches of America*, 246–250.

25. "Western Coffee House," *Daily Louisville Public Advertiser*, January 22, 1830, 3; "Our Friend's House," *Daily Louisville Public Advertiser*, September 21, 1830, 3.

CHAPTER 4. Fine Dining on the Brink of the Civil War

1. Walter J. Fraser Jr., *Charleston! Charleston!: The History of a Southern City* (Columbia: University of South Carolina Press, 1989), 220–222.

2. "The Charleston Hotel," *Charleston Courier*, Wednesday, January 25, 1837, 2; Maurie D. McInnis, *The Politics of Taste in Antebellum Charleston* (Chapel Hill: University of North Carolina Press, 2005), 100–103.

3. "The New Hotel," *Charleston Courier*, March 28, 1838, 2.

4. Fraser, *Charleston! Charleston!*, 216–217; "Extensive Conflagration," *Charleston Courier*, April 28, 1838, 3.

5. David S. Shields, *Southern Provisions: The Creation and Revival of a Cuisine* (Chicago: University of Chicago Press, 2015), 110; Tammis Kane Groft, *Cast with Style: Nineteenth Century Cast-Iron Stoves from the Albany Area*, rev. ed. (Albany, N.Y.: Albany Institute of History and Art, 1984).

6. McInnis, *Politics of Taste*, 104–108.

7. "Charleston County, South Carolina, Wills, Etc, 1818–1834," *South Carolina, Wills and Probate Records, 1670–1980*, 691–692, digital image, accessed via Ancestry .com.

8. "Jones' Establishment," *Charleston Courier*, October 15, 1843, 1; Larry Koger, *Black Slaveowners: Free Black Slave Masters in South Carolina, 1790–1860* (1985; rpt., Jefferson, N.C.: McFarland, 2011), 154.

9. "Cook for Sale," *Charleston Courier*, November 10, 1843, 3; "A Pastry Cook, &c.," *Southern Patriot*, February 23, 1846, 3.

10. "Proceedings of Council," *Charleston Courier*, July 26, 1838, 2.

11. Fanny Kemble, *Records of Later Life* (London: Richard Bentley and Sons, 1882), 122–123; Harriett P. Simons and Albert Simons, "The William Burrows House of Charleston," *South Carolina Historical Magazine* 70, no. 3 (1969): 155–176.

12. "Jones' Hotel To Be Reopened," *Southern Patriot*, October 29, 1847, 3; "Jones Hotel—Valuable Real Estate, at Private Sale," *Charleston Courier*, January 30, 1850, 1.

13. Philip N. Racine, ed., *Gentlemen Merchants: A Charleston Family's Odyssey, 1828–1870* (Knoxville: University of Tennessee Press, 2008), 211–212.

14. Eliza Lee to Henry Gourdin, in Racine, *Gentlemen Merchants*, 305.

15. "Concert at Hibernian Hall," *Southern Patriot*, February 16, 1848, 3.

16. "Bill of Fare of the Ladies' Restaurant," *Charleston Courier*, October 23, 1851, 2; "Mount Vernon Ice Cream Garden," *Charleston Courier*, April 2, 1852, 2.

17. Alexander Lovett Stimson, *History of Express Companies and American Railroads* (New York: Baker and Godwin, 1881), 107–108.

18. George R. Taylor, *The Transportation Revolution, 1815–60* (1951; rpt., London: Routledge, 2015), 115–117; "Charleston and New York Steam Packets," *Charleston Mercury*, January 28, 1858, 2.

19. "Exchange Cafe," *Southern Patriot*, September 15, 1846, 3; "Exchange Cafe," *Southern Patriot*, February 12, 1847, 3.

20. "Sheriff's Sale," *Charleston Courier*, August 6, 1827, 3. David Shields has inferred that one of three landowners named Fuller with property located west of the Ashley River—Christopher Fuller, Benjamin Fuller, or Thomas Fuller—was Nat Fuller's father. Shields, *The Culinarians: Lives and Careers from the First Age of American Fine Dining* (Chicago: University of Chicago Press, 2017), 124–125.

21. David S. Shields and Kevin Mitchell, *Nat Fuller, 1812–1866: From Slavery to Artistry* (Columbia: Institute for Southern Studies and McKissick Museum, University of South Carolina, 2015), 6–7.

22. "Charleston and New York Steam Packets," *Charleston Mercury*, January 28, 1858, 2.

23. "Fine Turkeys, Pheasants, Grouse and Capons," *Charleston Courier*, January 18, 1854, 2; "Just Received," *Charleston Courier*, March 26, 1856, 2.

24. "For Sale," *Charleston Courier*, June 12, 1855, 3; Shields and Mitchell, *Nat Fuller*, 37.

25. "What We Are to Eat," *Charleston Courier*, January 19, 1857, 1.

26. "The Subscriber," *Charleston Mercury*, January 2, 1860, 2.

27. "Notice," *Charleston Courier*, September 5, 1856, 3; "French and American Confectionery," *Charleston Courier*, November 19, 1856, 19; "Fancy Ball," *Charleston Mercury*, February 10, 1857, 2; "For Europe," *Charleston Courier*, April 22, 1857, 2; *Charleston Courier*, May 28, 1858, 2; "A. J. Rutjes," *Charleston Courier*, December 6, 1858, 2.

28. "Notice," *Charleston Courier*, June 9, 1860, 2; "Sheriff's Sale," *Charleston Mercury*, July 2, 1860, 3; Shields, *Southern Provisions*, 120.

29. "A. J. Rutjes," *Charleston Courier*, December 6, 1858, 2; "Mount Vernon Garden," *Charleston Courier*, December 21, 1858, 2.

30. 1850 United States Federal Census, Charleston, Charleston County, South Carolina, roll 850, page 14b, digital image s.v. "Thomas Tully," accessed via Ancestry.com; "Death of a Culinary Artist," *Charleston News and Courier*, rpt. *Macon Telegraph*, October 31, 1883, 1.

31. "Vanderhorst & Tully," *Charleston Courier*, September 16, 1859, 3.

32. Fuller v. Gatewood case records, Simons & Simons Papers, 431.02 (F) 06, Charleston Historical Society, Charleston, S.C.

33. "By T. A. Whitney," *Charleston Mercury*, March 21, 1864, 2; "Fifty Dollar Reward," *Charleston Courier*, October 25, 1862, 2.

34. "Notice," *Charleston Mercury*, October 10, 1860, 2.

35. "The Jubilee of Southern Union," *Charleston Courier*, May 30, 1857, 1; Shields and Mitchell, *Nat Fuller*, 41–43.

36. For a good overview of Richmond in the 1850s, see Gregg D. Kimball, *American City, Southern Place: A Cultural History of Antebellum Richmond* (Athens: University of Georgia Press, 2000), 4–36.

37. Obituary, *Richmond Whig*, May 29, 1872, 4; "Epicures, Attention!," *Richmond Dispatch*, May 15, 1852, 2; "Richmond Light Dragoons," *Richmond Whig*, July 12, 1850, 2.

38. "Local Matters," *Richmond Dispatch*, June 29, 1855, 2.

39. "American Saloon," *Richmond Dispatch*, October 29, 1853, 2.

40. "Pickled Oysters," *Richmond Dispatch*, February 12, 1857, 2; "American Saloon—Soft Crabs," *Richmond Dispatch*, June 8, 1855, 2.

41. "Open Confession," *Richmond Dispatch*, August 7, 1854, 2; "Local Affairs," *Richmond Whig*, August 8, 1854, 2; "Local Matters," *Richmond Dispatch*, August 9, 1854 2; "Came to My House," *Richmond Dispatch*, December 28, 1854, 2. In the original account of Thompson and Griffin's verbal exchange, the *Richmond Dispatch* saw fit to censor the middle letters in "damn" and "bitch." I've followed suit with the more offensive n—— term, which the *Dispatch* had no issue printing in its entirety.

42. "Alhambra House," *Richmond Enquirer*, February 11, 1845, 3. Allen alludes to his experience in New York and Washington in "The Arbour," *Richmond Dispatch*,

January 12, 1853, 4. It is possible that R. W. Allen employed Thomas Griffin before the latter opened the American Saloon. In June 1847, Allen advertised that patrons should "drop in and try one of Tom's frozen Cobblers, or Juleps" at the Alhambra. "The Fountain," *Richmond Enquirer*, June 29, 1847, 3. It is unknown where Griffin worked prior to opening his own establishment, but he had been in the city since the 1820s and very likely was hired out originally as an enslaved worker like many other African Americans in Richmond's restaurant industry.

43. "The Arbour," *Richmond Dispatch*, January 27, 1852, 3; "Snacks for Ninepence," *Richmond Whig*, September 24, 1852, 3; "Pleasure Retreat," *Richmond Dispatch*, March 17, 1854, 2.

44. "Norvell House," *Richmond Whig*, April 13, 1855, 3; *Richmond Whig*, December 19, 1856 3.

45. "Complimentary Dinner to Democratic Electors of Virginia at the Exchange Hotel," December 3, 1856, Library of Virginia.

46. "New French Eating House," *Richmond Daily Whig*, March 28, 1857, 3; "Zetelle's Eating Saloon," *Richmond Dispatch*, October 28, 1857, 3; "Les Rendevous," *Richmond Whig*, September 27, 1859, 3.

47. "Constable's Sale," *Richmond Dispatch*, September 18, 1857, 3.

48. "Free Lunch!," *Richmond Dispatch*, August 27, 1858, 3; "Soft Crabs!," *Richmond Dispatch*, May 25, 1859, 2; "Look Here, Epicures!," *Richmond Dispatch*, May 16, 1860, 2.

49. "Vauxhall's Island," *Richmond Dispatch*, August 20, 1860 2.

50. Philip J. Schwarz, "John Dabney," in *The Dictionary of Virginia Biography* and in *Encyclopedia Virginia*, https://EncyclopediaVirginia.org/entries/Dabney_John _ca_1824-1900; Wendell P. Dabney, autobiographical sketch, n.d., Mss qD115, Wendell P. Dabney Papers, 1904–1964, Cincinnati Museum Center, 34.

51. Kimball, *American City, Southern Place*, 23; David W. Blight, *A Slave No More: Two Men Who Escaped to Freedom, Including Their Own Narratives of Emancipation* (2007; rpt., New York: Houghton Mifflin Harcourt / Mariner, 2009), 33.

52. Qtd. in Blight, *A Slave No More*, 24. The practice of slave hiring has created quite a polarized historical debate in recent years. On one side, some, like Clement Eaton and Richard Wade, interpreted the practice as a step toward freedom that offered hired-out slaves more autonomy and the opportunity for income for over-work. Others have argued that hired slaves received inferior care, worked far harder, and were punished more frequently and severely. For a long time the hiring out of enslaved workers was assumed to be an anomaly in the southern slave economy, but after surveying a broad range of evidence, John J. Zaborney in *Slaves for Hire: Renting Enslaved Laborers in Antebellum Virginia* (Baton Rouge: Louisiana State University Press, 2012) concluded "slave hiring was integral to Virginia slavery because slave hiring touched upon *all* types of slaves, *all* locations and occupations, and *all* types of whites" (3). Zaborney argues that the

practice of slave hiring actually strengthened the institution of slavery in Virginia, as it allowed Virginia slave owners who did not have an immediate need for their labor to hire slaves out and earn income from them rather than selling them to states in the Lower South, where the expanding cotton culture was driving ever higher demand for slaves.

53. "Opening of the City Hotel," *Richmond Whig*, April 26, 1850, 4; "One of the Juleps," *Richmond Dispatch*, August 10, 1855, 2; Dabney, autobiographical sketch, 35. Dabney's discussion of his father's tips is intriguing, for it and other accounts that mention tipping in antebellum Richmond restaurants and resorts contradict what has been the standard line in accounts of the history of tipping. Most accounts assert that tipping didn't become a standard practice in America until the late nineteenth century, and it did so as a controversial import from the great houses of England and France. Clearly, though, hired-out enslaved workers in the antebellum South were receiving personal compensation—that is, money that they pocketed and did not have to hand over to their owners—in the form of tips. The linkage between this early southern practice of tipping enslaved workers and the later controversy over tipping waiters, porters, and other workers is a fertile avenue of inquiry for future researchers. For a representative account of the standard line on tipping, see Kerry Segrave, *Tipping: An American Social History of Gratuities* (Jefferson, N.C.: McFarland, 1998).

54. Early details of Fields Cook's childhood are taken from a fragment of a manuscript narrative that Cook wrote in 1847, which is one of the most unusual slave narratives to survive from the antebellum period. Unlike other narratives of the time, Cook wrote it not for a white audience and not to advance a cause such as the abolition of slavery. Instead, his stated purpose was to record a few things "for my owne benefit in future years." As such, it touches only briefly on the subject of slavery and omits vital details such as his parents' names, his master's name, and where he was born and raised. Most of the material on Cook's childhood days recounts his early religiosity and frightening encounters he had with horses, dogs, and other dangers. The manuscript was donated to the Library of Congress in 1902 and later transcribed. Mary Jo Jackson Bratton, ed., *Fields's Observations: The Slave Narrative of a Nineteenth-Century Virginian*, electronic edition, http://docsouth.unc.edu/neh/fields/fields.html.

55. *Fields's Observations*, 90.

56. For a survey of early Virginia resorts, see William Burke, *The Resort Springs of Western Virginia* (New York: Wiley and Putnam, 1846). For the history of the hailstorm julep, see Robert F. Moss, *Southern Spirits: Four Hundred Years of Drinking in the American South* (Berkeley: Ten Speed, 2016), 95–96.

57. "Bathing Establishment" and "Baths, Baths, Baths," *Richmond Dispatch*, May 18, 1854, 2–3; "A Big Treat," *Richmond Dispatch*, March 25, 1859, 3.

58. For a full account of the origin of the mint julep, see Moss, *Southern Spirits*, 90–103.

59. Qtd. in Moss, *Southern Spirits*, 96.

60. "Correspondence of the Dispatch," *Richmond Dispatch*, July 2, 1856, 1; "One of the Juleps," *Richmond Dispatch*, August 10, 1855, 2.

61. Blight, *A Slave No More*, 185–186.

62. Blight, *A Slave No More*, 185–186. In June 1862 Wendlinger advertised: "My servant Sam ran away from my saloon—Zetelle's—on Main Street." "Runaway," *Richmond Dispatch*, June 19, 1862, 2.

63. Dabney, autobiographical sketch, 23.

64. "A Great Sensation," *Richmond Whig*, June 24, 1859, 3.

65. "Richmond Correspondence," *National Police Gazette*, November 19, 1859, 3.

66. John DeFerrari, *Historic Restaurants of Washington, D.C.: Capital Eats* (Charleston: History Press, 2013), 54–56.

67. "Avenue Improvements," *Republic* (Washington, D.C.), May 19, 1853, 4.

68. "Gautier's," *Daily National Intelligencer*, October 31, 1853, 1.

69. Shields, *The Culinarians*, 132–133.

70. "He Has Served Great Men," *Washington Evening Star*, October 26, 1899, 14.

71. "National Eating House," *Semi-weekly Union*, June 27, 1851, 2.

72. Damani Davis, "Slavery and Emancipation in the Nation's Capital: Using Federal Records to Explore the Lives of African American Ancestors," *Genealogy Notes* 42 (2010). Available online at National Archives, https://www.archives.gov /publications/prologue/2010/spring/dcslavery.html.

73. "Circuit Court," *Washington Sentinel*, October 20, 1853, 3.

74. "National Eating House," *Daily National Intelligencer*, December 31, 1853, 4; "Mrs. Eliza Anderson Passes Away at the Age of Seventy-Five," *Washington Evening Star*, September 27, 1898, 2

75. *Constitution and By-Laws of the Washington Club* (Washington, D.C.: C. Alexander, 1853).

76. "The River," *States* (Washington, D.C.), July 3, 1857, 3; "Arrival of the Steamer Maryland," *States*, July 6, 1857, 3; "Wormley's Club House," *States*, August 21, 1858, 4; "Fresh Ortolan and Reed Birds," *Washington Evening Star*, August 27, 1858, 3..

77. "Notice," *Daily National Intelligencer*, November 19, 1859, 1; "Book Notes," *Magazine of American History with Notes and Queries* 12 (1884): 479; 1860 United States Federal Census, Washington Ward 1, Washington, District of Columbia, page 357, digital image s.v. "James Wormley," accessed via Ancestry.com.

78. J. Thomas Scharf, *History of Baltimore City and County* (Philadelphia: L. H. Everts, 1881), 513–517.

79. Charles Dickens, *American Notes for General Circulation*, 2nd ed. (London: Chapman and Hall, 1842), 2:25; Frances Trollope, *Domestic Manners of the Americans* (London: Whittaker, Treacher, 1832), 174.

80. Scharf, *History of Baltimore*, 516.

81. "Local Matters," *Baltimore Sun*, May 13, 1843, 2.

82. "Wise Saying," *Baltimore Sun*, January 14, 1845, 1. That's the entire joke, word for word.

83. U.S. Census Bureau, 1870, Baltimore Ward 12, Baltimore, Maryland, roll M593_576, page 263a; Family History Library, Salt Lake City, Utah, film 552075; *Baltimore Sun*, June 25, 1841, 2; "Alexander Butcher," *American and Commercial Advertiser*, December 7, 1850, 3.

84. "American Association for the Advancement of Science," *Baltimore Sun*, April 30, 1858, 1.

85. "The Picturesque and Memorable of the Baltimore and Ohio Railroad," *Baltimore Daily Exchange*, August 2, 1859, 3; U.S. Census Bureau, 1850, Baltimore Ward 11, Baltimore, Maryland, roll 284, page 186b; U.S. Census Bureau, 1860, Baltimore Ward 11, Baltimore (Independent City), Maryland, page 5603.

86. Ernest Ingersoll, *The Oyster Industry* (Washington: Government Printing Office, 1881), 167–168; "The Monumental City," *San Francisco Bulletin*m November 27, 1880, 1.

87. "The Very Last Municipal Excursion," *Washington Evening Star*, July 21, 1857, 2.

88. Turtle soup had been fashionable in London in the mid-eighteenth century and was still widely enjoyed there, thanks to British sailors bringing turtles to the city from the West Indies. The dish never made much headway in Paris, though. The great French chef Escoffier observed that "turtle soup is seldom appreciated in France and therefore rarely found on the menu." Qtd. in Sharon Stallworth Nossiter, "Turtle Soup," in *New Orleans Cuisine: Fourteen Signature Dishes and Their Histories*, ed. Susan Tucker (Jackson: University Press of Mississippi, 2009), 93.

89. "H.R.H. Prince of Wales," *Richmond Dispatch*, October 2, 1860, 1.

90. "Arrival of the Prince of Wales," *Richmond Whig*, October 9, 1860, 1; Robert Cellem, *Visit of His Royal Highness the Prince of Wales to the British North American Provinces and United States* (Toronto: Henry Rowsell, 1861), 375–376.

91. Cellem, *Visit of His Royal Highness*, 375–376.

CHAPTER 5. Fine Dining Heads West

1. "Editor's Table," *Knickerbocker* 43 (1854): 101.

2. Business Directory, *Tennessean* (Nashville), February 20, 1846, 1.

3. "The 'Davis Eating Palace,'" *Tennessean*, November 13, 1850, 3.

4. "Sad Warning to Boys," *Tennessean*, October 14, 1850, 2.

5. "The City Arcade," *Tennessean*, September 23, 1852, 3.

6. "A Veteran Dead," *Tennessean*, October 19, 1858, 3.

7. "Messrs. E & A Jonnard," *Nashville Union and American*, December 25, 1855, 3; "Fresh Arrivals," *Nashville Union and American*, May 11, 1856, 4; "Sheriff's Sale," *Daily National Patriot*, June 23, 1858, 2.

8. "Our Friend Walker," *Louisville Daily Journal*, September 3, 1836, 2; "Walker's Eagle House," *Louisville Daily Journal*, September 19, 1839, 2. This is the earliest reference I have found to a julep being served in the state of Kentucky, and notably it is found, contrary to the typical moonlight-and-magnolias mythology, not on a plantation but in a city bar.

9. "Shell Oysters! Shell Oysters!," *Louisville Daily Journal*, December 23, 1839, 2; "Turtle Soup Lunch," *Louisville Daily Courier*, June 20, 1844, 2; "Walker's Restaurant Hotel," *Louisville Daily Courier*, October 1, 1844, 2.

10. "Walker's New City Exchange," *Louisville Daily Courier*, September 4, 1845, 2.

11. "Fresh Oysters," *Louisville Daily Democrat*, November 25, 1845, 4; "40 Brace Grouse," *Louisville Daily Democrat*, November 29, 1845, 4; "Old Port Wine," *Louisville Daily Democrat*, December 5, 1845, 4.

12. "City Exchange," *Louisville Daily Democrat*, April 27, 1846, 3.

13. "Walker's City Exchange," *Louisville Daily Democrat*, September 30, 1846, 2; 1840 United States Federal Census, Louisville, Jefferson County, Kentucky, page 137, digital image s.v. "W. H. Walker," accessed via Ancestry.com.

14. "Hyman's Coffee-House," *Louisville Daily Journal*, April 24, 1837, 2.

15. "Hyman's," *Louisville Daily Journal*, January 7, 1837, 2; "White Hall," *Louisville Daily Journal*, September 21, 1839, 2.

16. "Shad, Shad, Shad," *New Orleans Picayune*, June 16, 1837, 4.

17. "Marble Hall," *Louisville Daily Courier*, April 30, 1849, 2; "Marble Hall," *Louisville Daily Courier*, January 21, 1851, 4.

18. "Look First Upon This Picture," *Louisville Daily Courier*, November 28, 1850, 4; "Something Extra!," *Louisville Daily Courier*, March 22, 1851, 3; "Marble Hall Restaurant," *Louisville Daily Courier*, April 11, 1851, 2.

19. "Marble Hall," *Louisville Daily Courier*, May 29, 1851, 3.

20. *Louisville Merchants Mechanics & Manufacturers' Business Register for 1850* (Louisville: Brennan and Smith, 1850), 36.

21. "Mr Hyman," *Louisville Daily Courier*, April 9, 1851, 3; lunch menus from *Louisville Daily Courier*, May 24, 1852–April 5, 1853.

22. "For Sale!," *Louisville Daily Courier*, April 29, 1853, 21; "Super Liquors, Wines, Cordials," *Louisville Daily Courier*, August 1, 1853, 2; "Liquors, Wines, & C.," *Louisville Daily Courier*, October 3, 1853, 2; "For Hire," *Louisville Daily Courier*, January 2, 1854, 2.

23. See, for instance, "Stock Wanted," *Louisville Daily Courier*, March 20, 1854, 2.

24. "Charles C. Rufer—Death of a Well Known and Popular Citizen of This City," *Louisville Courier-Journal*, March 31, 1883, 8.

25. "American Express Company," *Louisville Daily Courier*, July 27, 1857, 2; John F. Stover, *History of the Baltimore and Ohio Railroad* (West Lafayette, Ind.: Purdue University Press, 1987), 127.

26. "St. Charles, Fifth Street," *Louisville Daily Courier*, May 8, 1858, 2; "Recipes by the River," *Louisville Daily Courier*, May 8, 1858, 4; "Clams! Clams! Clams!," *Louisville Daily Courier*, July 21, 1858, 4; "St. Charles," *Louisville Daily Courier*, September 14, 1858, 1; "Charley Rufer," *Louisville Daily Courier*, November 19, 1858, 1.

27. "The Grand Union Festival!!!," *Louisville Daily Courier*, January 25, 1860, 1.

28. "Victor's Restaurant Burned," *New Orleans Daily Picayune*, January 11, 1874, 1.

29. "Charles Rhodes," *New Orleans Daily Picayune*, March 22, 1894, 3; "Moreau's Restaurant," *New Orleans Daily Delta*, November 2, 1850, 1; "Moreau's Restaurant," *New Orleans Crescent*, November 17, 1858, 1.

30. "Restaurant du Cardinal," *New Orleans Daily Picayune*, July 16, 1847, 3; David S. Shields, *The Culinarians: Lives and Careers from the First Age of American Fine Dining* (Chicago: University of Chicago Press, 2017), 153–155.

31. "The City," *New Orleans Daily Picayune*, August 21, 1859, 6.

32. "Correspondence of the Intelligencer," *Concordia Intelligencer*, January 5, 1850, 2.

33. National Archives, Washington, D.C., *Passenger Lists of Vessels Arriving at New Orleans, Louisiana, 1820–1902*, roll 30, s.v. "Frederic Huppenbauer," accessed via Ancestry.com.

34. "Document for sale of slaves Moses, Louis, Alfred, and Jake, 1860 January 17," roll 89, Oregon Historical Society Research Library. The finding aid for the Oregon collection speculates that Auguste Pino was "possibly a slave trader," missing the connection between Pino and Huppenbauer in the sale of the United States Restaurant.

35. *L'Abeille de la Nouvelle-Orleans*, September 12, 1877, 1; "Alciatore," *New Orleans States*, September 15, 1917, 8; Antoine's Restaurant advertisement, *New Orleans Times-Democrat*, September 1, 1888, 22. Antoine Alciator (the family changed the spelling to Alciatore in the late nineteenth century) would have been fifteen years old in 1840, a rather precocious age to be living alone and owning one's own restaurant. But is it possible? His 1855 marriage certificate is the first documentary evidence of an Antoine Alciator living in New Orleans. His death notice, published in the city's French-language newspaper in 1877, notes that Alciator had been a resident of New Orleans for twenty-four years, placing his arrival around 1853. His wife's obituary in 1917 states that she had been a resident of New Orleans for sixty-five years, placing her arrival in New Orleans at essentially the same time as her future husband's. That date is supported by the passenger list for the bark *Olivia*, which includes one Frederick Freise and his twenty-year-old daughter Julie arriving in New York on May 10, 1853. That Julie Freise is likely the future wife of Antoine

Alciator. The restaurant's own advertising in the nineteenth century consistently stated that "Antoine's Hotel and Restaurant" was "Established 1859." The 1860 census shows the young family living in the city's Ward 5, with the thirty-five-year-old Antoine Alciator working as a cook and his twenty-five-year-old wife Julie at home with eight-month-old Alex. In *Antoine's Restaurant Cookbook*, rev. ed. (New Orleans: Carbery-Guste, 1979), Roy F. Guste Jr., Antoine Aliciator's great-great-grandson, includes a photograph of an advertisement for Restaurant Antoine that supposedly appeared in an opera program in 1852, but that date seems erroneous. Adjacent to the Antoine's ad are notices for ladies' hairdresser Felix Saron at 14 Baronne Street and engraver A. H. M. Peterson which make clear that the program could not be from 1852. Saron did not immigrate to the United States until 1859, and city directories show that his shop was not located at 14 Baronne until 1867. Peterson took over his shop from C. Bellenot around 1866, so their ads place the likely date of the opera program sometime in the late 1860s.

36. "Restaurant," *Daily Union* (Washington, D.C.), February 21, 1857, 3; "The Great Delmonico Chef," *Springfield (Mass.) Republican*, November 5, 1899, 15; Shields, *The Culinarians*, 319–321; Lately Thomas, *Delmonico's: A Century of Splendor* (Boston: Houghton Mifflin, 1967), 87.

CHAPTER 6. Conflict and Commerce

1. "Military and Civic Reception," *Charleston Mercury*, November 10, 1860, 1; Margaret Middleton Rivers Eastman, *Hidden History in Civil War Charleston* (Charleston: History Press, 2012), 25–28.

2. David W. Blight, *A Slave No More: Two Men Who Escaped to Freedom, Including Their Own Narratives of Emancipation* (2007; rpt., New York: Houghton Mifflin Harcourt / Mariner, 2009), 186.

3. Robert F. Moss, *Southern Spirits: Four Hundred Years of Drinking in the American South* (Berkeley: Ten Speed, 2016), 129–131.

4. "Movements and Spirit of the War," *Richmond Examiner*, September 24, 1861, 2.

5. Blight, *A Slave No More*, 186.

6. Blight, *A Slave No More*, 194–195.

7. "News from the Confederacy," *New Orleans Daily Picayune*, June 7, 1863, 4.

8. "Proclamation," *Richmond Examiner*, March 3, 1862, 2; "In Limbo," *Richmond Dispatch*, June 17, 1862, 2.

9. "Senate-House Restaurant," *Richmond Dispatch*, July 25, 1862, 2; "Supposed Liquor Shops Closed," *Richmond Dispatch*, November 20, 1862, 1; "Special Notice," *Richmond Examiner*, October 8, 1862, 2. Robert Taylor was an African American man who went on to run his own restaurant briefly, and he seems to have left Richmond by 1871.

10. "Closing the Liquor 'Inlets,'" *Richmond Examiner*, November 20, 1862, 1.

11. "A Feast," *Richmond Whig*, December 9, 1862.

12. Wendell P. Dabney, autobiographical sketch, n.d., Mss qD115, Wendell P. Dabney Papers, 1904–1964, Cincinnati Museum Center, 18.

13. "The Courts," *Richmond Examiner*, April 20, 1863, 1. "Congress Hall," *Richmond Examiner*, May 1, 1863, 2; *Richmond Examiner*, June 11, 1863, 2.

14. Carol Gelderman, *A Free Man of Color and His Hotel: Race, Reconstruction, and the Role of the Federal Government* (Washington, D.C.: Potomac Books, 2012), 14–16; Terry L. Jones, *Historical Dictionary of the Civil War*, 2nd ed. (Lanham, Md.: Scarecrow, 2011), 2:1562–1563.

15. Sketches of the city of Washington on the eve of the war and after are collected in Marcus Benjamin, *Washington during War Time: A Series of Papers Showing the Military, Political, and Social Phases during 1861 to 1865* (Washington, D.C.: National Tribune Company, 1902), 3–11, 209.

16. "Closing of Hotels and Restaurant," *Daily National Republican*, March 2, 1863, 2.

17. Anthony Trollope, *North America* (New York: Harper and Brothers, 1862), 323.

18. "Boulanger's Restaurant for Sale," *Daily National Intelligencer*, July 16, 1862, 2; "Death," *Daily National Intelligencer*, August 22, 1862, 1; "By J.C. McGuire & Co, Auctioneers," *Washington Evening Star*, September 15, 1862, 2.

19. Trollope, *North America*, 309; Donet D. Graves, "Wormley Hotel," White House Historical Association, https://www.whitehousehistory.org /wormley-hotel-1.

20. "Buhler's," *Washington Evening Star*, December 21, 1861, 3; John DeFerrari, *Historic Restaurants of Washington, D.C.: Capital Eats* (Charleston: History Press, 2013), 46–47.

21. "Restaurants," *Daily National Republican*, May 11, 1864, 3, and February 6, 1864, 4; DeFerrari, *Historic Restaurants of Washington*, 25–26.

22. "Departure of the Orleans Cadets," *New Orleans Daily Picayune*, April 12, 1861, 1.

23. "The City," *New Orleans Daily Picayune*, November 6, 1861, 2.

24. "Restaurant of the Confederate States," *New Orleans Daily True Delta*, May 26, 1861, 4.

25. "Victor's Restaurant, On Boulevard Street," *Baton Rouge Advocate*, November 16, 1860, 1; David S. Shields, *The Culinarians: Lives and Careers from the First Age of American Fine Dining* (Chicago: University of Chicago Press, 2017), 313.

26. G. Howard Hunter, "Fall of New Orleans and Federal Occupation," in *Encyclopedia of Louisiana*, ed. David Johnson, July 27, 2011, http://www.64parishes .org/entry/fall-of-new-orleans-and-federal-occupation.

27. "Talk on the Flags," *New Orleans Crescent*, May 2, 1862, 1.

28. "The St. Louis Hotel," *New Orleans Daily Picayune*, December 31, 1865, 2; "Pompano," *New Orleans Daily Picayune*, July 27, 1862, 2; *New Orleans Daily Delta*, August 6, 1862, 1; "The St. Charles Hotel," *New Orleans Daily Picayune*, December 5, 1862, 2.

29. "Cassidy's Restaurant and Supper Rooms," *New Orleans Daily True Delta*, November 29, 1863, 3; "Communicated," *New Orleans Times-Democrat*, July 21, 1864, 1.

30. *Duncan & Co.'s New Orleans Business Directory for 1865* (New Orleans: Duncan, 1865), 95.

31. "Richelieu's Hotel, Bagdad, Mexico," *New Orleans Daily Picayune*, June 13, 1865, 6; "Victor's Restaurant," *Baton Rouge Tri-Weekly Gazette and Comet*, April 29, 1865, 4.

32. "City Intelligence," *Richmond Examiner*, June 11, 1863, 21; "Jim Cook," *Richmond Dispatch*, December 22, 1863, 2; "Jim Cook," *Richmond Examiner*, April 6, 1864, 1.

33. "Jim Cook Makes His Acknowledgments," *Richmond Examiner*, January 15, 1864, 1.

34. "A Wonder," *Richmond Whig*, May 3, 1864, 3; "At the Chickahominy," *Richmond Whig*, April 19, 1864, 2.

35. "Jim Cook, Julep Maker to the Prince of Wales," *Wilmington (N.C.) Journal*, September 29, 1864, 1.

36. Rutledge and Young records, 1860–1871, South Carolina Historical Society, Charleston, S.C..

37. William Howard Russell, *My Diary North and South* (Boston: T. O. H. P. Burnham, 1863), 98.

38. Walter J. Fraser Jr., *Charleston! Charleston!: The History of a Southern City* (Columbia: University of South Carolina Press, 1989), 253–255.

39. "A First Class Boarding House," *Charleston Mercury*, May 26, 1862, 2.

40. Fraser, *Charleston! Charleston!*, 261–269.

41. "Turtle Soup," *Charleston Mercury*, August 5, 1863, 2; "At the Bachelor's Retreat," *Charleston Mercury*, August 30, 1863, 2.

42. Mrs. St. Julien Ravenel, *Charleston: The Place and the People* (New York: Macmillan, 1906), 505.

43. "XCVII Anniversary of the German Friendly Society," *Charleston Mercury*, January 20, 1864, 2; "Fellowship Society," *Charleston Mercury*, March 9, 1864, 2; *Charleston Courier*, June 28, 1864, 1; "Turtle Soup and Wild Turkey," *Charleston Mercury*, September 21, 1864, 2. It is possible that by July of 1864, Tully and Vanderhorst had closed down their catering operation and left town. The list of unclaimed letters at the post office on July 8 included Tully's name. *Charleston Mercury*, July 8, 1864, 2.

44. Fraser, *Charleston! Charleston!*, 269. Details about the fire damage and the death toll were not captured in the local papers, since both the *Charleston Courier*

and the *Charleston Mercury* had ceased publication on February 17, their editors leaving town along with the retreating Confederate army. The best details about the Union occupation of Charleston can be found in the account of the *New York Tribune*'s special correspondent, who was traveling aboard the U.S. transport *Arago*. "The Fall of Charleston," *New York Tribune*, March 2, 1865, 1.

45. "The Fall of Charleston," 1.

46. "The Fall of Charleston," 1.

47. Fraser, *Charleston! Charleston!*, 272.

48. "From Charleston," *Edgefield Advertiser*, March 15, 1865, 2; "Nat Fuller," *Charleston Courier*, April 6, 1865, 3.

49. Mrs. Francis J. Porcher to Mrs. William McKenzie Parker, March 29, 1865, Smith Family Papers, South Caroliniana Library, University of South Carolina, Columbia, S.C.

CHAPTER 7. Reconstructing Southern Commercial Dining

1. "Notice," *Charleston Daily News*, April 20, 1866, 1; "Notice," *Charleston Daily Mail*, June 23, 1866, 4. What happened to Vanderhorst is uncertain, but she does not appear to have been involved in the culinary business after the Civil War.

2. Rutledge and Young records, 1860–1871, South Carolina Historical Society, Charleston, S.C.

3. Peter Gaillard Gourdin IV, comp., *The Gourdin Family* (Easley, S.C.: Southern Historical Press, 1980), 497.

4. "Mortuary Notice," *New York Herald*, July 10, 1874, 3.

5. "Notice," *Charleston Daily News*, June 11, 1866, 4.

6. "Our Firemen at Charleston," Augusta *Daily Constitutionalist*, May 1, 1866, 3.

7. Fuller v. Gatewood case records, 431.02 (F) 06, Simons & Simons records, 1714–1879, South Carolina Historical Society, Charleston, S.C.

8. "City of Charleston Death Certificates," *South Carolina Death Records, 1850–1874*, South Carolina Department of Archives and History, December 16–22, 1866, digital image; 1870 United States Federal Census, Charleston Ward 4, Charleston, South Carolina, roll M593_1486, page 112, digital image s.v. "Diana Fuller"; *Registers of Signatures of Depositors in Branches of the Freedman's Savings and Trust Company, 1865–1874*, Records of the Office of the Comptroller of the Currency, National Archives, Washington, D.C., RG 101, series M816, roll 23, Charleston, South Carolina, February 25, 1871–July 2, 1872, number 6629, digital image s.v. "Diana Fuller," all accessed via Ancestry.com.

9. "The Mansion House," *Charleston Daily News*, May 30, 1868, 3; "Hotels," *Charleston Daily News*, June 2, 1868, 2.

10. "A Grateful Present," *Charleston Daily News*, July 3, 1867, 3; "Tully," *Charleston Courier*, December 24, 1869, 1.

11. "First Class Restaurant," *Charleston Courier*, April 19, 1865, 2; advertisement, *Charleston Courier*, May 24, 1865, 2. We can assume that Johnston, like many hotel workers before Emancipation, was enslaved. Free persons of color were listed in the Charleston city directories, but enslaved persons were not, and Johnston does not appear in any of the extant directories before 1865.

12. "Twenty Dollars Reward," *Charleston Courier*, May 25, 1855, 2; "William H. Wigg vs. Charles H. Simonton," *Reports of Cases at Law and in Equity: Argued and Determined in the Court of Appeals and Court of Errors of South Carolina* vol. 12, *Jan 1859–May 1860* (Charleston: McCarter, 1860), 583–594. William H. Wigg sued Simonton for $3,000, the amount he claimed the attorney's interference in his efforts to sell his two half brothers had cost him. He lost in both the lower court and the court of appeals, which ruled Simonton's actions were nothing more than the good-faith obligations of an attorney representing his clients.

13. "Sheriff's Sale," *Charleston Mercury*, March 28, 1858, 3.

14. "George's Restaurant," *Charleston Courier*, October 18, 1865, 2; "Wigg & Co. Restaurant," *South Carolina Leader*, December 9, 1865, 3.

15. "Burglar Arrested," *Charleston Daily News*, May 14, 1866, 5.

16. Wm. H. Grimshaw, *Official History of Freemasonry among the Colored People in North America* (New York: Broadway, 1898), 263–264; "To All Whom These Presents May Come, Greetings," *Charleston Courier*, September 9, 1865, 2.

17. *Charleston City Directory for 1867–68* (Charleston: J. Orrin Lea, 1867), 56; *Jowett's Illustrated Charleston City Directory and Business Register, 1869–70* (Charleston: Walker, Evans, and Cogswell, 1869), 75; "Office of Clerk of Council," *Charleston Courier*, January 12, 1857, 2; "Our House," *Charleston Courier*, July 31, 1867, 2; "Christmas," *Charleston Mercury*, December 22, 1860, 2; "Mr. Charles Litschgi Dead," *Charleston Evening Post*, April 13, 1906, 5; "Fehrenbach's Temperance Restaurant," *Charleston Courier*, December 14, 1859, 2; "Full List of the Losses," *Charleston Mercury*, December 14, 1861, 1; "Billiards! Billiards! Billiards!," *Charleston Mercury*, March 3, 1868, 2.

18. "The Fire at Milneburg," *New Orleans Daily Picayune*, June 3, 1865, 2.

19. "Observations by Rambler—No. 12," *New Orleans Times*, November 19, 1865, 6.

20. Edward H. Hall, *Appleton's Hand-book of American Travel: The Southern Tour* (New York: D. Appleton, 1866), 108.

21. Virginius Dabney, *Richmond: The Story of a City*, rev. ed. (Charlottesville: University Press of Virginia, 1990), 189–191; John Leyburn, "The Fall of Richmond," qtd. in John T. O'Brien, "Reconstruction in Richmond: White Restoration and Black Protest, April–June 1865," *Virginia Magazine of History and Biography* 89 (July 1981): 261.

22. Private Journal No. 2, David Dixon Porter Papers, Library of Congress. Online at https://www.civilwarrichmond.com/written-accounts/archival-sources /library-of-congress/639-1865-library-of-congress-david-dixon-porter-papers -excellent-contemporary-recollection-of-lincoln-s-visit-to-richmond.

23. Qtd. in O'Brien, "Reconstruction in Richmond," 264.

24. "The Reception of the News of the President's Murder in Richmond," *New York Herald*, rpt. *Belvidere (Ill.) Standard*, April 25, 1865, 2.

25. O'Brien, "Reconstruction in Richmond," 271–274. Black Richmonders chafed under the daily harassment they received at the hands of Union troops, but their appeals to military authorities fell on deaf ears. In early June, Mayor Joseph Mayo, who had held office since 1853, was allowed to resume power, and he returned the old civic police force to the streets. This was a direct affront to black Richmonders, since Mayo had for years ordered harsh punishments for trifling offenses against slave laws, and the very same white police officers who had executed those punishments were once again patrolling the city's streets.

26. "The Richmond Freedmen," *New York Tribune* June 17, 1865, 1.

27. "Condition of the Colored People of Richmond," *National Republican*, June 19, 1865, 1; "Reception of the Colored Delegation by the President," *Wilmington Herald*, June 23, 1865, 1.

28. "The Convention of Colored Men at Alexandria," *Richmond Whig*, April 11, 1865, 4.

29. "Turtle Soup!," *Richmond Whig*, August 25, 1865, 2; "Sora," *Richmond Whig*, September 5, 1865, 3; "Oysters," *Richmond Whig*, September 29, 1865, 3.

30. "Dabney's House," *Richmond Whig*, September 22, 1865, 3; Wendell P. Dabney, autobiographical sketch, n.d., Mss qD115, Wendell P. Dabney Papers, 1904–1964, Cincinnati Museum Center, 37.

31. "Zetelle vs. Meyers," *Richmond Whig*, June 14, 1867, 3; "The City," *Richmond Whig*, March 15, 1872, 1.

32. Arthur F. Loux, *John Wilkes Booth: Day-by-Day* (Jefferson, N.C.: McFarland, 2014), 190.

33. John DeFerrari, *Historic Restaurants of Washington, D.C.: Capital Eats* (Charleston: History Press, 2013), 25–26.

34. George Alfred Townsend, *Washington, Outside and Inside* (Hartford, Conn.: James Betts, 1874), 176.

35. "'Fourth' in Washington," *Daily National Republican*, July 5, 1865, 1.

36. S. A. M. Washington, *George Thomas Downing: Sketch of His Life and Times* (Newport, R.I.: Milne Printery, 1910), 3–10; "September's Last in Newport," *Springfield (Mass.) Republican*, October 11, 1860.

37. Washington, *George Thomas Downing*, 8–10; "George T. Downing: A Sketch of His Eventful Life," *Cleveland Gazette*, May 2, 1885, 1.

38. "Mr. Downing Makes His Retiring Bow as an Agitator," *Providence Evening Press*, August 29, 1860, 2.

39. "Convention of the Colored People of New England," *Boston Herald*, December 2, 1865, 2; "The Cause of the Freedmen," *Newark Daily Advertiser*, December 13, 1865, 2.

40. *Detroit Free Press*, January 24, 1866.

41. "Important Expression of Views by the President," *Washington Evening Star*, February 7, 1866, 3.

42. LaWanda Cox and John H. Cox, *Politics, Principle, and Prejudice, 1865–1866: Dilemma of Reconstruction America* (New York: Free Press, 1963), 163. This remarkable encounter with the president has been captured by numerous historians of Reconstruction, but they tend to omit Downing's name from the account, describing the delegation as consisting of "Frederick Douglass and several other black leaders." Contemporary newspaper accounts, however, make it clear that Downing was the leader of the group and spoke first, with Douglass chiming in second.

43. Eric Foner, *Reconstruction: America's Unfinished Revolution, 1863–1877* (New York: Harper and Row, 1988), 159–161; "The Colored Men's Protest," *New York Evening Post*, February 19, 1866, 2. In October, Commissioner Howard of the Freedmen's Bureau informed a gathering of African Americans on Edisto Island, who during the war had settled on confiscated land on the South Carolina coast, that after harvesting their crops they would have to give the land back to its former owners. The Bureau shifted its efforts to urging African Americans to sign labor contracts, which usually meant working for their old masters on the same land where they were formerly enslaved. Throughout the South, both federal and local officials tried to compel many of the African Americans who had flooded into the cities to return to agricultural labor, enforcing provisions that Blacks had to have written proof of employment or leave for the countryside.

44. "The Proposed Third of April Celebration," *Richmond Examiner*, March 27, 1866, 3; "The Negro Celebration the Third of April," *Richmond Examiner*, March 31, 1866, 3; Virginia Museum of History and Culture, "Broadside, from the Committee, 2 April 1866," https://virginiahistory.org/broadside-committee-2-april-1866; "Freedmen's Celebration in Richmond," *Alexandria Gazette*, April 4, 1866, 2; "A Bugbear Disposed Of," *Philadelphia Inquirer*, April 6, 1866, 4.

45. "Views of Ex-Governor Wise," *Richmond Whig*, April 20, 1866, 1.

46. "At the Anniversary Meeting of the Richmond Blues," *Alexandria Gazette*, May 12, 1866, 2.

47. Dabney, autobiographical sketch, 12–13. The Dabneys lived next door to "the Old Church," which is to say the African Baptist church, which had been built in 1802 as the First Baptist Church and originally housed a white congregation. Over the years, more and more African Americans had begun attending—many

of them accompanying their owners to Sunday services—until the congregation was more Black than white. In 1841 the church split, with the white First Baptist Church constructing a new building and the Black members retaining occupancy of the old one.

48. "Honorable," *Richmond Enquirer*, rpt. *Alexandria Gazette*, September 26, 1866, 1; "An Honorable Negro," *Richmond Examiner*, rpt. *Tarboro Southerner* October 20, 1866, 2; "John Dabney," *Weekly Freedman's Press*, July 18, 1868, 3.

CHAPTER 8. Positions Lucrative, Commanding Respect

1. "Negro Impudence," *Harrisburg Patriot*, May 24, 1866, 8; "Utterly Repudiated," *Lancaster Intelligencer*, rpt. *Southern Aegis*, June 8, 1866, 3.

2. "The Negroes Dissatisfied with the Reconstruction Committee's Report," *Charleston Daily News*, May 22, 1866, 8; "Meeting of the Colored Folks," *New York Daily Herald*, May 11, 1866, 10. Frederick Douglass echoed Downing's sentiments in even stronger terms, calling the plan "a criminal abandonment of the colored people of the South to the 'tender mercies' of their old masters." Across the South, African Americans flocked to political rallies and joined their local Union Leagues, which were emerging as the political voice of poor, newly emancipated southerners. Convening in churches, schools, and private homes, the League's local members pledged loyalty to the Republican Party and the cause of civil rights, and they threw their energies into political education as well as raising funds for building new schools and churches. See Eric Foner, *Reconstruction: America's Unfinished Revolution, 1863–1877* (New York: Harper and Row, 1988), 285.

3. "Local Department," *Daily National Republican*, December 14, 1867, 3; "A Word in Season," *Virginian-Pilot*, January 18, 1868, 2. In December 1867 the *Weekly Sentinel* of Raleigh reported that the National Union League was meeting "in session (secret) in Washington several days last week. This, we presume, accounts for the presence there of Fields Cook and other negroes from this and other Southern States." The National Council of the Union League was indeed meeting in Washington, but its sessions were hardly secret. The Council published the minutes for the sessions in multiple D.C. newspapers, including the detail that Fields Cook was appointed the council's chaplain. "The National Loyal League," *Weekly Sentinel*, December 24, 1867, 2.

4. "Fields Cook, Negro," *Staunton Spectator*, April 27, 1869 2; "The Canvass in Virginia," *New York Herald*, May 24, 1869, 5. Hunnicutt was something of a chameleon when it came to his political convictions. In 1860, as the editor of the *Christian Banner* in Fredericksburg, he had been a Democrat and a vocal opponent of secession, but for a rather odd reason: he maintained secession would lead to war, which in turn would cause the end of slavery, for which he was a vocal proponent. Hunnicutt's Unionism alienated him from Fredericksburg's white

population, and he hightailed it to Philadelphia, where he spent the remainder of the war advocating for the Union and supporting Republican candidates. In the fall of 1865 he made his way to Richmond and launched the *New Nation*, a Republican newspaper, and immersed himself in local politics. He was the featured speaker at the controversial 1866 celebration of the first anniversary of the fall of Richmond to Union troops. See Matthew S. Gottlieb, " Hunnicutt, James W. (1814–1880)," in *The Dictionary of Virginia Biography* and in *Encyclopedia Virginia*, http://www.encyclopediavirginia.org/entries/hunnicutt-james-w-1814-1880.

5. "Virginia Elections," *Richmond Whig*, July 20, 1869, 2; "A Card," *Richmond Whig*, July 13, 1869, 1.

6. "Through the South," *New York Times*, June 10, 1867, 2; "In Trouble," *Richmond Whig*, May 4, 1869, 4. An editor's note about Fields Cook in the *Alexandria Gazette* in 1873 mentions his brother Jim's making juleps for the Prince of Wales and adds, "Jim, poor fellow, 'sleeps in the valley'" ("Personal," March 20, 1873, 3). In June 1867 a correspondent for the *New York Times* noticed a man tending the bar at the railroad depot in the small town of Burkesville, some fifty miles southwest of Richmond. A placard behind the bar announced, "The celebrated new drink by JIM COOK—Squint you foolishness." When the reporter asked Cook why he had given it that name, the bartender replied cryptically that he had "wanted to get it right." Less than two years later, Cook had moved further west to Harrisonburg, where he found work at Hill's Hotel. That May, Cook got into an altercation with Sam Garnet, one of the hotel's teamsters, who "applied offensive epithets" to him. Cook seized a butcher knife and stabbed Garnet several times in the arm and side, leaving a six-inch wound between Garnet's shoulder blade and ribs. The injury was not fatal, and Cook was released on a $250 bond from the hotel's owner. Within three years Jim Cook was dead, but where and how he died is not known. "Provost Court," *Richmond Whig*, September 29, 1865, 3.

7. "George T. Downing," *Anamosa (Iowa) Eureka*, April 30, 1868, 4; "The Levee of the Knights Templar," *Washington Evening Star*, April 16, 1868, 4; "Personal," San Francisco *Elevator*, June 19, 1868 2.

8. "The Well-Known Geo. T. Downing" and "The Senate Saloon," *Washington Daily Critic*, March 26, 1869, 4; "Washington Gossip," *New York Daily Herald*, February 21, 1870, 8. In February 1870, after temperance newspapers ran editorials condemning the presence of alcohol in the Capitol building, the House and Senate sergeants at arms ordered the two restaurateurs to cease and desist the sale of "strong coffee." They appear to have complied for a brief period until the controversy blew over.

9. *Springfield (Mass.) Republican*, February 10, 1869, 4.

10. "Downing and the Kitchen Cabinet," *New York Tribune*, February 19, 1869, 5.

11. "A Negro Applicant for the Position of Minister to Hayti," *New York Herald*, March 16, 1869, 3; "Visitors at the White House," *Boston Daily Advocate*, May 14,

1869, 1; "Address to the Colored People," *San Francisco Bulletin*, February 17, 1870, 1.

12. "Half Dozen on the Half Shell," *New York Herald*, June 2, 1869, 6; "From Washington," *Macon Weekly Telegraph*, April 12, 1870, 1; "An Austere Oyster Vendor," *Missouri Republican*, rpt. *Daily Milwaukee News*, January 22, 1871, 4. Amid all this criticism, Downing remained undeterred, and he continued to expand his activities and his network of influence. When Hiram Revels, the African American senator-elect from Mississippi, arrived in D.C., he stayed as guest in Downing's residence on Capitol Hill. In February 1870, Downing and Frederick Douglass were among the incorporators of the New Era Printing and Publishing Company, whose *New National Era*, under Douglass's editorship, was the first national newspaper aimed at an African American audience.

13. "Not Correct," *Washington Chronicle*, rpt. *Baltimore Sun*, August 4, 1868 1;

14. "In the Supreme Court of the District of Columbia," *National Republican*, December 12, 1868, 4; "*Providence Evening Press*, November 6, 1868, 1; advertisement, *Washington Evening Star*, January 11, 1869, 2; "The Wedding Last Night," *Washington Evening Star*, September 25, 1868, 2; "Washington News and Gossip," *Boston Journal*, December 23, 1868, 2.

15. Benjamin Perley Poore, *Perley's Reminiscences of Sixty Years in the National Metropolis* (Philadelphia: Hubbard Brothers, 1886), 2:247–248; George Alfred Townsend, *Washington, Outside and Inside* (Hartford: James Betts, 1874), 176.

16. "Minor Notes," *Washington Capital*, April 4, 1875, 4. In *The Culinarians: Lives and Careers from the First Age of American Fine Dining* (Chicago: University of Chicago Press, 2017), David Shields incorrectly describes Wormley as "notoriously reticent about politics (aside from the simple attestation that he was a Republican)" (198). Unlike Downing, Wormley had been born and raised in slaveholding Washington, D.C., and in the 1830s he witnessed firsthand the violence that could be visited on those who dared to buck the order of things—including the economic ruin that contributed to the premature death of his brother William. As late as the 1880s, the schoolhouse that William had built for their sister—the one that had been ransacked during the Snow Riots and later repaired—was still standing in the rear of James Wormley's restaurant. For details about the schoolhouse, see George W. Williams, *History of the Negro Race in America from 1619 to 1880* (New York: G. P. Putnam's Sons, 1883), 2:205–206.

17. "Colored Schools! ," *Daily National Republican*, January 8, 1870, 4; "Local Politics," *Daily National Republican*, April 1, 1870, 4; "The Fifteenth Amendment," *Washington Evening Star*, April 2, 1870, 4. Wormley was among the attendees at a meeting of the Republican Party in April 1870 that became so raucous that police had to be summoned to restore order. At issue was the process for appointing delegates to the upcoming Republican convention, but the meeting ended on a positive note when Wormley was tapped to plan the celebration of the pending

ratification of the Fifteenth Amendment to the Constitution, which guaranteed the right of all men to vote. The following day, the 1st Ward Republicans gathered at Stevens Schoolhouse for a brief meeting, at the conclusion of which "Mr. James Wormley requested that all give three cheers for the President of the United States." The members then proceeded to the White House, where they serenaded President Grant and listened as the president, Charles Sumner, and others delivered remarks upon the importance of the amendment and its guarantee of the franchise to all men.

18. *Laws of the Corporation of the City of Washington* (Washington: Chronicle Print, 1869), 22; "Social Equality," *Charleston Daily News*, December 24, 1869, 3; "Medical Department Howard University," *Washington Evening Star*, March 3, 1870, 4; Carol Gelderman, *A Free Man of Color and His Hotel: Race, Reconstruction, and the Role of the Federal Government* (Washington, D.C.: Potomac Books, 2012), 18–19. The "Negro Theatre Imbroglio" got picked up in newspapers as far away as New York and San Francisco. The *Charleston Daily News* on December 24, 1869, offered the incident as a lesson to South Carolina's Republican legislature as it considered its own civil rights measures, one that captured the catch-22 position of African American restaurateurs in a white-dominated economy. "The point of the joke," the *Daily News* sneered, "is that . . . Wormley, the famous colored caterer, will not allow a colored person to be served in his restaurant at any price. . . . The colored people should themselves desist from discriminating against their own color in barber shops and restaurants, before they attempt to prevent the whites from managing their own business in their own way." Apart from this one claim, there is no evidence that Wormley denied service to African Americans in his hotel or dining rooms.

19. Katti Gray, "Respecting the Black Family Story," *Howard Magazine*, Winter 2017, https://magazine.howard.edu/categories/features-sesquicentennial /respecting-black-family-story. The month following his defeat in the alderman race, William Wormley was appointed by Mayor Emery to be one of the three members of the Board of Trustees of Colored Schools. He united with William Syphax, the president of the board, and over the year that followed he was embroiled in constant controversies over the management of the schools, ranging from the training of teachers to selecting the recipients of building contracts.

20. "Colored Men of Washington," *Washington Capital*, April 16, 1871, 4.

21. William Henry Charlton, *Four Months in North America* (Hexham, Northumb.: J. Catherall, 1873), 50.

22. "Current Notes," *Boston Journal*, March 10, 1868 2; "The Marriage of Paul Gerard and the Pretty Octoroon," *Washington Evening Star*, December 8, 1869, 5; *New York Tribune*, November 27, 1869, 6. Many newspapers outside of Washington incorrectly identified Maria Wormley as "the daughter of the well-known negro caterer and restaurant keeper," but she was in fact his niece.

23. "Notes and Comments," *Detroit Free Press*, July 22, 1870, 2; "An Outrage on Downing," *New York Herald*, July 18, 1870, 7.

24. "A Visit to the South by a Northern Colored Man," *New York Times*, January 14, 1871. There has been some confusion over whether Downing ever resumed operating a restaurant in the Capitol building. In *The Culinarians* David Shields states, "When expelled as keeper of the House Restaurant in 1876, President pro tempore of the Senate Thomas W. Ferry, gave George Downing the position of Keeper of the Senate Restaurant" (255). Newspaper accounts, however, make clear that Downing actually lost the House position in 1870, not 1876. A frontpage article in the *Daily National Intelligencer* on July 27, 1876, titled "A New Keeper of the Senate Restaurant" indeed announced that Ferry had given the position to Downing. The following day, however, the newspaper ran a correction: "There seems to be some mistake about the disposition of Mr. Dempster from the proprietorship of the Senate restaurant and the installment of Mr. Downing." Dempster was having legal difficulties and had been out of town recovering from an illness, and Mr. Ferry had stated his intention to make a change after that season, but Downing was just one of several candidates, the strongest of whom was Mr. George DeShields.

25. "George T. Downing on the Radical Party," *New York Herald*, April 29, 1871, 6; "The Colored Troops Abandoning the Republican Camp," *Schenectady Reflector*, February 23, 1871, 2; "The Duty of Colored Voters," *New York Tribune*, rpt. *Weekly Louisianian*, November 2, 1871, 2.

26. "Barely Eleven," *Daily National Republican*, August 2, 1872, 2; "The Political Outlook," *Brooklyn Daily Eagle*, August 19, 1872, 2. The *Daily National Republic* offered to publish the names of all the African American men in the city who supported Sumner's course. They received just one letter, signed by eleven men. Two of them were James Wormley and William H. A. Wormley, and caterer John A. Gray was a third.

27. "The Late Charles Sumner," *Daily Graphic*, March 12, 1874, 6. George Downing and Frederick Douglass never fully patched things up after their falling-out over the election, and in 1874 Downing again got sideways with the *New National Era*, which was by that point under the editorship of Douglass's two sons. The *Elevator* of San Francisco suggested that at least part of the problem was personalities. The editors insisted upon their affection for Downing, stating that "a purer, nobler man never lived, and generous withal." At the same time it admitted, "He had his foibles, imperative, vain." Things continued to escalate. In May, newspapers reported that Downing had asserted that Frederick Douglass's sons "haven't inherited the brains of papa." The younger Douglasses responded in the *New Era* that Downing was "a petulant, notoriety hunting, vain old man" and ripped him as a "colored demagogue" and "champion egotist of our race." "The New National Era," *Elevator*, May 2, 1874, 2; *Newport Mercury*, May 9, 1874, 2.

28. Foner, *Reconstruction*, 558; "A Colored Man's Letter," *Boston Pilot*, rpt. *Congregationalist*, March 25, 1875, 2. In the South, armed bands of whites roamed the countryside intimidating voters, murdering dozens of African Americans in the process. The Republican Party, meanwhile, was evolving away from being the party of civil rights and toward championing the causes of northern business, and white Republicans increasingly saw Reconstruction as a political liability.

29. For a detailed account of the Hayes-Tilden drama and the Wormley Conference, see Gelderman, *A Free Man of Color*, 93–109.

30. Gelderman, *A Free Man of Color*, 108.

31. "Let Politics Alone," *People's Advocate*, rpt. *New York Globe*, July 28, 1883, 1.

32. "Local Affairs," *Newport Daily News*, May 25, 1877, 2; "George T. Downing: A Sketch of His Eventful Life," *Cleveland Gazette*, May 2, 1885, 1; "New York City," *New York Tribune*, October 9, 1878, 8.

CHAPTER 9. Augusta, Georgia

1. "Civil Rights," *Augusta Chronicle*, March 9, 1875, 4.

2. Leroy Davis, *A Clashing of the Soul: John Hope and the Dilemma of African American Leadership and Black Higher Education in the Early Twentieth Century* (Athens: University of Georgia Press, 1998), 3–4.

3. *Freedman's Bank Records*, 1865–1874, Augusta, Georgia, roll 7, November 23, 1870–June 29, 1874, image 82, National Archives and Records Administration, Washington, D.C., s.v. "Lexius Henson," accessed via Ancestry.com.

4. "Notice," *Loyal Georgian*, March 17, 1866, 4. One historian called the Terri "an oasis of freedom for ex-slaves seeking a new life in Augusta." The noted African American educator John Hope, who was born into Augusta's elite Black community in the 1860s, described many of the residents of the Terri as "human wrecks of swift emancipation. People left too old and helpless or too ignorant, though young, to discharge a freedman's obligation to society. . . . They were poor, but they were individual people." Davis, *A Clashing of the Soul*, 26–27.

5. *Haddock's Augusta, Ga. Directory and General Advertiser* (Augusta: E. H. Pugh, 1872), 192; "Turtle Soup," *Augusta Chronicle*, April 15, 1873, 2; "Fresh Oysters on Shell!," *Augusta Chronicle*, October 8, 1873, 3; "A New Feature in the Saloon Business," *Augusta Chronicle*, October 25, 1872, 3.

6. *Haddock's Augusta, Ga. Directory*, 14, 21, 47; *Hand Book of Augusta: A Guide to the Principal Points in and about the City* (Augusta, Ga.: Chronicle and Constitutionalist Book and Job Printing, 1878), 74–75.

7. *Haddock's Augusta, Ga. Directory*, 105; "Atlantic Saloon," *Augusta Chronicle*, October 15, 1872, 3; "Attention!," *Augusta Chronicle*, June 4, 1873, 3; "Henry Heitsch," *Camden Journal*, October 23, 1879, 9; "The City Fathers," *Augusta*

Chronicle, August 3, 1875, 4; "Globe Hotel Bar," *Augusta Chronicle,* October 4, 1878, 2; "Personal and General," *Augusta Chronicle,* September 24, 1885, 8.

8. "Co-Partnership," *Daily Constitutionalist,* July 19 1866, 3; "To Rent," *Augusta Chronicle,* November 9, 1878, 3; Meg Monthan, "Woodson Wood," Find a Grave, https://www.findagrave.com/memorial/147001856. James F. Heuisler launched the Shades restaurant on Ellis Street in November 1864. In July the following year, he and O. K. Hilliard opened the Office restaurant. By the end of 1865, Heuisler was back on Ellis Street at what he was calling the Old Shades Saloon, which he sold in May 1866 and the new proprietors renamed the Alhambra. He was a partner in a firm called Heuisler & Brady for a few years, which may have operated a restaurant, before moving to the Opera House Arcade at the end of 1871. See "Restaurants," *Daily Constitutionalist,* November 4, 1864, 3; "The Office Restaurant," *Daily Constitutionalist,* July 23, 1865, 4; "Old Shades Saloon," *Daily Constitutionalist,* December 1, 1865, 2; "Alhambra Restaurant," *Augusta Chronicle,* May 6, 1866, 2.

9. "Civil Rights at the Atlanta Theatre Monday Night," *Macon Weekly Telegraph,* March 16, 1875, 4; "The Civil Rights War," *New Orleans Daily Picayune,* November 16, 1875, 2; George C. Wright, *Life Behind a Veil: Blacks in Louisville, Kentucky, 1865–1930* (1985; rpt., Baton Rouge: Louisiana State University Press, 2004), 57.

10. "Exchange Saloon and Restaurant," *Augusta Chronicle,* November 28, 1875, 3; *Hand Book of Augusta,* 75; "Handsome Set of China," *Augusta Chronicle,* December 8, 1878, 4.

11. *Hand Book of Augusta,* 75; "Handsome Set of China," *Augusta Chronicle,* December 8, 1878, 4; "Brevities," *Augusta Chronicle,* June 28, 1883, 6.

12. "The National Dental Association," *American Journal of Dental Science* 13 (1880): 154; "A Welcome to Mr. Randall," *Augusta Chronicle,* July 8, 1879, 4; "First of the Season," *Augusta Chronicle,* September 22, 1877, 8.

13. "Our House Restaurant," *Augusta Chronicle,* November 4, 1877, 2; *Sholes' Georgia State Gazetteer and Business Directory for 1879 & 1880* (Atlanta: A. E. Sholes, 1879), 917.

14. Davis, *A Clashing of the Soul,* 30–37; autobiographical sketch, John Hope Collection, AUC Robert Woodruff Library Archives, Atlanta University.

15. *Hand Book of Augusta;* Edward J. Cashin, *The Story of Augusta* (Augusta: Richmond County Board of Education, 1980), 149–154.

16. "The Windsor Cafe Is a Concern," *Augusta Chronicle,* October 1, 1882, 6; "The Windsor Cafe," *Augusta Chronicle,* November 30, 1882, 4.

17. "Brevities," *Augusta Chronicle,* October 7, 1882, 4; "Caufman's Banquet," *Augusta Chronicle,* October 18, 1882, 4; "Independent Firemen," *Augusta Chronicle,* November 14, 1882, 4.

18. "The Bartenders' Sunday Night," *New York Herald,* November 24, 1885, 9; "Personal," *Augusta Chronicle,* December 20, 1887, 8.

19. Population statistics calculated by the author from data sets downloaded from the IPUMS National Historical Geographic Information System, https://www.nhgis.org/user-resources/datasets-overview.

20. 1880 United States Federal Census, Augusta, Richmond County, Georgia, roll 163, enumeration district 098, digital image, accessed via Ancestry.com.

21. Ibid., page 293; *Sholes' Augusta City Directory, 1882* (Augusta, Ga.: Sholes, 1882), 356; "John Sancken, 86. Augusta Leader, Taken by Death," *Augusta Chronicle*, December 19, 1946, 1.

22. "The New Windsor," *Augusta Chronicle*, June 3, 1883, 6; "An Auspicious Opening," *Augusta Chronicle*, September 8, 1885, 5.

23. "Who They Are! The Men at The Head of the Augusta Exposition," *Augusta Chronicle*, January 8, 1888, 5.

24. Advertisement, *Augusta Chronicle*, August 18, 1889, 7.

25. "Significant Signs, Wherein There Is Evidence of Our Progress," *Augusta Chronicle*, October 29, 1888, 4; "A Royal Spread," *Augusta Chronicle*, October 11, 1889, 8.

26. "Connelly's Restaurant," *Augusta Chronicle*, October 26, 1889 5.

27. "Lexius Henson," *Augusta Chronicle*, August 29, 1883, 6; "Distinguished Visitor," *Augusta Chronicle*, October 5, 1883, 6.

28. "Old Chronicle Building Sold," *Augusta Chronicle*, June 4, 1885, 8; "Commercial House [advertisement]," *Augusta Chronicle*, January 27, 1887, 6.

29. "The Colored Race. The Wonderful Progress Which It Has Made in Money Getting Its Capacity," *Cleveland Gazette*, October 23, 1886, 1; Richmond County, Georgia Tax Digests, 1890, Georgia Archives, Morrow, Ga.

30. "Lexius Henson Fails," *Columbia State*, January 21, 1892, 1; "Affairs in Augusta," *Charleston News and Courier*, January 21, 1892, 2nd ed., 2; "Henson Closed Up," *Atlanta Constitution*, January 21, 1892, 1.

31. "Sued on Open Accounts," *Louisville Courier-Journal*, March 31, 1887, 7.

32. "The New Delmonico," *Aiken (S.C.) Standard*, March 23, 1892, 4.

33. "Death of Lexius Henson," *Atlanta Constitution*, October 11, 1892.

34. Richmond County Marriage Records, 1828–1978, page 193, Georgia Archives, Morrow, Ga.; "John Sancken, 86. Augusta Leader, Taken by Death," *Augusta Chronicle*, December 19, 1946, 1.

35. "Charles Henson at the Windsor," *Augusta Chronicle*, December 1, 1901, 16; "A Rushing Business—Charlie Henson Continues to Grow in Favor," *Augusta Chronicle*, January 26, 1902, 8.

36. "The Metropole Finest Cafe in the South," *Augusta Chronicle*, October 18, 1903, 13; "Charles W. Henson Died Yesterday," *Augusta Chronicle*, October 23, 1908, 2.

1. Bobby L. Lovett, *The African-American History of Nashville, Tennessee: 1780–1930* (Fayetteville: University of Arkansas Press, 1999), 107–108; *King's Nashville City Directory* (Nashville, 1868), 203.

2. Conservatives insisted that nonresident African Americans were flooding into the city to vote illegally, and they charged Sumner and Harding with keeping in their saloons stacks of voter registration certificates, already presigned by the registrar, to hand out to the newcomers. The court testimony from the case paints wildly contradictory pictures, but it seems that instead of widespread fraud there were just a handful of voters who, through simple error or ignorance of the rules, tried to vote without valid certificates. "The Election Frauds," *Tennessean*, August 6, 1867, 4; "City Affairs," *Nashville Union and American*, January 16, 1868, 1.

3. "How It Will Work—The Civil Rights Law in Its Practical Bearings," *Tennessean*, March 2, 1875, 4. Sumner did, however, believe that the Black populace would take full advantage of integrated railroad cars, for African Americans—even women and children—were currently forced to ride in the smoking car.

4. "Smith & Harding," *Tennessean*, January 21, 1871, 2; "In Chancery at Nashville," *Tennessean*, August 27, 1872, 2; "Death of Henry Harding," *Tennessean*, March 9, 1888, 4; "Estate of Henry Harding," *Daily American*, June 20, 1888, 5; "The Lincoln Colonization Society," *Tennessean*, February 22, 1877, 4.

5. "George & Dan Restaurant," *Louisville Courier-Journal*, December 21, 1873, 4.

6. "Assignees Sale in Bankruptcy," *Louisville Courier-Journal*, July 25, 1876, 4; "Old Dan Clements Dying," *Louisville Courier-Journal*, May 9, 1884 8. Between restaurant stints, George Brown took a federal government job as a Treasury "storekeeper" inspecting the record keeping and tax filings of the city's many whiskey distilleries and wholesalers. He ran into legal trouble in 1877 when he was arrested for allegedly stealing property worth ten dollars from the Conservatory of Music. After securing his release, Brown wrote a letter to the *Courier-Journal* expressing dismay at his treatment. "It is true that I am but a very humble colored man," Brown wrote, "but my honesty was never before questioned. . . . It is hard enough for a laboring man to earn a living any way, but it is next to impossible for him to do so if he is arrested without probable cause and his guilt is assumed and declared in the newspapers, when he is entirely innocent of crime." "George Brown's Innocence," *Louisville Courier-Journal*, February 1, 1877, 4.

7. "Lt. Browning Wins His Suit," *Louisville Courier-Journal*, October 28, 1884, 7; "George Brown," *Louisville Courier-Journal*, August 28, 1884, 8; "George Brown Dead," *Louisville Courier-Journal*, June 9, 1898, 6. Shortly after returning from Chicago, Brown secured a food concession at the Second Southern Exposition, operating a dining room in the northeast corner of the exhibition hall. At a press dinner held there, he wowed the delegation of visiting journalists with a spread of

fruit, "golden soup," salmon "a la Geo. and Dan," frog legs and peas, sweetbreads, and young prairie chicken with salad. Brown had overextended himself to purchase the concession, though, which forced him to declare bankruptcy two months later.

8. "Mr. James Wormley," *Daily Critic*, April 3, 1882, 2.

9. Carol Gelderman, *A Free Man of Color and His Hotel: Race, Reconstruction, and the Role of the Federal Government* (Washington, D.C.: Potomac Books, 2012), 117–118.

10. "James Wormley," *Boston Journal*, October 21, 1884, 4; "The Late James Wormley," *Philadelphia Press*, rpt. *Harrisburg State Journal*, October 25, 1884, 1.

11. "The Golden Opportunity," *Chicago Tribune*, May 26, 1894, 13.

12. Colonel Goodbody, "Our Daily Food: A Meal in the Nation's Capital," *Pittsburgh Courier*, May 7, 1932, 7. The author has been unable to determine whether there is an actual relationship between Colonel Goodbody and his possible descendant Slim.

13. "Cool and Refreshing," *Richmond Whig*, July 21, 1868, 3.

14. Wendell P. Dabney, autobiographical sketch, n.d., Mss qD115, Wendell P. Dabney Papers, 1904–1964, Cincinnati Museum Center, 17, 53.

15. Dabney, autobiographical sketch, 46–47.

16. "How Dabney Bought His Freedom," *Lexington Leader*, rpt. *Springfield (Mass.) Republican*, October 16, 1894, 8; Dabney, autobiographical sketch, 35–36.

17. Dabney, autobiographical sketch, 97. In his autobiography, Dabney relates the origin of his name. When Elizabeth Dabney was pregnant with Wendell in 1865, two women passing through Richmond stayed at the Dabney home. They were Jane Eckles, a pioneering northern schoolteacher, and Edmonia Lewis, the first professional African American sculptor. Lewis had just achieved her first commercial success selling portrait medallions and busts of abolitionists such as William Lloyd Garrison and Charles Sumner and was using the funds to finance her first trip to Europe. At the two women's suggestion, the Dabneys named their son Wendell Phillips Dabney.

18. Dabney, autobiographical sketch, 41–42. When John Dabney later told his son about this exchange, Wendell was baffled. "Why should the fact that I belong to one race make me inferior to a person of another race if I know as much as he does and can do as much?" His father replied, "Well, that's what I'm sending you to school to learn."

19. "Little Jack," *Century Illustrated Monthly Magazine* 33 (March 1887): 800.

20. Dabney, autobiographical sketch, 23.

21. Dabney, autobiographical sketch, 33.

22. Dabney, autobiographical sketch, 35, 66.

23. Dabney, autobiographical sketch, 57–58.

24. "How Dabney Bought His Freedom," *Lexington Leader*, rpt. *Springfield (Mass.) Republican*, October 16, 1894, 8.

25. "Dabney," *Richmond Dispatch*, June 8, 1900, 2; John Dabney Dead," *Richmond Times*, June 8, 1900, 7; "Famous Julep Mixer Dead," *Baltimore Sun*, June 8, 1900, 9. For detailed descriptions of nineteenth-century barbecues and political rallies, see Robert F. Moss, *Barbecue: The History of an American Institution*, 2nd ed. (Tuscaloosa: University of Alabama Press, 2020).

CHAPTER 11. The Decline and Fall of Southern Restaurant Cuisine

1. "A Card," *Alexandria Gazette*, March 21, 1873, 3.

2. "Death of a Culinary Artist," *Charleston News and Courier*, rpt. *Macon Telegraph*, October 31, 1883, 1.

3. "City Improvements," *Charleston Daily News*, September 17, 1872, 4; 1880 United States Federal Census, Charleston, Charleston County, South Carolina, roll 1222, enumeration district 066, page 291B, accessed via Ancestry.com; Savannah, Georgia, Cemetery and Burial Records, January 1883–December 1889, page 175, s.v. "Archibald Wigg," accessed via Ancestry.com; *Sholes' Directory of the City of Savannah 1888* (Savannah: Morning News, 1888), 373. In 1880 Archibald Wigg achieved the rare feat of being listed twice in the federal census, recorded with his wife Susan in their house on Henrietta Street in Charleston on June 11 and then again six days later in the Moultrieville district on Sullivan's Island, having presumably just moved out to the beach for the summer season. In a curious coda, the year he passed away, his daughter Annie married Robert Smalls, a former blockade runner turned Republican politician. It was Smalls's second marriage—his first wife died in 1883—and the *Atlanta Constitution* noted: "A feature of the wedding was the large attendance of whites." Between 1875 and 1887, Smalls had served five terms (not all consecutive) in the United States House of Representatives. The year Smalls and Annie Wigg married, President Benjamin Harrison appointed Smalls collector of the Port of Beaufort, a post he held until 1913. Smalls remained active in South Carolina politics and was one of the most forceful though ultimately unsuccessful voices against the efforts of white Democrats to disenfranchise Black citizens in the infamous Constitution of 1895, which effectively ended African American voting in South Carolina politics until the civil rights movement of the 1960s.

4. In 1862 an advertisement in the *Charleston Courier* offered a $100 reward for the return of "a black fellow by the name of Frank (calls himself Francis Moultrie) belonging to E. Vanderhorst and well known as his cook." Whether Moultrie was captured and returned to Vanderhorst is unknown. "One Hundred Dollars Reward," *Charleston Courier*, November 14, 1862, 2. See also "The Social Swim," *Washington Colored American*, April 4, 1903, 12; Booker T. Washington, *The Negro in Business* (Chicago: Hertel, Jenkins, 1907), 43–47.

5. The one notable exception in Charleston was William G. Barron, one of Tom Tully's several assistants who later undercut his former teacher on catering gigs. Barron remained prominent as a caterer, and he operated a restaurant on State Street until his death in 1900.

6. "Restaurants Needed," *Charleston Evening Post,* June 7, 1899, 5.

7. "A Golden Wedding," *New Orleans Times-Picayune,* September 1, 1900, 8.

8. It seems likely that this turn toward dialect and mockery of European-born chefs was tied in with American nativist tensions, reflecting a growing anxiety about the presence of "foreigners." The exact causes are uncertain, but the change in treatment is noticeable when looking across such stories in the aggregate.

9. "Mrs. Rutjes' Woe," *Durham (N.C.) Globe,* May 28, 1892, 1. Rutjes's second wife managed the best she could on her own, operating a boardinghouse in Raleigh until the early years of the twentieth century.

10. Herbert T. Ezekiel, *The Recollections of a Virginia Newspaper Man* (Richmond, Va.: H. T. Ezekiel, 1920), 111–112.

11. "John Welcker," *Daily National Republican,* March 29, 1875, 5; "A Patriotic Letter," *Richmond Dispatch,* May 6, 1900, 8.

12. "Briefs," *Tarboro Southerner,* April 7, 1881, 3; "Zetelle," *Atlanta Constitution,* November 5, 1881, 7; untitled, *Atlanta Constitution,* March 18, 1883, 9; "Mons. Spiro Zetelle," *Richmond Dispatch,* August 29, 1888, 1; "Zetelle in Paradise," *Richmond Dispatch,* February 6, 1891, 3; "Death of Mr. Spiro Zetelle," *Richmond Dispatch,* January 14, 1894, 10.

13. "Gastronomy in Maryland," *Cincinnati Daily Star,* March 3, 1880, 3; "The Monumental City," *San Francisco Bulletin,* November 27, 1880, Supplement 1.

14. Menu collection, New York Public Library, http://menus.nypl.org, accessed January 18, 2018.

15. "Destruction Decided as Only Cure for Stately Old Charleston Hotel," *Charleston News and Courier,* November 13, 1958, 10.

16. Qtd. in David S. Shields, *The Culinarians: Lives and Careers from the First Age of American Fine Dining* (Chicago: University of Chicago Press, 2017), 17; Wendell P. Dabney, autobiographical sketch, n.d., Mss qD115, Wendell P. Dabney Papers, 1904–1964, Cincinnati Museum Center, 37.

17. E. A. McCannon, *Commanders of the Dining Room: Biographic Sketches and Portraits of Successful Head Waiters*#123# (New York: Gwendolyn Publishing, 1904), 63.

18. Brian J. Rothschild, Jerald S. Ault, Philippe Goulletquer, and Maurice Héral, "Decline of the Chesapeake Bay Oyster Population: A Century of Habitat Destruction and Overfishing," *Marine Ecology Progress Series* 111 (1994): 29–30.

19. "Salty, Slippery, and Delicious," *Virginia Living,* October 2008, 137–142; David S. Shields, *Southern Provisions: The Creation and Revival of a Cuisine* (Chicago: University of Chicago Press, 2015), 101–103.

20. Alexander Filippini, *The Delmonico Cook Book* (London: Brentano's, 1890), 6.

21. "Western Game," *Washington Daily Globe*, January 31, 1856, 1.

22. "Interstate Commerce in Birds and Game," *Threshermen's Review*, September 1902, 18.

Afterword. The Legacy of the Lost Southern Chefs

1. *South Carolina: The WPA Guide to the Palmetto State* (1941; rpt., Columbia: University of South Carolina Press, 1988), 152.

2. David S. Shields and Kevin Mitchell, *Nat Fuller, 1812–1866: From Slavery to Artistry* (Columbia: Institute for Southern Studies and McKissick Museum, University of South Carolina, 2015), 3–4.

Index

Washington, George, 13, 46, 148, 150

Washington, John, 93–94, 130–133, 136, 144

Washington Club (Washington, D.C.), 100

Washington Hall (hotel, Louisville, Ky.), 60, 120, 252n23

Washington Monument, 136

Webster, Daniel, 45

Webster, Joseph Dana, 150

Welcker, John, 138–139, 168, 184

Wells, Henry, 72

Wendlinger, Caspar, 94, 130–131, 163, 257n62

Whig Party, 113, 179

White House, 25, 49, 96, 98, 100, 136, 166, 172, 183, 271n17; stewards, 35, 46, 182

White Sulphur Springs (Va.), 91–92

Wigg, Alfred R., 159, 160

Wigg, Archibald, 157–160, 229–230, 278n3

Wigg, John, 158–159

Wigg, William H., 157

Wigg, William H., Jr., 158–159, 265n12

Willard, Henry, 95

Willard, Joseph, 95

Willard, Orasmus, 92

Willard's Hotel (Washington, D.C.), 95–96, 137

Williamsburg, Va., 80, 81

Wilson, Henry, 169

Wilson, John Lyde, 24

Wise, Henry A., 174–175

Wondrich, David, 107

Wood, James, 119

Wood, Woodson, 197–198

Wormley, James, 39, 100, 168–170, 183–187, 189–191, 216–217, 272n16; politics and, 184–191, 270nn16–17; Wormley Conference, 189–190

Wormley, James, Jr., 185

Wormley, Lynch, 38–39

Wormley, Mary, 39

Wormley, William (James Wormley's brother), 39, 41, 100, 270n16

Wormley, William (James Wormley's son), 185, 271n19, 272n26

Zanone, James, 110

Zetelle, Spiro, 83–86, 87, 94, 107, 130, 167, 231–233